THE BEGINNER'S GUIDE TO
Starting a Garden

THE BEGINNER'S GUIDE TO
Starting a Garden

326 Fast, Easy, Affordable Ways to Transform Your Yard One Project at a Time

Sally Roth

Timber Press
Portland, Oregon

Frontispiece: 'Red Ribbons' daylily, by Elizabeth McWilliams

Photography credits appear on page 260.
Illustrations by Karla Beatty and Anna Eshelman

Published in 2017 by Timber Press, Inc.
The Haseltine Building
133 S.W. Second Avenue, Suite 450
Portland, Oregon 97204-3527
timberpress.com

Printed in China
Text design by Julianna Johnson and Kate Giambrone
Cover design by Benjamin Shaykin and Patrick Barber

Library of Congress Cataloging-in-Publication Data

Names: Roth, Sally, author.
Title: The beginner's guide to starting a garden: 326 fast, easy,
affordable ways to transform your yard one project at a time/ Sally Roth.
Description: Portland, Oregon: Timber Press, 2017. | Includes
bibliographical references and index.
Identifiers: LCCN 2016017920 | ISBN 9781604696745 (pbk.)
Subjects: LCSH: Gardens—Design.
Classification: LCC SB473 .R647 2017 | DDC 635—dc23 LC record
available at https://lccn.loc.gov/2016017920

IN LOVING MEMORY

OF *my mother*

CONTENTS

A LIFETIME OF LEARNING 8

A BUILDING BLOCK GARDEN PRIMER 17

TWELVE EASY, SMALL GARDENS

FIRST IMPRESSIONS
At the Lamppost 56

A WELCOME GARDEN
At the Entrance 72

A PRETTY FRAME
At the Corners 86

DRESS UP A TREE
Shady Spots 102

BETWEEN NEIGHBORS
Private or Pretty? 118

CHEERFUL COLOR
In the Lawn 132

AN EVER-EXPANDING GARDEN
Extending the Edges 146

A BECKONING BENCH
Gathering Places and Sitting Spots 159

SIDEWALK STRIP
Creating Curb Appeal 176

LOTS OF POTS
A Can't-Miss Container Garden 192

ARTIST'S CANVAS
Gardening on Slopes 209

NOW YOU SEE IT, NOW YOU DON'T
Dealing with Eyesores 224

GARDENING SECRETS
Top Ten Ways to Save Time and Money 236

Resources 255

Further Reading 258

Photography Credits 260

Index 261

A Lifetime of Learning

△ The author in her garden in the high Rockies of Colorado, where a combination of frigid winters, lack of water, and about two and a half months between spring thaw and first snow makes her grateful for all the gardening tricks that she's learned over the years— and the new ones she's still learning.

I learned how to garden at my mother's knee—literally.

"I'm going outside for a while," she'd announce, and I'd follow along, hurrying to get my little red wagon, so I could help haul plants or weeds or rocks.

Her gardens were gorgeous. And ever changing, as she transplanted things a few inches left or right, or all the way across the yard. I can still see her standing back, squinting, to check the look of what she was creating.

"Needs more yellow, right there," she'd say, pointing. Then she'd reach for the shovel to move a blooming clump of coreopsis daisies then and there.

Every year, her flower beds got bigger, and the lawn got smaller. Meanwhile, I absorbed the art of gardening, and the how-tos of transplanting, dividing, and otherwise making more of a good thing.

Garden centers were almost unheard of back then, so Mom got most of her plants from friends and neighbors. Oh, you could send away for plants

▽ My mother could usually be found outside, in her "natural habitat," as we joked—her gardens.

through the mail, but that cost money, and Mom was a penny-pincher. Having gone through the Great Depression, she never took money for granted.

Sixty years later, I still remember which precious plants she had sent away for, because those words became part of their name: "The smokebush I sent away for." "The 'Peace' rose I sent away for." "The climbing 'Don Juan' [rose] I sent away for." That was the grand total, until I grew up and visiting the garden centers and nurseries then springing up all over became a weekly outing for Mom and me.

Some plants were growing around the hundred-year-old house when my parents bought it in the 1930s, like peonies, old "lemon lily" daylilies (*Hemerocallis flava*), lily-of-the-valley, and a few pink "live forever" sedums. And Mom made more of those plants, as well as plants she'd received from friends, saving seeds, slicing off starts, and rooting cuttings. She managed to plant our whole acre with lush gardens that probably cost her a total of $100 over the decades.

It was a gardening education, but I didn't realize that until I left home and started my own garden. Then I was the one talking the leg off anyone who stopped to admire what I was doing. "The hollyhocks? Those came from

◁ Every summer, my mom broke off a spray of her beloved smokebush to put in the old white ironstone pitcher. "Smell," she'd urge me. "Doesn't it smell good?" I can still conjure the distinctive scent.

Mom's yard—she always called them 'outhouse flowers,'" I'd say, laughing. "See these babies? The big ones seed themselves! Here, let me dig you a few.

"And those are the columbines I started from Katie's seeds. Hers were pink and white, but some of mine came out dark purple! Don't you love that color?"

Then I'd stand back and squint at the bed. "Needs more yellow. . . ."

Passing on the Gift

Unlike my mom, who lived in the same house most of her long life, I've moved around. Pennsylvania, Oregon, Indiana, Washington, Colorado—wherever I've lived, I've made gardens that got bigger every year. And I still rely on the tricks I learned at my mother's knee to make fast, cheap, beautiful gardens.

Sharing the know-how—and the plants—is a big part of the fun! This year, my husband, Matt Bartmann, and I got to do that with his dad and stepmom, Lou and Lila. Lou is an artist, who creates stunning illuminated letters, like those in the famed *Book of Kells*, combining his calligraphy with precise dabs of vivid color and gold leaf.

And Lila loves color even more than Lou does. While I throw on whichever T-shirt is handy on top of my usually grubby jeans, she creates perfectly coordinated outfits of orchid, salmon, and turquoise, complete with just the right

△ I love to see which plants in the garden get the hummingbird seal of approval. Columbines, like this yellow one I grew from seed passed along by an eighty-year-old friend, are always a hit.

▷ Lou and Lila's front yard was a sad-looking wasteland when I first laid eyes on it.

△ Purple is Lila's signature color, so of course the trellis Matt built for their yard had to be purple. She was delighted to help paint it—and just happened to be wearing raspberry overalls that day.

hat, shoes, and jewelry. Even the chef coats she and Lou wear in the kitchen are bright lime green, not basic white.

Color is such a huge part of who Lila is that I was taken aback the first time I saw their front yard. A bright purple door, and a deep purple pot beside it, yes, that's Lila. But the rest was dismal. Exposed gray weed barrier fabric flapped sadly in the breeze. Red lava rock outlined every bed, clashing horribly with the purple and making the yard so busy, my eyes didn't know where to look. Three randomly placed big, round, white rocks just added to the visual confusion. "Too much! No focus!" my brain complained.

The front of the house, a simple 1960s ranch-style, was stark and bare—not even a foundation shrub in sight. As for flowering plants, except for a few along the sidewalk and driveway, there were none. The yard had beaten all their attempts to pretty it up. Why? A glorious old Siberian elm tree, with a trunk 3 feet across, completely dominated the yard.

Recognizing defeat, artist Lou and artistic Lila had focused most of their efforts along the perimeter of the yard. They'd edged the driveway with a tapestry of groundcovers and a few perennials. They'd put in clumps of daylilies at one corner of the yard, around a prized daphne shrub that was fighting for its life in a big circle bed of variegated goutweed, a horribly aggressive, hard-to-eradicate groundcover the previous owner had planted.

But mainly, Lou and Lila had poured their love of color into the backyard, an exuberant riot of red and purple flowers, where they spent most of their time.

Still, the neglected front yard nagged at them. The neighborhood was full of beautiful gardens, and they felt theirs just didn't measure up.

One Christmas, we gave Lou and Lila a makeover of their front yard as a present, complete with "after" pictures of what we had in mind, done via computer manipulation. We'd do all the work. We'd supply all the plants. All they had to do was trust us. And then sit back and enjoy. They loved the idea, and accepted gratefully.

As usual, our wallet was mighty thin, so we planned to spend a grand total of $35 for lumber to build a trellis and to buy a vine to grow up it.

Figuring out how to make the yard look good, with that giant tree in the picture? Finding the hundreds of plants we'd need? That was a gift, too. The gift I'd gotten from my mother when I was a kid. The gift Matt and I were now going to pass along—the gift of creating what I like to call building block gardens.

Painting a Masterpiece

Lou and Lila stayed out of the way when we began work on their yard. But after we put in the first plants, Lou came out to investigate.

"Oh! I see what you're doing!" he said, pausing to look at a pair of red-leaved heucheras we'd nestled beside a sweep of silvery lamb's-ears. His face lit up in recognition—not of the plants but of the process. "You're painting with plants!"

With half a day of work about once a week, for two months (with time out for late Colorado snowstorms), Lila and Lou's once unloved front yard became a favorite stopping place for the many folks who stroll the quiet streets of their neighborhood.

I love a quick payoff, too. I don't want to wait years for my gardens to look good. I can hardly wait the few days it will take for those tantalizingly plump bearded iris buds to bloom. "Beautiful from the beginning," that's my motto.

But biting off more than we can chew is a common malady among gardeners. And my mom knew her limitations and had it down to a science. Instead of digging up half the yard at once, only to run out of energy long before it was planted, she'd make a small garden. A garden that she could do start to finish—getting rid of the lawn grass, setting plants around to see how they'd look, then putting them in—in just a few hours.

▷ Lila and Lou's front yard is not quite finished. We're waiting to make sure the goutweed is completely vanquished before prettying up the foreground corner.

△ Violets and Johnny jump-up violas sow themselves generously, quickly filling in cracks to block weeds from sprouting.

"I made a new garden!" she'd announce proudly to my father, whose main role outside was a vital one: the Appreciator.

Hand in hand, they'd spend an hour admiring, with Mom explaining why she'd put which plant where, and how it was going to look when everything filled in.

"Looks beautiful already, Mary," he'd say. And it did.

A couple of weeks later, she'd say again, "I made a new garden!" And so on, for years, until the lawn had dwindled to nothing more than graceful paths leading us through the flowers.

Labor of Love

Taking care of all those plants was never a problem for Mom, either. She had tricks for minimizing time spent on those tasks, too. I laughed when the term "low maintenance" became the new concept in gardening a few decades ago. Low maintenance? It was already a way of life for Mom, and for me.

I remember watching a nearby neighbor, bare headed and sweaty in the baking summer sun, wrestling a rototiller through his tomato and gladiolus plantation. He was red-faced and irritable—not an attitude I'd ever associated with gardening. I eventually asked timidly (I was a kid and he was a scary grown-up), "Why don't you use mulch?"

"You have to get the weeds," he said with a self-satisfied snort, "and it's either the tiller or the hoe." I wasn't about to tell him that what he was doing would only bring thousands more weed seeds to the surface to eagerly sprout. And the funny thing was, my mom used the grass clippings from his yard to mulch her plants so she wouldn't have to weed.

Artists in the Making

Every garden is different. And so is every gardener. We all have our personal favorites—the colors and plants that make our heart sing. We all have different conditions in our yards, too, and different climates. But we have one big thing in common: we love beauty.

I'm always peering into yards, wherever we go, whether it's a trip to the supermarket or a journey across the country. I love to see what people have planted, and think about what works and what doesn't. If the gardener is out in the yard, I'll wave and call, "Beautiful!" They know what I'm talking about, and they always smile. Garden Appreciator is an important role, for all of us who play with plants.

▷ What better way to make friends with a neighbor than to share the joy of gardening—and to share a garden? An expanse of silvery lamb's-ears and other easy plants contrasts with the dark red shrubs, trees, and iris that both neighbors use as accents.

In crisscrossing the country to take pictures for this book, my photographer husband, Matt, and I not only found beautiful gardens filled with thousands of dollars' worth of plants, but we also saw beautiful gardens that were nothing more than a patch of sunflowers around a mailbox, as well as the many beautiful gardens in between. Looking at those gardens not as finished gardens, but imagining how they got there, we realized they shared another big trait besides beauty: they could be done in small blocks.

One small, doable, affordable piece at a time, to create a finished masterpiece.

All the tricks I've learned over a lifetime of dirty fingernails are in this book. So is lots and lots of down-to-earth advice on how to make your garden look like a masterpiece, without spending a fortune or giving up every minute of each precious weekend.

I've never used graph paper to plan a garden, and you don't need to, either. Put away the pencils and the measuring tape, and instead, pick up some plants you love. It's way more fun to depend on your own eye for beauty.

Hold off on the plant encyclopedia for now, too. Sure, you'll find lots of plant names in these pages, because I'm a plant nut, and these are my friends—as familiar as the human pals I hang around with. But if plant names

△ I've never had an all-white garden, not even a mostly white garden, because I'm just too enamored of color. But I still sigh with pleasure at the cool elegance of plain white, like this show-stopping assembly of Shasta daisies.

aren't second nature to you, don't worry about them. You can learn how to put together a beautiful garden just by looking at the shapes and colors of plants.

As for all those gardens Matt and I discovered across thousands of miles, you'll see many of them in this book. "Your yard caught our eye," we'd say, over and over, which usually opened a wonderful conversation. "Thanks for having such a beautiful garden!"

And Lou and Lila's yard makeover? They're already adding their own touches, now that the majestic tree has been made a part of the yard rather than an overwhelming presence. You'll see their garden here and there in this book, too—just look for the purple.

Whatever your signature color—Lila's purple, my own blue, my mom's yellow, and on through the rainbow—we're all artists at heart. That's why we garden.

A Building Block Garden Primer

△ Reliable, easy-care plants
in a mix of colors and
shapes are the foundation of
what I like to call the "building
block garden."

I t took me a minute to get it, the first time I heard the saying, "Fast, good, cheap—pick two." Then it dawned on me: yes, you can have that job done fast and well, but it won't be cheap. Sure, we can do it cheap and make it good, but it's not going to be fast.

We laugh because we recognize the truth behind the saying. But by building your garden one project at a time—in blocks—we're going to make a lie out of it. You *can* have a fast, cheap, good-looking garden, even if you've never lifted a shovel before in your life, let alone studied garden design. Building block gardening is for everyone. It's based on common sense, with big payoffs every step of the way.

Building block gardening has another benefit, and it's a big one: it's easy. This approach to making your yard beautiful is easy to plan, easy to plant, and easy to care for. Anyone can do it, in any climate, in any conditions, on any budget. All you need to do is choose a spot, pick your colors and your style, round up your plants, and then dig right in to have a finished garden in just a few hours. A fast, cheap, easy garden that looks good right from the start.

Ready to rewrite that old saying? "Fast, cheap, good, easy—pick four!"

The Beauty of Building Blocks

Each chapter of this book focuses on a different area of the yard—the lamppost, the doorstep, the tree in your front yard, the corner by the neighbor, and so on—for a total of twelve small, related gardens you will make, one at a time.

▷ A lamppost garden, a garden on either side of the doorstep, and a hedge between neighbors—four easy pieces, and the whole yard is visually connected, thanks to the repeated colors of yellow and pink.

▷ Inexpensive creeping phlox, yellow alyssum, and dwarf irises blanket a spring garden in a blast of color that lasts for weeks.

△ One plant of salmon petunias is enough to make a splash in a small garden. Repeat it elsewhere, and the impulse buy won't get lost in the big picture.

Instead of looking at your whole yard and wondering, "What does it need?" you'll be looking at a small, specific area and saying, "What can I put here to pretty it up?" That's a big difference in perspective. Considering your yard as a whole can be daunting. Where should I start? Am I doing this right? How can I afford so many plants, let alone find the time to get them in the ground? Narrowing your focus to one small area eliminates all those worries.

FAST!

You'll start by focusing on one small area at a time, putting in a small garden you love in just an afternoon for as little as $20. Then you'll take your cues from that finished garden to make another, and another, and another, as your free time and budget allow. Each of the small gardens will include some of the same colors, and even some of the same plants, so all the pieces are tied together.

Making a garden in just a single small area makes it easier to decide what to plant. That saves plenty of time—and money—right away. And it saves even more time later, when you build on that single small garden to create the next one. You'll be using the same colors and some of the same plants, so you won't be starting from scratch.

△ Plant in multiples for big impact. The wow power here comes from a trio of dramatic red hot poker (*Kniphofia*) partnered with a shorter yellow variety and fronted with a pair of burgundy daylilies.

Yes, they're separate gardens, but they will be related, with each one visually tied to the others. Stop at just one or two, and your yard looks great already. Put them all together, and your yard will feel complete.

Every gardener loves instant gratification, and plant sellers certainly make it easy for us to indulge. Blooming six-packs fly off the shelves these days, while seed racks mostly gather dust. Why wait for flowers when we can have them right now? Why fuss with seedlings for months when we can have those velvety purple petunias for just a few dollars? Or those salmon ones? Or—oh! What are those blue flowers! We've all been there, carrying home treasures that are going to look gorgeous and transform our whole yard.

Except they don't. The purple petunias disappear from a distance. The salmon ones make just a lonely dab of color. The blue-flowered ones turn out to be too fussy. So let's do it a different way. Fast. That way, you can have a pretty, finished garden in just a few hours.

What's the secret? It's a trick every quilt maker knows well: to create a big, beautiful, finished bedcover, just make one small block of joined, colored, fabric pieces at a time. Each piece that's added to a block brings a pleasing sense of accomplishment, and each block makes the growing quilt look better. That sense of accomplishment is vital. It's what keeps us moving forward, encouraging us to make the next block.

Your life is busy. Your budget is limited. You want a yard that looks like the cover of a magazine. And it's entirely possible, when you tackle one small part at a time.

Free time is as precious as extra money. By starting small, we're not talking about weeks of work. We're talking about a few hours. And at the end of those few hours, you'll have a finished garden that looks great right from the get-go.

All you have to do is spend some time thinking about what you like, with a little help from this book. Then, make a trip to the garden center, carve out a few hours for planting, and you have it nailed. There's no pressure to hurry up, no angst over an unfinished or unsatisfying planting—you'll have a garden, and it's beautiful. And you'll do it again . . . when time and money allow.

CHEAP!

The very best gardeners—my mother and nature itself—taught me how to make beautiful gardens on a budget. I'm a penny-pincher, but I also know that saving money along the way lets me indulge when I see that special (read: pricey) plant I just have to have.

▷ Daylilies are dependable workhorses, but they're as stunning as a show pony. This one is 'Red Ribbons'.

△ Daisies are like basic chino pants—you can dress them up with wide spacing and controlled partners, or go casual, as in this group of golden coreopsis, classic white Shasta daisy, and lavender erigeron.

Observing nature has taught me plenty, too. Wandering the woods and fields all my life, I soaked up nature's teachings about plant combinations and colors, about shade and sun, and about multiplying those plants. I learned which plants hummingbirds and butterflies like best, and why; which ones can adapt when the soil gets swamped with rain, then dries brick-hard; and I used those lessons in my own yard.

Flowers—that's where we all want to start. When you visit a garden center, it's the flowering plants that draw you like a magnet. They're right up front, making it easy for customers to yield to the siren song of a plant in bloom.

But which flowers should you buy? First, focus on the workhorses: those dependable, trouble-free, low-maintenance, long-lived perennials, plants that survive over winter to come back in spring, year after year. Seems like a tall order, but many, many perennials match those requirements.

Old-time favorites such as bearded iris, coreopsis, Shasta daisies, veronica, daylilies, and tall garden phlox are still worth their weight in gold. And in the past fifty years, more sturdy perennials have become garden staples—velvety lamb's-ears, purple coneflower, threadleaf coreopsis, delicious colors of yarrow, daylilies that go way beyond old-fashioned rusty orange. These workhorse perennials, along with shrubs and ornamental grasses, are the backbone of the garden. You'll have plenty of room to try out all sorts of other flowers, too. But for building a foundation, pick plants you can rely on.

The perennial workhorses are widely available and are often the least expensive plants at the garden center or in the catalog. But don't be fooled by that low price—these plants offer plenty of beauty, color, and style. Every perennial suggested in this book is one that will live for decades with no special care, adapting to a wide range of climates and soil conditions. That's extra important in today's changing climate, when we can no longer count on the weather to behave as we expect.

▽ Long-blooming Jupiter's beard (*Centranthus ruber*) reinforces the color of the rose, but with a satisfying shift in shape and texture.

▷ An edging of grassy liriope fills in fast from small starter plants. Roses are fast growers, too. An unprepossessing— and inexpensive—bagged or potted shrub rose can reach 4 feet tall and wide its first year.

▷ A light-colored gravel path draws the eye through soft, mounded perennials to the spiky contrast of yucca and red-flowered hesperaloe.

MISTAKES NOT TO MAKE
Think Small

Plant growers know we love instant gratification, so they've taken to selling bigger and bigger pots of perennials. But big pots—the 3- to 5-gallon sizes—are a bad buy. Not only are they twice the price as typical 1-gallon pots, but they're heavy and hard to carry. You'll need to dig a much bigger hole, too. And once you take that plant out of the pot, it won't get much bigger its first year, or ever.

Instead, buy the smallest pots you can find. They're a real bargain. You can buy several 2¼- to 4-inch pots for the price of a single perennial in a big pot. And you can pop them into your garden with just a hand trowel; no shovel needed.

The eager roots of these young plants will quickly grow into the surrounding soil, and then you won't have to water as often. You may not get many flowers the first summer, but your perennials will reach full size by the end of their first season in the ground.

You'll be adding annuals, too—plants that delight you for only one gardening season, dying after they produce seeds or at the touch of frost. They'll be just as easy-care and dependable as the perennials. But, in the interests of saving your wallet, you'll focus on the plant-it-once perennials you can enjoy for years. I'll bet you already know most of them. And you may already have some of them growing in your yard.

WORKHORSE PERENNIALS

Artemisia 'Powis Castle', 'Silver Mound', 'Seafoam', and other cultivars

Asiatic lily (*Lilium* hybrids)

Basket-of-gold, gold alyssum (*Aurinia saxatilis*)

Bearded iris (*Iris* hybrids)

Bergenia (*Bergenia cordifolia*)

Black-eyed Susan (*Rudbeckia* species and hybrids)

Brunnera (*Brunnera macrophylla*)

Candytuft (*Iberis sempervirens*)

Catmint (*Nepeta* hybrids)

Daylily (*Hemerocallis* species and hybrids)

Hardy geranium (*Geranium* species and hybrids)

Heuchera, both coral bells and fancy-leaved (*Heuchera* hybrids)

Jupiter's beard (*Centranthus ruber*)

Lamb's-ears (*Stachys byzantina*)

Lanceleaf coreopsis (*Coreopsis lanceolata*)

Oriental poppy (*Papaver* hybrids)

Purple coneflower (*Echinacea purpurea*)

Red hot poker (*Kniphofia uvaria*)

Shasta daisy (*Leucanthemum ×superbum*)

Siberian iris (*Iris sibirica*)

Snow-in-summer (*Cerastium tomentosum*)

Tall garden phlox (*Phlox maculata, P. paniculata*)

Threadleaf coreopsis (*Coreopsis verticillata*)

Tiger lily (*Lilium lancifolium*)

Veronica, both creeping and upright (*Veronica* species and hybrids)

Yarrow (*Achillea* species and hybrids)

Yucca (*Yucca* species)

Another budget-friendly aspect of the building block garden is that it serves as a nursery bed, holding plants that you can make more of without spending a dime. A quick slice with a trowel or shovel will give you at least a few starter plants for your next garden. Those starter plants will take a year or two to reach full size, but knowing they didn't cost a cent seems to make it easier to be patient. In fact, it's fun to watch your new starts gain girth. It is another accomplishment to feel good about.

△ A couldn't-be-simpler trio of red barberry and blue spruce packs a punch of year-round color. Japanese barberry is unwelcome in some areas, where it's escaped to the wild; if so, substitute a dark-leaved weigela.

Starting new plants from seeds you collect, or transplanting self-sown seedlings, will expand your gardens, too, without depleting your wallet. And for sheer magic, nothing beats starting plants from cuttings. Just clip a few stems, strip the lower leaves, poke them into the soil, and you'll have all the blue catmint (*Nepeta ×faassenii*), cardinal flower (*Lobelia cardinalis*), mums, hydrangeas, and dahlias your yard can hold.

GOOD!

It's good looks you're after. A garden that pleases your eye, that makes you smile to see it when you pull up in front.

Whether you're making a new garden or improving an existing one, creating those good looks begins days, weeks, a lifetime before you even reach for the shovel. And it has nothing to do with gardening. It's that eye for beauty and for style that you already have.

What? You say you don't have an eye for style? Sure you do! You use it every day, when you choose which clothes to wear. You're showing the world your style, whether it's jeans and a T-shirt or night-on-the-town glamour. Many of us are swamped by insecurity when it comes to putting plants together in a garden. Yet we know what styles we like, we know what colors look good on us, and we know what we feel comfortable in.

So set aside any feelings of insecurity you might have about making a garden. You already have a good eye for design, and you'll find all sorts of easy tips in this book to transfer that skill to plants. Just think of it as satisfying your own sense of beauty and showing your sense of style to the world.

Planning for continual bloom, so there are no dead spots while we're waiting for the next flower to kick in, requires lots of plants and a careful study of bloom times. Or does it? Not in the building block garden! Here are some tricks:

→ You'll plant perennials that bloom for a month or longer, not just a couple of short weeks.
→ You'll include plants that are eye-catching even when they're not in bloom.
→ You'll add a different plant of a similar color but an earlier or later bloom time beside a brief bloomer, so that the color continues.
→ You'll fill in with inexpensive annuals to keep the flowers coming.
→ You'll include annuals, perennials, grasses, and shrubs with burgundy, silver, orange, or golden leaves, to add even more long-lasting color.
→ You'll discover the money-saving benefits and the beauty of shrubs.
→ You depend on evergreens and "ever-silvers" to keep the garden looking good in winter.

Let's consider shrubs. Hardly anyone, except for garden designers, gets excited about shrubs at a nursery or garden center. Unless they're loaded with bloom, we tend to walk past them without a second glance. But those shrubs are exactly what you'll want to add to your garden.

Shrubs grow fast, and they cover a lot of space in a garden—a nifty money-saving trait. In a couple of years, a hydrangea will be about 5 feet in diameter; a mugo pine, 4 feet wide; a lilac, 5 feet tall. A groundcover-type juniper can swiftly spread to cover a 2- to 3-foot circle of bare soil in just one year.

Summer gardens are easy, because they're splashed with pretty flowers. Winter is a different story, however, and that's when shrubs, especially evergreens, and ornamental grasses earn their keep. These permanent plants add to the garden in spring, summer, and fall, too. But in winter, long after the first hard frost, shrubs keep contributing their beauty to the garden. They give a sense of structure and permanence, making it look solidly established.

Common shrubs like forsythia, heaths and heathers, hydrangea, weigela, and spirea don't cost much more than a gallon-pot perennial, and you don't need many of them. You can find shrubs for as little as $10, especially when they're not in bloom. And you won't have trouble finding flowering shrubs at the garden center. Just like perennials, they're moved up front at bloom time to catch our eye and loosen our wallet. And in fall, that prominent spot will be loaded with shrubs and trees with bright foliage or berries.

Ornamental grasses are as hard working as shrubs. They look good long into winter and often all the way until spring, when we clip down the bleached blades to make way for new growth. Their personality is much different from that of shrubs, though. Grasses are graceful. Even those that grow stiffly upright, like 'Karl Foerster' feather reed grass (*Calamagrostis acutiflora* 'Karl Foerster'), have a fine texture and airy plumes that soften the garden.

▽ Beauty's a big reason to plant a hydrangea, but practicality is part of it, too. These vigorous shrubs fill a big space, fast, and their huge clusters of flowers show off from a distance.

▷ Depend on shrubs, evergreens, and ornamental grasses to keep bold color going, even in the off-season.

△ Bright pink diascia (foreground), roses, and agastache flowers glow among contrasting cool gray grasses and deep red foliage.

EASY!

For creating a building block garden, all you need to know before you dig into the soil is which colors you like best, which shapes appeal to you, and what style of garden makes you feel at home. That's design, done by common sense and creativity.

You can get overwhelmed when you're trying to decide what to plant in your yard. With tens of thousands of plants in cultivation, it's hard to know where to start, let alone how to put them together. So, we're going to narrow down the selection to the basics, annual and perennial plants you can find at just about any garden center. Limiting your choices eliminates the stress of making lots of decisions, too, which goes a long way in making gardening easy.

PLANT HARDINESS ZONES

USDA plant hardiness zones are based on average annual minimum temperatures. Knowing a plant's hardiness zone rating will help you to determine whether it will survive in your climate. The lower the zone number, the colder the winter temperatures.

To see temperature equivalents and to learn in which zone you garden, see the US Department of Agriculture Hardiness Zone Map at *usna.usda.gov/Hardzone/ushzmap.html.*

For Canada, go to *planthardiness.gc.ca/* or to *atlas.agr.gc.ca/agmaf/index_eng.html.*

For Europe, go to *uk.gardenweb.com/forums/zones/hze.html.*

For the UK, search for "hardiness" at *rhs.org.uk.*

AVERAGE ANNUAL MINIMUM TEMPERATURE

Zone	Temperature (°F)	Temperature (°C)
1	Below −50	Below −46
2	−50 to −40	−46 to −40
3	−40 to −30	−40 to −34
4	−30 to −20	−34 to −29
5	−20 to −10	−29 to −23
6	−10 to 0	−23 to −18
7	0 to 10	−18 to −12
8	10 to 20	−12 to −7
9	20 to 30	−7 to −1
10	30 to 40	−1 to 4
11	40 to 50	4 to 10
12	50 to 60	10 to 16
13	60 to 70	16 to 21

◁ Vivid painted daisy (keeping the yellow iris company here) is hardly "perennial"—it lives only a few years. Plant seeds yearly, to keep those vivid daisies coming.

I like plants that aren't too needy: perennials that live a long time, instead of petering out unless I coddle them; plants that won't suffer if rain is scarce and I forget to water; flowers that bloom a long time; plants that insects aren't too interested in chomping; and plants that shrug off diseases.

"Plant it and forget it" is how I think of perennials, because I can depend on them to look good with minimal attention. We'll focus on such perennials and annuals in this book, because undemanding plants free up hours of time. Building block gardens are beautiful, but they won't make you spend every Saturday taking care of them. Unless you want to.

Another factor in choosing plants for your garden is the climate of your region. The US Department of Agriculture Hardiness Zones chart (see hardiness zones table on previous page) presents the climate zones of the United States, which helps you to know what plants will thrive in your area. Just take a look at the plant tags at nurseries and garden centers, which indicate what hardiness zone(s) each plant thrives in.

The selection of plants for gardens in Zones 5 through 9 is practically endless. Those zones, defined by lowest winter temperature, cover the giant stretch of temperate area around the globe, where most garden plants originated. But Zones 2 through 4 are a different story. Plant choices are much

MISTAKES NOT TO MAKE
A Short but Lovely Life

Some "perennials" don't live up to that name, even with the best of care. They can fade in a few years instead of growing more robust, or die over winter without warning. Some are short-lived by nature. Those marked with an asterisk in the following list are biennials, which normally live only two years, but are sometimes sold as perennials. All are beautiful and well worth growing, as long as you're aware that you may not get to enjoy them for decades, or even for more than a couple of years. They do self-sow, however, dropping seeds that sprout into plants to replace the parent.

*Canterbury bells
  (*Campanula medium*)

Delphinium
  (*Delphinium* species and hybrids)

*Hollyhock (*Alcea rosea*)

*Forget-me-not (*Myosotis sylvatica*)

*Foxglove (*Digitalis purpurea*)

Iceland poppy (*Papaver nudicaule*)

Indian blanket, gaillardia
  (*Gaillardia* species)

'Limerock Ruby' coreopsis
  (*Coreopsis* 'Limerock Ruby')

Lupine (*Lupinus* hybrids)

Maltese cross
  (*Lychnis chalcedonica*)

Painted daisy
  (*Tanacetum coccineum*)

*Rose campion (*Lychnis coronaria*)

Snapdragon (*Antirhinnum majus*)

*Sweet William (*Dianthus barbatus*)

more limited in the coldest areas, and many favorites are not able to thrive there. Lots of familiar plants won't survive in Zones 10 and 11, either—the hottest areas of the country. But that heat opens up lots of other plant possibilities from tropical areas or deserts around the world.

If you live at one of the extreme ends of the hardiness zone scale, depend on your local nurseries and read catalogs with care to find plants that like to grow in your region.

Like everyone else, I sometimes don't heed the warnings about what *not* to plant, especially when it comes to invasive plants. And some perennials can take off running, too. I wouldn't be without beebalm or goldenrod, for instance, but I know that one of my early spring chores will be lifting out those wayward spreading roots. The time to decide whether you want to do those kinds of chores is before you plant.

Many plants drop seeds to start the next generation. Plants that sow themselves modestly, such as columbines (*Aquilegia* species), Virginia bluebells (*Mertensia virginica*), and old-fashioned tiger lilies (*Lilium lancifolium*), are a plus. But annuals and perennials that sow themselves extra enthusiastically can be a boon or a bane. If you appreciate the free-for-all effect of a cottage garden, you'll smile when you see all those hundreds of seedlings of bachelor's buttons, California poppies, cleome, feverfew (*Tanacetum parthenium*), garden balsam (*Impatiens balsamina*), and other generous self-sowers. But if your

▷ Deciding which colors you like best and putting them together in a variety of shapes is all it takes to make a gorgeous garden. Annual petunias, lantana, and verbena will carry the show until frost.

△ In fall, the moody color of big, bold clumps of New Zealand flax (*Phormium* species) lets the zingy purple door show off, while providing a sharp contrast to the delicacy of the feather grass (*Nasella*, formerly *Stipa* species) in this low-maintenance garden.

garden isn't so laissez-faire, you'll want to think twice before putting them in. Choosing plants that stay in their allotted space, rather than sending out runners or dropping seeds willy-nilly, can cut way down on maintenance chores.

You will find recommendations in the book for plants that are aggressive spreaders. They are perfect for areas where that eager-beaver trait is a desirable one, such as covering a hillside or extending a garden. You can decide for yourself whether you want a pushy plant. Other recommended plants in the book may spread, too, such as mat-forming 'Georgia Blue' veronica or silvery soft lamb's-ears, but they'll be easy to control with a once-a-year uprooting of unwanted stems.

Checking the Look—And Fixing It

When creating a garden, it's vital to stand back and assess what you're putting together. Just as you check your look in the mirror before you leave the house, you'll be gauging your garden to see if it's great as is, or if something isn't quite right.

Here's where trusting your eye is crucial. If that garden looks like something is missing, well, you can just assume that something is missing. If you don't like the look of that red rose next to that orange daylily, you're right. If that spiky yucca doesn't look perfect in that spot, it's not. Your eye is the best gauge of your design. Give it credit, and listen to what it's telling you.

If your eye isn't delighted by your garden, chances are the problem lies in one of the following areas:

→ **"It Needs Something"** Almost every time, that "something" that's needed is a place for our eyes to light upon. We crave a focal point— an attention-getter that catches the eye immediately. Plants with spiky or vertical form, like yuccas or tall grasses, or tall plants with big flowers, loudly say, "Look here!" Human-made objects are even more powerful focal points. Adding a tall pot of flowers or a birdhouse on a post to a garden bed will calm down the "don't know where to look" issue in an instant.

→ **Colors aren't right** No, they probably aren't, if your eye says so. Some easy fixes: insert a foliage plant to calm the war between the clashing colors. Greens, gray-greens, and silver-leaved plants give the eye a bit of resting space between colors that don't go well together. Or, if the problem is "too much of the same," add a contrasting color between hues that are too similar.

→ **Dead spots** Each perennial has its own bloom season, and sometimes there's a gap before the next show. Solution: add petunias and other easy annuals that bloom for ages, to distract the eye from perennials that have finished blooming or haven't started. Plant them in the ground, or put them in a container for even more impact.

→ **Some flower colors disappear from a distance** Blue, blue-purple, burgundy, and other deep hues tend to blend into the surrounding greenery from a distance. Simple fix: add white, yellow, or hot colors of pink, red, or orange to make the garden pop.

If you still can't figure out what is bothering you about the garden, take a picture. It's often easier to see what's wrong in a photo.

Your first small garden will give you all the basics you need to feel confident about putting plants together to please your eye. And the gardens that

△ A dash of red, even dark red like this rock rose (*Helianthemum nummularium*), and the contrast of a tuft of blue fescue go a long way to liven up a garden.

follow will build on that knowledge, until you, too, can say, "That garden needs something . . . and this is what it is!"

Building on the Basics

With building block gardening, you're creating one workable section at a time, not the whole yard. That means no big areas of torn-up lawn. No special tools. No several days of muscle-aching labor. Your only decisions will be which plants you like best. You'll learn painlessly how to put them together. And that's when gardening becomes a pleasure, instead of a chore that's riddled with uncertainty and insecurity.

Tunnel vision is a big help when it comes to building block gardening. Each garden focuses on the most important effects for that particular location. Making a garden along a fence, for instance, calls for a different look than planting around your front steps.

In each chapter of the book—each garden—you'll find out what the most important effect is for that special area, and how to create it. Then you'll use your same color scheme, and some of the same plants, to make that garden look good. Ultimately, instead of treating each garden as a separate piece,

△ Spiky gray plants instantly say "desert," but they mean "low maintenance," too, not to mention "money-saving." A few plants, widely spaced in gravel mulch, plus rocks, are all you need to get this look.

you're using a lot of the same colors, and often some of the same plants, for the next one.

With the next garden, the hardest part—deciding what you like—is done. You've chosen plants that satisfy your own eye for beauty. With the basics in place, it becomes simply a matter of adding more, in another spot. And you can do that as time and money allow.

Garden designers call this repetition, and you'll be doing a lot of it. Repeating a color, repeating a form (tall and skinny, low and creeping), repeating the same plants—all of this creates a cohesive look.

Your gardens may be separated as far as location, but they all belong together. Your eye will skim over the lawn grass in between to alight on the repeated pinks or yellows, or the spiky iris or tall hollyhocks or other eye-catching forms. Your yard has become a united whole. It all belongs together, because you've repeated colors and forms. Your eye will notice.

The Best Yard on the Block

Get ready for compliments on your new gardens. Your plantings are going to be conversation pieces for your neighbors, and maybe even traffic-stoppers for those walking or driving by.

What a great opportunity to pass along what you've learned! I love to chat with passersby when I'm working in the front yard. It's even more fun to share plants, so I often give them a sample of whatever caught their eye, right then and there, by tearing off a rooted piece of lamb's-ears, or grabbing my shovel to lift a chunk of coneflowers.

Spreading beauty and know-how is one of the best things about gardening. And, who knows, your new gardening buddy may bring you a sample of one of their own treasures in exchange.

Enjoy your own new appreciation for your garden, too. That pride you're feeling is only natural. "I did it myself!" You did. And it's beautiful.

Simple As It Gets: Shape, Color, Style

I can still see the photo of my high school choir in my mind: all of us in matching robes, lined up perfectly by height. That arrangement may work well in a photo in which faces are the focus. But in a garden? Not at all.

▷ Romance is in full bloom in this simple planting of shrub roses, lavender, and lamb's-ears along a cottage picket fence.

△ The simple, good-sized leaves of silvery lamb's-ears are a bold note among dainty sedums and fine-bladed grasses in this colorful mix.

Variety is the name of the game in the garden. Take those plants you've selected and mix them up: a tall one here, short one there, mid-height elsewhere, and something reclining among them. And put a yellow one here, an orange one there, a tall red one, a low white one, a delicate blue one flying in the breeze—whatever combination of shapes and colors you like best. Simply think in terms of color and shape, whether you're planting flowers, shrubs, or grasses, and go for a variety of both.

SHAPE

"Shape" covers a lot of ground, once you start looking at plants. There's the overall shape of a plant, which is easy to see at a glance. But there's also leaf shape and flower shape. And we want to plant a mix of all of these. The simple trick: just use your eyes when you pick out plants, and include a variety of those shapes. That'll make your planting interesting. And an interesting garden is a good garden.

Take a look at any plant, and you can tell its general shape, or form, in an instant. Some are low and sprawling. Some are tall and skinny. Some are fountain-shaped. Some are spiky. Some are mounded in a neat dome. And some—make that, most—are clumps. Their form is nothing special, although their flowers may be gorgeous. Black-eyed Susans, purple coneflowers, Oriental poppies—they're just clumps. Clump forms are perfect for a garden,

▷ Blue veronica, with its upright posture, complements the sprawling roses, while a dense evergreen shrub provides a quiet backdrop that makes the bright colors pop.

△ Maybe the most versatile perennial of all, bearded iris is even more valuable in the garden for its spiky, upright foliage than its glorious flowers. Long after the luscious blossoms are finished, the foliage remains a strong vertical accent.

because plants with dramatic form are best used in small numbers, as accents or focal points. Clump-shaped plants will be the big majority of the garden.

One plant form is a particularly powerful attention grabber: spiky. Our eye goes in an instant to an upright yucca, a stand of bearded iris leaves, or other spiky characters. Spiky plants are like exclamation points. Use spiky shapes to draw attention, and surround them with less forceful plant forms, like clumps, mounds, and sprawlers.

Height goes hand-in-hand with plant form. It's the adjective in front of the plant's overall shape: a tall clump, a knee-high mound, a low sprawler.

When describing plants, there's no need to get too specific about height. Keep it simple with three general categories: low, mid-, and tall. Your eye (or the plant label) will tell you which is which.

Also notice leaf shape. When describing leaves, start by focusing on size: big, medium, small, tiny. Leaves are the main feature that gives a plant its texture. Plants with tiny to small leaves, or with thin, grassy blades instead of leaves, have a fine texture. Increase the size of the leaves, and you may have bold, striking texture. In the garden, you want a mix, to keep things interesting. Big leaves are as strong as spiky plant form—they stand out among small and medium leaves, making us look at them.

You'll see other differences in leaves, too, but as usual, let's keep it easy. Just name it "plain and simple," or "ferny," or "long and skinny, tapering to a point."

When you're putting plants together, take a look, and go for a variety of leaf sizes and shapes. By mixing the forms of the leaves and of the overall plants, you're instantly getting contrast, and that makes the eye look twice. You can build a beautiful conifer collection as easily as a pretty flower garden, for instance, just by combining a variety of different plant forms and leaf shapes.

And when describing the flower shape of plants, make it easy by using your own vocabulary. Is that a daisy? A big daisy, like a black-eyed Susan? A giant daisy, like a sunflower? A little daisy, like a fall aster? Or maybe it's a vertical spike of fuzzy flowers, like liatris, or blazing star (*Liatris* species), or a low splash of small flowers, like creeping phlox.

With flowers, again we want a mix of both size and shape in the garden. A bed of all daisy shapes would be uninspired. Liven it up with spiky liatris flowers, and add low clusters of annual sweet alyssum. You're becoming a garden designer already!

COLOR

You won't need a plant encyclopedia to have a beautiful garden, although those books are mouthwatering to look at. You will find plant names in this book that you may want to look up, to get an idea of their appearance. But with building block design, you can stop thinking about flowers by their names altogether.

Instead, think of the plant as a splotch of color, while keeping its form in mind. That's not a 'Caradonna' salvia; it's a blue-purple clump of spiky flowers. Golden alyssum? Let's think of it as a low patch of bright butter yellow. 'Georgia Blue' veronica spreading like a pool of blue? "Pool of blue" is all we need to know. Using this trick makes arranging your plants as simple as child's play.

Then all you have to do is mix them up: mix colors, while you simultaneously mix forms and shape. Tall spiky red guy, check. Knee-high clump of yellow daisies, got it. Low pool of blue, you bet. It's a garden!

In nature, hardly any color combinations look bad. But some look better than others. And since "good" is what we're going for, those better combinations are our goal.

You want to use contrasting colors: plant colors that are so different that when combined, they stand up and shout for attention, such as rich dark purple next to white, orange-red or maroon with silver, yellow with red.

△ Jazz up the relaxed shapes of perennials and groundcovers with the excitement of spiky yuccas and grasses. But use them sparingly, for special effect.

▷ Similar size, similar overall plant shape, but a big difference in color: as long as one attribute is quite different, even the simplest combinations, like this shrub rose and dwarf blue spruce, can be powerful.

▷ A low, tidy bed of marigolds adds vivid color at the house entrance. A tall fountain of rosy pink cosmos, another super easy annual to grow from seed, is free to spill over in a bed away from foot traffic.

△ Pick your favorite colors, repeat in a variety of plant and flower shapes, and presto— you have an eye-pleasing arrangement. Rusty yarrow holds center stage here, complemented by rosy purple coneflowers.

And you want to use complementary colors: plant colors that harmonize with each other and create restful combinations. Contrast demands a lot from viewers, so these softer complementary combinations provide rest for the eye. But with too many complementary, harmonizing colors, the garden can look blah: for example, pastel blues and pinks are lovely, but when you add a splotch of burgundy foliage among them—that all-important contrast—they come alive.

So use the two together: contrast for pizazz, and complementary colors to calm things down, providing balance.

The Big Bang Effect

Choosing plants with eye-catching flowers that can be seen easily from a distance gives you more bang for your buck, because you need fewer of them to create a show. The annuals and perennials you love can fill that role in three ways:

→ They have colors that stand out like spotlights
→ They have big blossoms, about 2½ inches across or more
→ They blanket themselves in flowers of any size, creating a solid splotch of color

For maximum punch, look for plants that combine two or all three of these showy traits. White color, big flowers, and abundant bloom make Shasta daisies shine like a spotlight. Lavender petunias are a gentle color, but their prolific good-sized flowers hit two marks. A 'Lemon Gem' marigold is diminutive in the size of both the plant and blossoms, but those itty-bitty flowers cover it in a bright splash of lemon yellow.

Spotlight Colors

When we came home after a big wildfire burned near our mountain canyon, we instantly spotted fluttering strips of bright tape decorating every property. Some places had red strips of tape; others, hot pink; and a few spots had orange ribbons. They weren't surveyor markers. They were code, meaning "house up here" or "checked for livestock" or whatever signals the firefighters were sending to each other.

Those colorful strips stood out dramatically. The colors were super bright, and they were uncommon in nature. So, whether they're firefighter signals or Oriental poppies, they yell, "Look at me!" And we do. In the yard, our eye zeroes in on that clump of red geraniums or the bright orange California poppies or those flamboyant bright pink petunias.

If hot colors warm your heart, go ahead and make a spicy salsa garden. If you prefer mild to hot, save the jazzy reds, oranges, and hot pinks for accents, just as you'd put on a bright scarf to liven up a subdued outfit.

White and yellow stand out strongly, too, and they're much more versatile than the spicy hues. They go with any other color, and they brighten the overall effect of your yard. Most of us enjoy white for its congeniality: it gets along with everything. But white can be elegant, especially if you play up that elegance to an extreme with an all-white garden. You simply can't go wrong with white as your spotlight color.

Yellow stands out like sunshine on a cloudy day, and, like white, it goes with just about everything. Yellow comes in a range of shades, from sulphur yellow to butter to rich gold, and these hues are a cinch to match up with other partners.

To get the most bang out of your spotlight colors, intersperse them among your secondary colors to create a satisfying rhythm that the eye can't help but follow as it moves from one highlight to the next.

Secondary Colors

The vast majority of garden flowers aren't showstoppers. Favorites such as lavender, catmint (*Nepeta ×faassenii*), gaura, and many of the warm-colored agastaches such as 'Desert Sunrise' have softer personalities and make

△ Long-lived and long-blooming, gold alyssum glows for months, starting in spring. Plant a scattering of pale blue grape hyacinths to poke up through the cloud of yellow for a charming spring surprise.

excellent quiet partners in the garden. Plants with dark foliage also provide a relaxing contrast to vivid colors, which is good because a garden of nothing but bright, lively show-offs can get tiresome. It makes us want to rub our eyes after that initial "Wow!" response. Everywhere we look, something is demanding our attention.

Softer partners allow our eyes to relax, and so our mind and body relax, too. And quieter plants make showy plants stand out even more. They're the backup singers that let the soloist soar. The black skirt that transfers attention to the special top we're wearing. The neutral sofa we brighten with bold throw pillows.

These plants have soft shapes, as well as smaller flowers. Their leaves aren't big and glossy or stiff and spiky; they have a finer texture. Their form is nothing special—a loose mound or clump that mingles easily with its neighbors. Up close or at a medium distance—say, from the bench in the arbor—they're treasures to admire as you stroll your yard. And, thanks to them, your gardens will be lush, with a romantic sense of abundance. From a distance, they become part of the background, which allows the show-offs to truly show off.

Use this chart—or your own artistic eye—to quickly pick great combinations of spotlight, secondary, and accent colors for your garden.

◁ This gardener's signature color is purple, with accents of red and yellow. Petunias and an edging of annual sweet alyssum carry the theme into fall, when the leaves of the Virginia creeper redden to complement the colors.

Spotlight Color **PICK 1**	*Secondary Colors* **PICK 2 OR 3**	*Accent Colors* **PICK 1 OR 2**
butter yellow	blue, blue-purple, orange-red, pink, purple, red, sulphur yellow, white	deep red, bright red, burgundy
sulphur yellow	blue, blue-purple, hot pink, pale pink, butter yellow, white	orange-red, bright orange, red-purple (magenta), burgundy
golden yellow	hot pink, blue-purple, melon orange, pale pink	burgundy, deep pink
white	pink (any shade), blue-purple, light blue, butter yellow, sulphur yellow, pink-purple	red-purple (magenta), true blue, orange, purple, red-orange
bright orange	blue, white, pale rose-pink, hot pink, melon orange, apricot (pale peach), rusty red-brown	red-purple (magenta), blue-purple, burgundy, lime green
hot pink	pale pink, blue (any shade), white, sulphur yellow, melon orange, apricot (pale peach), rusty red-brown	red-purple (magenta), butter yellow, red-orange, burgundy, lime green
bright red or red-orange	sulphur yellow, true blue, pale blue, blue-purple, purple, butter yellow	white, burgundy, lime green

▷ Look at all the colors in this single spectacular bearded iris. You can choose an entire palette, just by picking up a few of these hues in other plants. Peach, apricot, gold, burgundy, cool deep blue— the choice is yours.

Big Flowers

Some hibiscus plants have flowers so huge, I wonder if the astronauts on the space station can see them. As for so-called dinnerplate dahlias, well, yes, that moniker is an exaggeration, but not by much. Such gigantic blossoms certainly do catch your eye, but you won't need to go to such extremes in your gardens. A more basic 2½- to 3-inch blossom is big enough to command attention from a distance.

Perennial daisies of almost any kind will fill the bill, and you'll find dozens to pick from, from the delicious new warm-hued coneflowers to familiar annual sunflowers. Daylilies and bearded iris come in enough colors to suit any garden. And shrub roses are now everblooming workhorses, thanks to the 'Knockout' series.

Dense clusters of much smaller blossoms, like those of tall garden phlox or pink Jupiter's beard (*Centranthus ruber*), create a substantial show of color from a distance, too. That's the effect we're looking for—flowers of big enough size, whether a single blossom or a cluster, to be easily visible from across the yard. Following are some examples:

FLOWER POWER: BIG-FLOWER EFFECT

Asiatic lily (*Lilium* hybrids)

Basket-of-gold, gold alyssum
   (*Aurinia saxatilis*)

Bearded iris (*Iris* hybrids)

Black-eyed Susan
   (*Rudbeckia* species and hybrids)

Daffodil (*Narcissus* hybrids)

Dahlia (*Dahlia* species and hybrids)

Daylily
   (*Hemerocallis* species and hybrids)

Gladiolus
   (*Gladiolus* species and hybrids)

False sunflower
   (*Heliopsis helianthoides*)

Hibiscus
   (*Hibiscus* species and hybrids)

Jupiter's beard (*Centranthus ruber*)

Petunia (*Petunia* hybrids)

Purple coneflower and
   warm-color coneflowers
   (*Echinacea* species and hybrids)

Red hot poker (*Kniphofia uvaria*)

Rose (*Rosa* species and hybrids)

Shasta daisies
   (*Leucanthemum* ×*superbum*)

Sunflower, annual and perennial
   (*Helianthus* species)

Tall garden phlox
   (*Phlox maculata, P. paniculata*)

Marigold
   (*Tagetes* species and hybrids)

Tulip (*Tulipa* hybrids)

Zinnia (*Zinnia* species and hybrids)

Bring On the Annuals

Annuals exist to make flowers, lots of flowers. Seeds are their reason for being, and the more they can produce, the happier they are. So they bloom their hearts out. Many don't quit until the frost, so their splashes of color can brighten the garden all season. All annuals at your garden center will be easy growers and generous bloomers, so just pick your favorites. Petunias, marigolds, blue ageratum, calendula—scores of common, inexpensive annuals will fill your garden with color that lasts all season.

For the strongest effect from a distance, plant in groups that cover at least 2 feet across with a splash of the same color. A group of three plants is a good rule of thumb; for 'Wave' and other spreading petunias, just one plant is plenty. If your yard is a large one and the viewing distance is greater, just increase the number of plants to make a bigger patch of color.

PENNY-PINCHER TIP
Shrubs for Color

Use shrubs with show-off foliage—moody maroon, golden yellow, lime green, orange, variegated—just as you would flowers, for a patch of pure color. That trick saves money and time, by creating a good-size spot of color with a single plant. One shrub can easily cover the same space as three to six perennials.

Your Garden Style

Next time a photo of a garden—or a real live garden—makes you ooh and ahh, think about what it is that's caught your eye. Try to leave the house in the photo out of the equation, and focus on the yard.

The following multiple-choice quiz will help you pin down what appeals to you most, and how that translates to your garden style. Choose the answer that comes closest to your feelings.

Most gardeners fall somewhere in the middle when it comes to style. We may like a neatly clipped hedge, but we also enjoy a wild billow of perennials. There's no need to stick to strict style guidelines when you plant your garden, but do keep maintenance time in mind.

The gardener's guiding hand is instantly visible in a formal garden. Plants of tidy shapes create a firm sense of control. While most of us can appreciate formal style in public gardens, few of us are willing to put in the time these high-maintenance plantings require.

▷ Alternating colors create a semiformal effect because the gardener's hand is so evident. The bright chartreuse shrubs against the quiet colors of the house add a lively, contrasting touch.

What Is Your Garden Style?

Results

Add up your answers: 1 point for each "a" and 3 for each "b."

7 to 10: You lean toward a more formal style of gardening. You prefer an orderly look, with a yard that instantly shows that there's a strong guiding hand behind the garden.

11 to 18: An informal garden is more your style. You prefer a casual look, although you also like to mix it up, adding a clipped hedge, say, to please your own sense of what works for you.

19 to 24: Informal all the way. No clipped shrubs for you.

1. **Neatly clipped forsythia or unclipped natural growth?**
   a. Get out the shears.
   b. Hands off—I like shrubs that grow naturally.

2. **Garden beds and borders edged with straight lines or with curved edges?**
   a. I like the sense of order and control that straight lines give.
   b. I like the romantic look of curved lines.

3. **Open space of bare ground around each plant, or no bare space between plants?**
   a. I like to see each plant individually, with mulch or bare soil between it and the next plant. That way, I can better appreciate each one.
   b. I like to see plants shoulder-to-shoulder or weaving among each other, with no bare ground between. That way, I can admire the garden as a whole.

4. **Bed of pink tulips, or a rainbow mix?**
   a. Oh, that all-pink would be pretty.
   b. Mix! The surprise is half the fun.

5. **Artistic combination of conifers, or cottage-garden jumble of self-sowing flowers?**
   a. Evergreens.
   b. Cottage garden.

6. **Birds plant sunflowers in your flower beds. What do you do?**
   a. Weed them out as soon as you recognize them.
   b. Let them grow wherever they sprout.

7. **You planted beebalm. It's spreading into your other plants. What do you do?**
   a. Remove every straying bit to keep it in the place it's supposed to be.
   b. Let it go where it wants. The more the merrier!

8. **Garden ornament (assume that money is no object): large marble figure or old wooden chair painted purple?**
   a. Fine art. It's a focal point, after all.
   b. Artsy, that's me. Though I might paint that chair yellow instead of purple.

If you like order and want your gardens to show it, borrow some stylings from formal gardens to use in your semiformal yard. Space your plants widely, with open ground between them, and keep the hedge clippers handy. Boost the presence of broad-leaved evergreens, change that garden gnome to a classic urn, keep the edges of beds and lawn sharply defined, and you've stamped your garden semiformal.

The informal style has an air of romance, thanks to a sense of abundance and lushness, curving lines, plenty of flowers, and an overall casualness about the arrangements—even though you may have spent an hour placing them carefully. You'll still spend time on maintenance, but not nearly as much as you would maintaining a more formal style.

An all-natural style goes even farther. This approach may earn you questioning looks from neighbors, because a garden that looks like nature went wild can look neglected. Balance the wild look with the human touch of wide, tidy paths and arbors, and keep your plants confined to the boundaries of

▽ Casually jammed full of all sorts of plants, this garden reminds us of a walk on the wild side surrounded by the abundance of nature.

△ Simply scrumptious, the warm colors of creeping sedums, coreopsis daisies, and rich red roses are planted in multiples so each kind makes a bigger splash.

your own yard. A sign that announces "Wildlife Habitat" can also help put the neighbors at ease.

Be careful when you're picking out garden features for a house with an emphatic design. A split-rail fence or a formal red brick wall won't go with a long, sleek California-modern house with lots of glass.

Luckily, many houses, from 1940s ranch-style to subdivision modern, have a fairly neutral style. So do most of the fences, trellises, arbors, and benches we may want to add to the yard. Many of those outdoor structures have a timeless classic style that looks great with many types of architecture. But beware of garden structural additions that do have strong personalities, like a white picket fence, for instance, or a log bench, or a rustic twiggy arbor. Keep your house's style in mind to prevent a culture clash and, instead, create the perfect tone.

The style of a garden can go a long way in shifting the effect of your home's overall style. You can play up or play down existing features by using garden style to emphasize them or to counteract them (see table below).

Front Yard Versus Backyard

Our front yards are where we show off—our lovely house, our best sweep of lawn, our neat-as-a-pin tidiness. Our backyards are where we live. They may be cluttered with toys and tools, pocked with holes dug by our dogs, or have a weedy corner, because we're not showing them to the world.

SHIFTING THE STYLE	Adds Formality	Adds Casualness
	Brick wall topped with clipped hedge	Russian sage (*Perovskia atriplicifolia*) spilling over a brick wall
	Straight-edged bed along straight walk	Curving bed along straight walk
	Circular bed	Oval bed with curving outline
	Line of daffodils	Drift of daffodils in lawn
	Large, unbroken expanse of lawn	Freeform oval bed of shrubs in lawn
	No vines on house	Trellises of vines against house
	Row of ornamental grasses	Ornamental grasses in flower bed or in a group of three (two behind, one in front)
	Single evergreen shrub in container	Mix of colorful plants in a container, including trailing types
	All-white garden	A mix of colors
	A bed of tea roses	Climbing roses and shrub roses in perennial beds

▷ A DIY fence and arch, crafted from graceful branches, announces country cottage charm. It would be out of place in front of a sleek modern house or a stately Victorian.

△ Lead the way for friends to enter your front gate with an inexpensive welcome of two dozen daffodils, about $15 for a cheerful splash of springtime.

Still, we want beautiful gardens in both the front and back of our houses. In this book, you'll find specific areas that are clearly front yard concepts, others that are strongly backyard ideas, and some that can be either or both.

ENTER HERE

"We had to paint our front door red," mentioned a friend who'd moved to a new house. "No one could find it." That's one way to do it. But plants are a surefire solution, too. Gardens make it easy for visitors to see right away which way to go. The plantings can guide the eye to the front door.

If you have an obvious paved walk leading to the front door, small gardens at the beginning of the walk and at the doorstep of the house will emphasize the entrance even more. A fence along the front of your property, with a gate highlighted by an arbor, or a simple gap in the fence, helps to funnel visitors to the entrance to your place, while giving you some privacy.

If your front walk is hard to see, perhaps leading from the driveway instead of from the sidewalk, use standout plants with bright colors or striking form to instantly draw a visitor's attention to its location.

And if you have more than one door on the front of the house, mark the appropriate one with a big pot of flowers beside it.

PRIVATE LIFE IN THE BACKYARD

The backyard is for you. It's where you spend time relaxing, sipping lemonade on the patio, or puttering about, playing with your plants. And it's for your family and friends, for playing, sharing a meal around the grill, or just enjoying the outdoors.

Backyards are usually enclosed by a fence or hedge, because no matter how much we like our neighbors, we want to feel free to relax without being watched.

▽ Stout clumps of squash contribute striking contrast to the softer shape of neighboring blue *Caryopteris,* while making it easy to keep up with the harvest on daily strolls through the garden.

The backyard is also an extension of the house. It's the place where we live when we're outside. You'll find easy ways to make it welcoming with the backyard gardens in this book, so that your patio looks pretty, your tall wood privacy fence tends to disappear, and your garden bench actually gets used.

FRONT, BACK, OR BOTH

Bird feeders and birdbaths, hummingbird feeders, and butterfly gardens usually go in the backyard, because that's where we may enjoy them most. But they can add a special touch to our front yard gardens, as well.

Vegetable gardens usually go out back, too, but there's no need to relegate all our food plants to a separate patch hidden from public view. A dwarf apple tree is as pretty in bloom as a nonfruiting flowering cherry—and its fragrance is sublime—so it can be a perfect inclusion in a front garden. Blueberry bushes, which go flaming red in fall, take naturally to life in a garden, as long as you can reach the berries. A bold clump of rhubarb leaves, a bush squash, or a tepee of pole beans can make a fine focal point in either a front or back garden.

Where to Start

Making your front yard look beautiful is fun, and that's the logical place to start making your building block gardens. So the garden chapters in this book begin with your front yard and the entrance to your house. You will also see those gardens every time you come home. Being greeted with beauty can go a long way toward forgetting a stressful day.

Now that you've chosen your favorite plant colors, figured out your style, and know how to look at a plant as color and form, it's time to decide where you want to begin. Which garden do you want to start with? Choose any one you like.

TWELVE EASY, SMALL GARDENS

First Impressions

AT THE LAMPPOST

△ In this lamppost garden at the street, a significant patch of sturdy purple coneflowers are held within a filmy haze of blue Russian sage (*Perovskia*) and blue fescue in the front, and airy *Agastache*, just beginning to bloom, rises behind. The coneflowers self-sow to thicken and extend a planting.

"**W**elcome! A lover of beauty lives here!" That's the message you're sending with this garden at your lamppost, mailbox, or walkway from the street. It's the first planting that visitors and passersby will see. And behind its prettiness lies practicality—it shows guests where your yard begins.

It's a personal pleasure, too, because not only will you enjoy the beauty, but you'll feel rewarded by the looks and comments of appreciation from neighbors and passersby. Your lovely small garden may even inspire a neighborhood trend.

Small Is Beautiful

This garden is a small one, about 3 to 6 feet in diameter, but you're going to pack in plenty of punch. If you have a lamppost or a mailbox at the entrance, the garden will go around that. Otherwise, just choose one corner of the walk to your front door, where it joins the public sidewalk or street, and plant there. You can mirror this garden in the other corner later if you like, but a

▽ "Ever-silver" plants, like the lavender that anchors this entrance, and the permanent presence of rocks, make a garden look good even in late winter.

single-side planting is powerful enough to grab attention. And attention is what you want, since this is the "enter here" sign.

Perhaps you have a few steps at the opening to your yard. If that's the case, plant both sides of the stairs instead of one corner. You want to lead people in, as directly as you can, and plants lining the opening steps are a sure way to do that.

Small though it is, this garden establishes your signature style and your color scheme. Its plants become the basis for gardens in other parts of the yard, because you'll be repeating them.

Most important: unless you're going for extra-quick and simple, with a single attention-getting plant, be sure to mix it up. Even in this small space, you have plenty of room to plant a variety of plant forms, shapes of leaves and flowers, textures, and colors.

Goodbye Grass, Hello Garden

Removing the lawn grass is the first step in making any new garden. Here's how to make quick work of it:

1. Water the area thoroughly. Then, step on a shovel to slice around the perimeter of the area of lawn you want to remove.
2. Kneel, sit, or stoop within the area, about 1 foot back from the edge. Keep a forked dandelion digger and a trowel or hand hoe at your side.
3. Using the trowel, the hand hoe, or your hands, begin lifting the turf free of the soil all along that sliced edge. Peel it, roots and all, back toward you.
4. Continue peeling up the grass, rolling the turf onto itself as if you are rolling up a carpet. You'll be surprised how easily it lifts away from the soil.
5. If the turf balks, give it an extra lift with your trowel or shovel, and keep going.
6. Deeply rooted weeds usually stay rooted while the grass peels away. Remove them down to the bottom of the roots with your trowel or dandelion digger after the sod is off.
7. Dig out any bits of grass you may have missed with your trowel.

That's it. You now have a clean slate for planning a new garden! No need to turn the soil, which will bring weed seeds to the surface. Instead, just dig planting holes for your plants.

▷ In a lamppost garden, you can depend on low-growing shrubs to cover a big area without costing a bundle. A single plant of purple heather, or heath, is the perfect partner for a low, modern classic lamp.

Height Matters Here

Proportionate height is what you want to use in this garden. Start by looking at the lamppost or mailbox. You want to mix it up in this garden, mixing plant forms (tall and skinny, low and sprawly, and so on), and here you'll also include the lamppost as one of the players, which is usually a vertical element. Consider these ideas:

→ If your lamppost or mailbox is a short element, about 3 feet, then tall, skinny plants such as columnar junipers, hollyhocks, or annual sunflowers will look great with it. Their form adds a visual exclamation point, because they're higher than the lamppost or mailbox. The eye will go first to the tall plants, then to the lamp or mailbox, and then to the shorter plants in this garden.

→ Plants that are about one-third as tall as a shorter lamppost or mailbox (about 1 foot) are also just the right height. Skip the tall ones, if you like, and use these instead. Or plant both tall and shorter ones.

→ If yours is a tall lamppost, 5 to 8 feet high, tall "exclamation-point" plants will compete with it for visual attention. Instead, choose plants of mid-height, 2 to 3 feet tall, and clump form, or low sprawlers.

→ Do plant a vine to grow up a tall lamppost. That will make the post a stronger focal point, by visually reinforcing the height. And it's a great way to squeeze even more color into this garden.

→ Steps leading to the walk? Just choose plants of tidy habit that won't interfere with free access, in your signature colors.

△ The strong shape of purple coneflowers grabs the eye among soft-textured spreaders at the lamppost, and ties this yard together by appearing in other gardens.

Plant Shape and Color

Plants of clump form, such as Shasta daisies, purple coneflowers, or a loosely shaped smokebush (*Cotinus coggyria*), are a perfect fit in this garden. So are neatly mounded plants, such as fall mums, 'Purple Dome' aster, blue fescue, or ball-shaped evergreens. And for a third congenial form, look to arching, fountain-shaped plants, such as a weeping Japanese maple, blue Russian sage (*Perovskia atriplicifolia*), or pennisetum grass. These three shapes contrast well with the vertical post, and contrast is what makes a garden interesting to our eyes.

Include a spiky plant to add punch, if you like, but be sparing. This garden is too small, and viewed at too close a range, to accommodate several strong characters, which would look too busy.

This garden is also a great spot to showcase your favorite low-growing plants, such as 'Angelina' or 'Dragon's Blood' sedum or a whole flock of hens-and-chicks (*Sempervivum tectorum*). They won't get lost in the distance, because you're standing right next to them when you look at this garden. And, if you add a vivid yellow-striped 'Color Guard' yucca to the low growers, you've got an instant garden for about $15.

It's also the perfect spot to put a garden ornament. The lamppost already draws the eye, and then it's a simple step down to admire your welcoming ornament (gnome or concrete turtle?). No lamppost or mailbox? Your ornament will command attention all by itself.

The number of plants you'll need depends on their size, but you won't need many. A single hydrangea, Japanese maple, or 'Knockout' rose can hold court all by itself (though, if you're like me, you won't be able to resist tucking other small plants into every inch of bare space). The pleasure of making a garden is in combining plants, so let's aim for a mix. This garden is going to set the tone for future plantings.

Coming and Going

Keep in mind that you'll view this garden from two sides, both coming and going. You can arrange your plants so that lower growers are on all sides, or, if you prefer, spotlight them on two sides only. Put them at the front of the garden—the side that faces the street, from which people enter or view the garden as they drive by—and along the walkway.

Choosing Plants

Plants that make passersby look twice—that's what you want in this garden. Bright patches of color and good-size blossoms are the stars here, with a supporting cast of softer characters.

Keeping your color scheme and plant forms and shapes in mind, head for the garden center or nursery and start shopping. Pick out a perennial plant in your main color. Next, choose two or three annual or perennial companions in your secondary colors. And finally, tuck an accent-color annual or perennial into your cart.

▷ In this living art gallery of succulents, sedums, and other creepers, a mix of colors and shapes makes it intriguing.

▷ Foliage colors are just as much fun to play with as flowers, and they last much longer. Go for a mix of shapes and colors, like this intriguingly curly 'Seafoam' artemisia, upright fescue, and moody barberry. With only three plants, you can achieve big beauty.

◁ A billow of blue Russian sage, golden 'Karl Foerster' feather reed grass, and white daisies make a satisfying—and inexpensive—trio. Planted elsewhere in the yard, the same colors and some of the same plants, spiced up with a dash of red, create continuity through repetition.

PENNY-PINCHER TIP
Annuals and Evergreens

Buying annuals instead of perennials saves money, but you'll have to replant them next year, or invest in perennials later. Still, if your wallet is anemic at the moment, it's a fine way to get the color you crave until you can afford more permanent plants.

You can eliminate the cost of a shrub entirely by substituting an evergreen perennial, such as white candytuft (*Iberis sempervirens*), or an ever-silver plant that holds its gray foliage all year, such as lavender or 'Powis Castle' artemisia.

And you want this area to be beautiful all year round, so add some permanent plants, maybe an ornamental grass and a shrub, to the cart.

The total cost will depend on your choices and the prices where you shop. But if you go for common plants at a big-box store garden center, you should be able to check out for about $25, even with the grass and shrub. If you stick to flowers, you can get away with spending even less.

Another option for a garden at the beginning of the front walkway, especially if you lean toward the formal style, is to plant this area in shades of green. Evergreens are one of the big elements of formal style, so you'd be establishing the tone of your garden right from the opening.

An assortment of three small- to medium-size shrubs of different forms, textures, and shades of green will be plenty. Include a broad-leaved type (everything that doesn't have needles), such as a rhododendron, with conifers, such as creeping juniper, to vary the texture. Add a colored conifer, such as 'Golden Mop' dwarf threadleaf cypress, for extra zing, or keep it elegant and traditional with a quiet palette of greens.

Attention Getters

Now add a focal point. Our eyes notice a thing that just doesn't belong. Strongest of all, for a garden focal point, are human-made objects. They don't belong in a big way; they're not plants. That makes them extra powerful, so use them with restraint.

Certain plants are as dominant to the eye as garden ornaments. A handful of plants have such striking form that they stand out like a spotlight:

→ Contorted hazel, curly willow, fantail willow, weeping trees, and oddball ornamental conifers holler for attention.
→ Ordinary shrubs that have been sheared or pruned into extraordinary shapes draw attention: a ball of forsythia, a square-topped privet, a Pfitzer juniper pruned into "clouds" at the tips of its branches.
→ Yucca, agave, hesperaloe, prickly pear, barrel cactus—desert plants—have distinctive, powerful plant shapes.

The front garden is the perfect spot to showcase your favorite "oddball" plant. Grabbing attention is what this garden is all about, so bring on the unusual. One is enough, for the most clarion characters—the unusually shaped trees and shrubs that cost big money and pack a huge visual punch.

Turn Up the Lights

A plant that becomes a spot-light—that's the first thing to add if you feel your front garden is lacking something. Go for a big splash of bright color, or a dash of white or yellow. No room for another perennial? Annuals are easy to squeeze into tight spaces.

MISTAKES NOT TO MAKE

Less Is More

Dotting your entrance with do-dads will make it look cluttered and busy, because the eye can't resist going back and forth from one to the next. A single garden gnome or whirligig, or a closely spaced family of resin turtles, can be successful. We notice it quickly, for sure, but then the eye moves on.

Whichever ornament you choose, keep in mind that it makes a strong statement about your own personality. A touch of whimsy—one painted birdhouse, or one metal praying mantis sculpture—is plenty to get the point across, without stealing the thunder from your beautiful garden.

In the case of desert plants, their effect is less heavy-handed, and it becomes blunted with repetition. If you plant one at the front, plant it in other areas, too, to strengthen the visual connection among your separate gardens.

Trial Run

Before you move your plants out of their pots and into the ground, set them where you think they'll look good. Redo the arrangement often, until your eye is satisfied. Moving a plant as little as 6 inches backward, forward, or sideways can make a big difference in the overall effect. Keep in mind, too, the eventual size of the plant, especially if you're starting with smaller sizes. Half an hour of time now will save you hours later. So play with your pots until you're happy, before you get out the shovel. And, as always, trust your eye.

Rocks

When I moved to the deep clay soil of southern Indiana many years ago, the first thing I noticed was that there were no rocks. I could dig freely, without a rock ever stopping the shovel. That was great, for sure. But once my bed was dug, I wanted rocks to use as garden accents, and there simply weren't any. Now I live in the Rockies, which, as I keep reminding myself every time my shovel sends sparks, were certainly well named. Luckily (or unluckily, depending how you look at it), most areas of the country have rocks aplenty. If your yard isn't personally blessed with them, you can find all shapes and sizes at landscaping supply yards.

△ The solid visual strength of rock, accented with a young hesperaloe spike, stands out among a spill of blue hardy geraniums and lavender.

◁ At this front walkway, a serene symbol of compassion, the standing Buddha gets a place of honor before a few low-key plants that remain in the background rather than compete for attention.

Why do we want rocks? They're attention-getters. Even though rocks are natural objects, they still make us look at them in a garden bed—because they're not plants. And they are a great way to make plants look even better. The contrast of the rock with the plants nearby makes an instant *ahhh* spot.

Rocks are also a trick for artfully filling a space without investing in plants. Not only does the rock itself take up room in the bed, but you'll want to leave some open space around it on at least one side to show it off. In a more formal garden, rocks can save you many dollars on plants, because they stand alone, taking up even more room.

You'll be using rocks in other gardens, especially when you're extending plantings. And, as with particular plants and colors, the place to start is with that very first garden: at the beginning of the front walkway. As your yard progresses, the rocks will add another element of that all-important repetition, just like the plants.

A giant boulder at the front walkway (or in the lawn) is a popular garden element, or maybe it was just hard to remove once it was there. But it's not

▷ Don't forget to smell the roses—and appreciate how their colors are repeated in the coneflowers and yellow yarrow elsewhere in this yard.

▽ Color in winter is a sight for starved eyes until flowers start to bloom. Include some fancy conifers to brighten the winter garden and welcome you home.

necessary to hire a backhoe to put an accent rock at your lamppost, or anywhere else. Smaller rocks, about breadbox-size, are much more appealing, because they look more natural.

Smaller doesn't necessarily mean easy to handle, though, when it comes to rocks. These rocks can be mighty heavy. Enlist a helper, even if you think you can manage it all by yourself. No sense risking your back.

Long Bloomers

The sad truth about perennials is that most are in bloom for only two weeks. Fifty weeks of the year, that clump of glorious Oriental poppies is only green leaves, or sleeping below ground. That's not okay for a front garden. In that important spot, we want flowers that keep on going and going.

Annuals are the easy answer. Once they start in late spring, most don't quit until frost lays them low. But some perennials are extra-generous with their length of bloom, too, and you won't have to replant them each spring as you do with annuals.

LONG-LASTING FLOWERS

These dependable, easy-care perennials bloom for at least one month, and many bloom all season:

'Autumn Joy' sedum
　(*Sedum* 'Autumn Joy')

Anise hyssop (*Agastache foeniculum*)

Basket-of-gold, gold alyssum
　(*Aurinia saxatilis*)

Black-eyed Susan
　(*Rudbeckia* species and hybrids)

Catmint (*Nepeta* ×*faassinii*)

Columbine
　(*Aquilegia* species and hybrids)

Coneflower
　(*Echinacea* species and hybrids)

Coreopsis (*Coreopsis* species and
　hybrids)

Hardy geranium 'Rozanne'
　(*Geranium* 'Rozanne', hybrid)

Hollyhock (*Alcea rosea*)

Hummingbird mint
　(*Agastache* hybrids, warm colors)

Purple rockcress (*Aubrieta deltoidea*)

Russian sage (*Perovskia atriplicifolia*)

Shasta daisy
　(*Leucanthemum* ×*superbum*)

Sweet William (*Dianthus barbatus*)

Tall garden phlox
　(*Phlox maculata, P. paniculata*)

Veronica (*Veronica* species
　and hybrids, especially 'Sunny
　Border Blue')

Winecup (*Callirhoe involucrata*)

▷ Yellow is one of the strongest spotlight colors, and hearty *Rudbeckia*, or black-eyed Susan, blooms for months.

△ Grow a large-flowered clematis up the lamppost to squeeze more flowers into the limited space and to vary the height of the display.

▷ The cheerful welcome of a patch of sunflowers costs just the price of a packet of seeds—or nothing at all, if you plant a handful of birdseed.

Vines

It's amazing how strongly a small front garden can set the scene for an entire yard. It's a beauty by itself, of course, but it also gives us the colors and the plants that we'll repeat throughout other gardens around the yard. So this is the place to pick a vine that you'll use again, in other settings. For beauty and versatility, nothing beats clematis, which generally have big flowers in rich colors that go with any color scheme, and a relatively tame growth habit.

Large-flowered clematis vines are more suited to this garden than their small-flowered cousins, the sweet autumn clematis (*Clematis terniflora*) and virgin's bower (*Clematis virginiana*). Unlike those vigorous species, which are rampant growers, the vines of most large-flowered clematis reach only about 10 feet long. Cut back the plant to about 6 inches above ground level in late spring, to make way for the new flush of growth and flowers.

Most large-flowered clematis, with the exception of old-fashioned dark purple 'Jackmanii', won't cover an arbor or pergola, but they will add gorgeous color on a wood or wire trellis—or a lamppost or mailbox post. They are perfect with climbing roses in other areas of the yard, another trick to strengthen repetition.

For a completely different effect that will make your hummingbirds happy, consider coral honeysuckle (*Lonicera sempervirens*). It's more vigorous than clematis, and it'll hug a lamppost as well as cover an arch. You may need to help it climb at first, by tying the stems to the support. Be ruthless about snipping back errant stems—this vine responds to pruning with a flush of new growth, becoming denser and more compact, with a new burst of bloom.

Finishing Touches

How's it look? That's the big question with any finished project, so take your time looking at your new garden from all sides. Stand at a distance, too, to gauge the impact of the colors and forms. It's a cinch at this point to lift any plant that seems to be in the wrong spot and give it better placement.

When your front garden suits your eye, put down a layer of mulch around all the plants, to about 1 inch from the edge of the walk, sidewalk, and lawn. Taper the depth of the mulch near the walk, so that it's about ½ inch lower than the paving. The paving will act as a barrier to keep bits of gravel or bark from straying. Dig out some soil if necessary along the edges to create a shallow trench to hold the mulch.

First Impressions

AT THE LAMPPOST

This front garden, about 4 by 5 feet, is the first thing passersby see. A long-blooming, trouble-free 'Sunny Knockout' rose sets a cheerful tone, with complementary light, bright whites and a touch of moody blue. Plant daffodils and tulips in fall for early spring color.

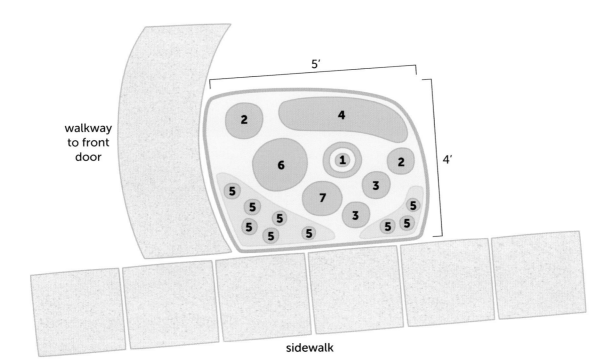

walkway to front door

5′

4′

sidewalk

1. 'Ramona' large-flowered clematis (*Clematis* 'Ramona'),
   1 plant
2. Shasta daisy (*Leucanthemum ×superbum*),
   2 plants
3. 'May Night' salvia (*Salvia ×sylvestris* 'May Night'),
   2 plants
4. 'Blue Star' juniper (*Juniperus squamata* 'Blue Star'),
   1 plant

5. 'Carpet of Snow' annual alyssum (*Lobularia maritima* 'Carpet of Snow'),
   9 plants (or sow 1 packet of seed)
6. 'Sunny Knockout' rose (*Rosa* 'Sunny Knockout'),
   1 plant
7. 'Elijah Blue' blue fescue (*Festuca glauca* 'Elijah Blue'),
   1 plant

Welcome Home

AT THE ENTRANCE

△ A warm purple door and trellis, coppery coleus, and lime sweet potato vine hint at the artsy personality of this homeowner. Notice that the pot is set beside the stoop, not on it, to allow ample room for visitors.

T his doorstep garden is for you. It's also for visitors and guests. And it's for those who walk or drive past your house, and will enjoy taking a look. But mainly, it's for you, to admire whenever you see it.

The front-door area is a spot where you can put colors and plants that would get lost in other plantings. Instead of being sadly overlooked, they'll get plenty of attention, because this garden is the most private pleasure of them all. It's viewed from up close as you go in and out of the house a dozen times a day.

And if you have a front porch you spend time on, you'll love it even more. Not only do you get to delight in looking at this doorstep garden, but it's right there in handy reach. So go ahead—putter around to admire, tuck special treasures in wherever you like, and enjoy the anticipation of the next thing to bloom.

▷ Purple flowers echo the purple door and step, but in spring, all eyes go to the fabulous venerable flowering crabapple. Tulips bring the tree's color down to ground level.

Suitable Plants

Easy access. That's what you want in this garden area.

Start by pruning back the branches of your existing foundation shrubs so that your home's entrance is wide and welcoming, without twiggy branches that reach out. The haircut may look raw for a week or two, but the shrubs will quickly fill in along the new and better boundary.

Avoid plants that lean or keel over, such as miscanthus grass or old-fashioned peonies, unless there's a railing at the steps that will keep them from falling onto the entrance. Include plants that add beauty all year—evergreen shrubs and perennials and ever-silvers, such as lavender.

Use the same plants on both sides of the steps—the same colors, same flower shapes, the same plant shapes—so your entrance is symmetrical. Spiky plants are the strongest way to say, yes, we're a pair, because they have the most powerfully eye-catching form. Settle a spiky-leaved perennial, such as bearded iris, yucca or agave (at least 2 feet away from the touch of passersby), or an ornamental grass, on each side of the entrance, and it's instant symmetry—even if other plants aren't the same—because the eye goes there first. Not a fan of the spiky look? Go for tall, skinny plants as an accent, such as a pair of columnar junipers or hollyhocks.

If pairing up the same plants sounds too matchy-matchy, aim for similarity, not exact sameness. Similar colors, similar plant forms, similar heights, so that your entrance looks balanced, not lopsided. And plant just one tall or spiky accent, instead of a matched pair. It will still draw the eye to your entrance, and that's the goal here.

A SINGLE COMPELLING CHARACTER

Grab your wallet and head to the garden center, because the front entryway area is a perfect place to put in a single special tree or shrub, one with an attention-getting silhouette or bright winter bark.

In winter, with your house as a backdrop, the curled and twisted branches of Harry Lauder's walking stick (*Corylus avellana* 'Contorta') or the vivid color of coral bark Japanese maple (*Acer palmatum* 'Sango-Kaku') will show off better here than in open areas of your yard.

Character plants cost more than commoners, but if you can squeeze one into the budget, it'll delight your eye all through winter—and that's priceless.

△ Curly willow's gracefully twisting branches, bare of leaves, are an artistic accent from fall through early spring.

▷ Unexpected color is a treat at the doorstep. Lime green heather, or heath, adds a contrasting punch below the rusty red steps, and the soft red buds of pieris mirror the colors.

△ 'Blue Star' junipers complement the single lamppost, but the dramatic fan leaves of palms in mosaic pots pull the eye onward to the doorstep.

▷ You can't go wrong with good old geraniums for a super show from a single plant at the doorstep, or in any garden. The big, bright, prolific flower heads grab attention anywhere, even when planted in the Colorado State University Trial Gardens.

AVOID HAZARDS

You don't want dangers in this garden, because people and pets will be passing by. Keep all poky, spiny, thorny plants at a safe distance, about 2 feet, from the entranceway. You don't want passersby to accidentally get stabbed if they take a misstep, or reach for the handrail and grab a thorny rose.

Keep dropped leaves, berries, and petals in mind, too. They can be a hazard to passing feet, especially when wet. Camellias are lovely, but are not good next to the steps when their big, blowsy flowers fall. You also don't want these items tracked into the house.

No matter what your garden style, casual or semiformal, you want the entrance to look tidy. Stick with plants that don't require fussing to clip off dead flowers or prune back into bounds, and you're saving time on maintenance.

USE REPETITION

Repetition is our mantra, so you'll want to use some of the same colors you've chosen for other areas. That alone is enough to make the yard feel like it's all part of the same whole. Pink at the lamppost? Some pink at the entrance.

Depending on how big your doorstep area is, you may or may not decide to use some of the same plants you have used in the lamppost garden. But it's a nifty way to save pennies and time, and chances are, you can slice off a piece to use in this garden. Sunny yellow 'Happy Returns' daylily at the mailbox? It will look just as cheerful here, by the steps.

Long-blooming workhorse perennials are always welcome. So are easy-care evergreen shrubs and ornamental grasses, which will strengthen the harmonious effect of your yard even in winter.

COLOR CONSIDERATIONS

If your house is a definite color, not a goes-with-everything neutral, make sure your doorstep garden complements or contrasts with that hue. Pink, red, blue, purple, yellow houses, as well as red brick, all call for a little caution when selecting colors for your doorstep garden. Pay attention to the color of your trim, too, and choose plant colors that either echo it or contrast successfully with it.

Also consider the color of your entrance steps, if you have them, and of your porch floor, so you can adjust your colors accordingly. And don't forget

△ Simple is good—and usually much cheaper. Bearded iris edged by a tidy groundcover, highlighted with silvery lamb's-ears and a golden euonymus shrub, are a handsome combination nearly year-round.

the front door! If yours is a strong color, make sure to choose plant colors that stand out. You want contrast here, not matching colors that will disappear (white against white, for instance) or clashing colors that look dissonant anywhere, but especially in this garden.

If your house has a warm red brick façade, keep cool pinkish purple flowers away from that, for instance, or make sure there's plenty of neutralizing green or white between the flowers and the brick. Blooming redbud trees (*Cercis canadensis*) against bricks do catch the eye in early spring, but not in a good way. Color clashes at the doorstep are much more noticeable than in other areas of the yard. The house colors are the background for this garden, so keep them in mind when you're choosing plant colors. And, should you decide to repaint your house, you will want to select hues that go with the garden, so you won't have to change the plantings.

The doorstep is a strong player in the overall theme of your yard, so it needs a powerful garden. Highlight it with enough of your signature color to be easily seen from the street. Go for large, bright flowers, too, or plants with big, bold leaves. Or, as a simple alternative, try ornamental grass or an evergreen, and paint your front steps a bright color. If your doorstep garden still lacks punch, here's an easy fix: add a big container at the home's entrance, just below or above the steps. The bigger, the better—for most houses, a container that's about 2 to 3 feet tall will be just right.

LESSER LIGHTS

Once your spotlight colors have been selected—the eye-catching white, yellow, pink, red, or orange flowers that you want to repeat throughout the yard—you can add any color you please in this garden. Those high-power hues will satisfy the eye from a distance, reinforcing this garden as part of the bigger picture.

Continue the color theme if you like, by adding your secondary and accent colors. But if you're itching to expand your palette, this is the place to do it. You can skip the secondary and accent colors altogether, and go for something new and different. Or you can integrate additional colors into your standard assortment.

In other gardens, you may want to choose colors that stand out from a distance. But this planting is up close and personal. So, once you have your spotlight colors in place, have fun playing with colors that don't need to shout

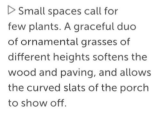
▷ Small spaces call for few plants. A graceful duo of ornamental grasses of different heights softens the wood and paving, and allows the curved slats of the porch to show off.

from across the yard. That luscious cobalt blue that disappears at a distance? It would be perfect here. And the same goes for the 'Domino Lime Green' flowering tobacco (*Nicotiana alata*) you fell in love with, or the green 'Envy' zinnia you've been wanting to try.

LITTLE TREASURES

Small plants and small flowers can get the attention they deserve in the doorstep garden. Snowdrops, crocuses, violets, Johnny jump-ups—you don't need to plant dozens to make a splash when you're going to be looking at them from just a few feet away.

Here's the place to experiment with new annuals or perennials, too. You can see for yourself how vigorous or satisfying they are before you invest in multiple plants and the time to plant them elsewhere. For example, 'Limerock Ruby' coreopsis certainly is pretty, but it may not come back the next year. The color of purple heliotrope (*Heliotropium arborescens*) may make your heart sing and the vanilla fragrance is divine, so you'll want to keep it right here— even if it does disappear from 20 feet away.

That's the beauty of the building block garden: you can add some special gems as your wallet and free time allow. In the meantime, a simple, basic planting will make this garden look good.

THINK SPRING

Spring-blooming plants brighten the garden and lift our spirits. Be sure to plant some at your doorstep, where you'll be able to enjoy them often.

The doorstep is also the ideal spot for spring-blooming shrubs. Azaleas are a classic, or you can try deciduous beauties, such as vivid orange-red flowering quince (*Chaenomeles* hybrids), a waterfall of white bridal wreath spirea (*Spiraea ×vanhouttei*), or flowering almond (*Prunus glandulosa* 'Sinensis'), whose bare stems are lined with fluffy pink bumbles. All are old reliables that are widely available at nurseries and garden centers in the spring.

If you have enough space in this area (and your budget) for a small tree, an ornamental flowering cherry could look beautiful here in spring. Save the flowering crabapple for a different location, though—its dropped fruit will make your entrance messy.

Snuggle in some spring bulbs, too. Tulips and daffodils fall into the "large flowers" category, so you can limit yourself to a clump of three to five here and

▷ A dozen tulips cost about as much as a fast-food meal, and you'll enjoy them for much longer. Plant in clumps of the same color instead of one by one, to boost the impact.

△ Give a stunning dark-colored shrub like this smokebush (*Cotinus coggyria*) the spotlight at the doorstep. A single clump of silvery blue oat grass (*Helictotrichon sempervirens*) enhances the drama.

there, and still make a big impact with only a few dollars. But spring bulbs are inexpensive enough, if you buy in wholesale quantities, to plant hundreds, even thousands, throughout your yard. (You can buy daffodil bulbs for as little as $25 for 100, if you order large quantities; check the Resources section at the end of this book for sources.)

Many favorite spring bulbs are small, including crocuses, snowdrops, Grecian windflowers (*Anemone blanda*), and charming miniature daffodils, such as 'Tête-à-tête' or 'Minnow'. So the doorstep garden is perfect for them. They can be easily seen as you enter and leave your home.

A Grand Entrance

We can't make a short flight of practical steps look like a romantic, sweeping staircase, but we can fool the eye with plantings that create a grander entrance. Continuing your doorstep garden along the walk for a few feet gives the entrance to your house the welcoming air of arms opened wide. It can also increase the overall visual width of even a narrow sidewalk, so visitors stroll along in a relaxed way, instead of scurrying up to the entrance.

You'll want plants with some height planted along the front of your house, so that the bare foundation isn't exposed. Most of them may already be in

△ Nothing says "Come on in!" like a walkway lined with pretty colors. Low-growing yellow alyssum and common, easy creeping phlox are the stars for more than a month in spring, with bearded iris leaves adding welcome vertical contrast.

place. But for the walk leading to the porch or front door, choose lower plants, from ground-huggers to a height of about 8 inches, which will echo the flatness of the walk. Break them up with plants of other forms, if you like, such as clumps of spiky bearded iris or dwarf shrubs. But don't solidly line the walk with shrubs; that feels like a chute and makes feet want to hustle along.

If you would like a formal touch, you may want to create a low, neatly clipped hedge lining both sides of the walk. Choose a plant you've used or plan to use in another garden for the hedge, to keep the continuity going— boxwood, lavender, or, in mild climates, rosemary. Follow the lines of the walk, curving or straight, and allow space for mulched ground between the hedge and walk, and hedge and lawn, to reinforce the orderly note and make the planting look wider.

With the doorstep garden in place, and perhaps the lamppost garden at the street, it's also an easy matter to extend the gardens to line the entire walkway, if you like.

Human-made objects are strong attention-getters, so you might want to put a big pot near your front door to boost the impact of your garden. If you have a shady porch, that container won't be instantly visible from the distance, so add a second one (or a pair) near the steps.

In this garden, your favorite gnome or turtle will disappear from a distance, but you can settle your "friends" here, too, for your own personal pleasure. If you'd rather use an ornament as a focal point instead of a container, choose one of substantial size, at least 3 feet tall.

Enjoy the Beauty, and Enter with Ease

A few plants can make a big difference in the welcoming look of your home. Start with early blooming spring bulbs for a cheerful kickoff to the summer flowers to come. Remember to plan ahead for winter, with ornamental grasses, interesting shapes, and the colors of evergreen foliage and bright bark. Highlight your favorite garden ornaments here, too, to greet your visitors with classic style or a bit of humor.

Keep the practical side in mind, too, by selecting plants that don't interfere with people coming and going. Pretty, with a purpose—that's the piece we're putting together in the doorstep garden.

A Welcome Garden
AT THE ENTRANCE

This welcoming garden is two sections about 3 by 6 feet, tapering to 1 foot wide. Two simple containers anchor the garden, and one serves double duty as a nursery bed. A bunch of fresh (not dried) curly willow (*Salix matsudana* 'Tortuosa') twigs, bought from a florist for about $1 a stem, are shoved into the lower pot to root; meanwhile, they add an accent of unusual twisting stems to the garden. Plant tulips and other spring bulbs in fall for early spring color at the entrance.

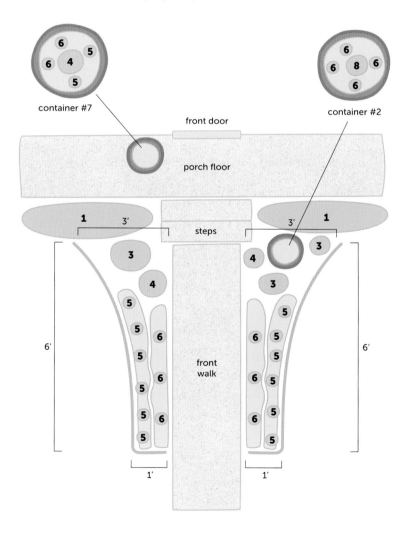

1. Existing foundation shrubs
2. Large glazed pot, holding curly willow twigs (*Salix matsudana* 'Tortuosa') with an edging of blue annual lobelia (*Lobelia erinus*, or other blue cultivar)
3. Shasta daisy (*Leucanthemum ×superbum*), 3 plants

4. Salmon geranium (*Pelargonium* species and hybrids), 3 plants
5. 'Lemon Gem' marigold (*Tagetes tenuifolia* 'Lemon Gem'), 14 plants, or sow 1 packet of seed in the garden and 1 packet in pots
6. Annual blue lobelia (*Lobelia erinus*, or any blue cultivar), 12 plants

7. Glazed pot, holding 'Lemon Gem' marigolds (*Tagetes tenuifolia* 'Lemon Gem'), annual blue lobelia (*Lobelia erinus*, or any blue cultivar), and a salmon geranium (*Pelargonium* species and hybrids)
8. Live curly willow twigs (*Salix matsudana* 'Tortuosa') from a florist, 6 to 8 stems

A Pretty Frame

AT THE CORNERS

△ A spread of lavender woodland phlox (*Phlox divaricata*), a spot of purple pansies, and the crowning glory of flame tulips to take over where fading daffodils left off—what a delightful and easy way to mark the corners of the yard!

▷ No need to cover every inch of a garden—mulch will make it look finished, even with empty space. Here, a super-simple combination: a mound of gold, a splash of silver, and upright iris leaves for vertical zest.

△ Deep shredded bark mulch keeps weeds down in the wide spacing of this pretty corner. Roses add height to serve as corner posts, while other plants contribute a variety of foliage shapes.

I'll bet you know exactly where your property stops and your neighbor's starts, even if there's no marker at the boundary line. We humans are doggedly territorial critters, whether we live on a tiny lot or a huge, rolling estate. In the backyard, fences are an easy way to mark our territory. In the front yard, however, a tall, stout fence between neighbors—or along the street—tends to be overkill. And it's usually not necessary, either.

All you need are corner gardens—plantings in each of the two front corners of your yard. Corner gardens are a friendly way to stake your claim, but they have bigger, better reasons behind them: beauty, of course, is number one. But they're also a powerful tool for focusing attention on your place, while making it feel even more welcoming.

Warm and Welcoming

Even though part of the reason for planting a pair of corner gardens is to mark your territory, you'll make your yard seem friendlier by defining those boundaries. Our ancient ancestors may have stalked the savannah, but we're a lot more comfortable when we feel cozy instead of vulnerable to the wide open spaces. Corner gardens limit the space of our front yard, whether it's a little city lot or an acre in a subdivision.

▷ Groundcover sedums are a quick way to fill a corner—if it has edging to contain them. Grasses add height and soften the brick wall, while geraniums add a dab of color.

MISTAKES NOT TO MAKE
Corners That Aren't

Beds of other shapes, such as squares or circles, can mark the corners, too, but they don't create a sense of enclosure. Instead of inviting the eye into the yard, they'll halt it right there. If you already have an existing square or circular bed at the corner, now's the time to turn it into a cozy-feeling L. Lengthen the legs to fashion an inviting, enclosing corner, and for strongest effect, curve the inside inward. If you change a convex curve on the inside to a concave line, you won't even have to buy any plants—those you remove when you're changing the shape will fill the new legs.

Corner gardens direct attention to the yard as a whole: the space between the corners. Once we take in the space between, then our eye goes to the corners themselves. Oh, how pretty!

Let's play a quick little game. Pretend you're taking a picture. Now, hold up your hands, and frame the scene you're going to snap. Look at your hands. What shape are they making? They're making Ls. They're corners. Outside corners, enclosing the space within—the part you want to focus on. That pair of Ls works just as simply for framing a yard. Even if you've already marked the front boundary of your yard with a fence, swinging the ends of that border around the corner will soften that straight line, and keep the eye moving through the yard.

The corner gardens are L-shaped: one leg goes along the front boundary, and one leg goes along the side. Make the legs roughly equal in length, for starters. Later, when time and money allow, you can extend the legs, if you like. But for now, we're just doing a short L, 6 to 8 feet long on each leg.

The outside of the L should be square and straight, because you're marking a boundary. The inside boundary of that L-shaped bed can be whatever you want. If your style is formal, a straight block-letter L reinforces the sense of control that appeals to your sensibilities. If your style is informal, you may

△ A California wildflower with an icon of genteel English gardens? Why not, when the colors of the California poppies and the clematis are so spectacular together. Scatter the poppy seeds in early fall, to get a head start on bloom time.

want to make your corner bed a triangle, with the inside curved for a touch of grace. A triangular bed lets you get more plants into the space, too.

Make a Pair

Even a single corner garden will help draw attention to the rest of the yard. But if you can, create a pair to make your point. Corner gardens work most powerfully in pairs. Like a pair of pillars marking the entrance of a driveway, they direct our eyes to the scene in between.

If we're outside the yard, looking in, we have a natural stopping point for our gaze: the house. It doesn't matter how that house is situated, or how far back from the street it is. The big solid structure says "Whoa." That's why we don't need four corner gardens, in either the front yard or the backyard.

We already have a boundary at the end of the view. From outside looking in, it's our dwelling we call home sweet home. If we're inside the yard or inside the house, looking out, the corner gardens create the stopping point of our gaze.

Most of us have already staked our territorial claim with fences in the backyard. Yes, it's tempting to plant along the fence, and you may have already done that. But corner gardens add color and beauty, because they're wider, deeper, and more graceful than a straight strip along the fence. Plus, you'll be curving the inside of that L, and curves are beautiful.

Your front yard isn't visible from the backyard, and vice versa. So you can treat the corner gardens in these areas separately. Sunlight or other conditions often are different in the front and the backyard, which is another good reason for planting in separate pairs. In a sunny front yard, you might liven up the corners with bright poppies, spiky bearded irises, a shrub rose, and a graceful fountain of 'Morning Light' miscanthus grass. In a shady backyard, your corners might hold shade-loving azaleas, hostas, and early blooming blue lungwort.

WEIGHT

Corner gardens are anchors. Their visual weight holds the yard in place like stakes at the corners of a tent. And that calls for some heft. Wispy, delicate plants, such as fountain grass (*Pennisetum* species) or 'Whirling Butterflies' gaura, and pastel colors are pretty, but they aren't heavy enough to anchor a whole yard.

Instead, think beefy. Make your anchoring corners heavier by including evergreens and other plants with dense foliage. Look for big-leaved bergenia, Oriental poppies, hostas, or other stout perennials, to provide even more solidity. A single breadbox-or-bigger rock, or a few of them if your back can handle it, contribute weight, too. It's all about balance: you are balancing the corner beds against the whole yard, so they need to be heavy and strong.

Once you have the heavy hitters in place, add some lightweights, too. Finer foliage, smaller flowers, pale colors—you need some dainty yin for all that beefy yang. Ornamental grasses are a quick way to add that feminine touch, so pop in a clump or three among the big brothers. Plan for each type of plant to cover an area of 2 feet or more in diameter. We want a solid swath of each plant, not a dainty little dab.

DON'T PLANT A PROBLEM
Stop Right There!

Avoid notoriously aggressive plants that could infiltrate your lawn or your neighbors' yards. Steer clear of bamboo, goutweed (*Aegopodium podagraria*), and Jerusalem artichoke (*Helianthus tuberosum*), the three most aggressive and impossible-to-remove offenders. Say no to plume poppy (*Macleaya cordata*) and cup plant (*Silphium perfoliatum*), too, which are also infamously pushy in many areas. All have deep, running roots that can travel a mile a minute, or so it seems. Use a bed edging along the neighbors' side for a neat, tidy line and to keep overenthusiastic plants from trespassing into their lawn.

△ Most early spring perennials aren't as big as summer bloomers, but they are every bit as welcome. Go for yellows for farthest visibility, and bolster the garden with tulips and other bulbs.

▷ A corner garden of cactus, yuccas, and other desert plants in gravel suits this gardener's personal style, even with lush green lawn and trees.

▷ An old concrete post
denotes this corner,
extending into a simple
boundary-marking chain line
that says "fence."

◁ A pedestal birdbath makes a strong, calming focus in a corner jumble of roses, delphiniums, and red hot poker.

You can mirror the planting in your second corner, if you like. But you don't have to use exactly the same plants or the same arrangement. Corner gardens work great as a complementary pair, not necessarily an exact match. Even if the plants are arranged differently, use plants with similarities.

Repeat the main colors you used in the lamppost and entrance gardens. Continue the color scheme and repeat some of the same plants, so that the corners become part of the whole. Salmon geraniums at the doorstep? Salmon geraniums in the corners—or salmon petunias or salmon coneflowers. Yellow 'Happy Returns' daylilies at the lamppost? Yellow daylilies in the corners.

STRETCHING THE HEIGHT

You want the corner gardens to stand out from other flower beds and borders, and boosting the height of the bed itself is an alternative to using tall plants. An alternative, mind you, not an addition! If you crown a raised bed with a clump of hollyhocks or a columnar juniper, your plants will look as if they're itching to go airborne.

To do this, it's easiest to dump several wheelbarrow loads of soil in the corner, after you remove the grass. No need to build Mount Everest. Even a low rise of, say, 8 to 10 inches will add sufficient emphasis. Settle a few rocks in the bed, and mulch it generously to keep rain from washing away the soil. As the soil settles, it will stay in place, especially once the roots of your plants spread.

If you want your corner beds higher than about 1 foot, you'll need to wall them in to prevent erosion. Readymade interlocking pavers, landscape timbers, or natural rock require more work and more money, but they're worth every penny over time. Landscape timbers are the cheapest approach, but they only make square edges. If you want that graceful curve on the inside of the corner, use bricks, rocks, or pavers there.

PUNCTUATE THE CORNER

Corners are the place to go bold! And an exclamation point is the perfect place to start. Columnar junipers, 'Sky Pencil' holly, and other evergreens that grow in a narrow, upright shape are about as close to a living exclamation point as you can get. They'll look stiff and unnatural, though, unless you give them some friends—also evergreens—of softer shape to counteract their unusual form.

Any tree will serve as a punctuation point all by itself because of its height. Plant punctuation marks come in a variety of shapes, but you'll know them

PENNY-PINCHER TIP
On a Slant

A sloped raised bed saves money. Simply slope the corner downward in a gentle descent until it meets the lawn, keeping the highest part at the back. You'll only need blocks or timbers on the backside of the L, because the front curve will flow right into the lawn. Edge the front with pavers, stone, or brick, if you like, or plant an edging of sweet alyssum, dwarf bearded irises, dwarf marigolds, or other tidy plants along the curve to define the line. Be sure to allow enough space for a lawnmower's wheel along the edge, to save time on maintenance later.

when you see them. Look for anything beyond the usual loose mound—ball shapes, such as 'Sunjoy Citrus' barberry; weeping flowering cherries; twisting, graceful Japanese maples.

We've been talking about trees and shrubs, but perennials add punctuation, too. Look for accent plants that grab the eye with their shapes—spiky yuccas, tall hollyhocks or red hot poker, fountains of miscanthus grass.

Another option, and it's a tempting one, only takes five minutes to get the effect: plant a trellis for a punctuation point. Inexpensive metal trellises, sold at garden centers for about $20, take just a few minutes to put up, because the legs serve as built-in supports when you push them into the ground. Keep the flat surface of the trellis parallel with the street or sidewalk for best visibility. Even in winter, when your morning glories, scarlet runner beans, or other vines have died back, the structure will still be a high point.

Whichever punctuation point you pick, put your choice at the corner itself, roughly centered at the angle of your L bed. It's your corner post.

▷ An outlined corner, anchored with a hefty rock and lilac and brightened with gold alyssum, proudly marks the end of this yard.

Add the Divas

Look for drama queens to jazz up your corner gardens—accents of loud color or arresting shape. For a quick fix to boring corners, pop in a pot of 'Wave' petunias, or a commanding clump of strappy, white-striped 'Cosmopolitan' miscanthus grass, or a spiky New Zealand flax or yucca. Presto!

ALL-YEAR BEAUTY

You'll want the corner gardens to look good year-round. That means evergreens and ever-silvers and ornamental grasses. All contribute a splash of color when the world is winter gray or blanketed in snow.

Small flowering trees, such as dogwood or redbud, have appealing forms even when their branches are bare. And so do clump-forming deciduous trees, such as birches or aspens.

Add more dabs of color to your winter palette with shrubs and trees that have colored bark or lasting vibrant berries. Sprawling heathers, red-twig dogwood, old-fashioned kerria, yellow-twig dogwood, shaggy cinnamon-bark river birch, elegant white-bark birches and aspens go way beyond brown and gray.

Summer's a cinch, with hundreds of great perennials to add color. Because the space is bigger than a doorstep or lamppost garden, here you can go for beebalm, creeping phlox, obedient plant, yarrow, and others of spreading habit.

BE KIND TO YOUR BUDGET

A triangular corner garden with legs about 6 feet long covers about 18 square feet. Lengthen those legs to 8 feet, and you'll be covering about 32 square feet. Ten feet on each side of the L? Now we're talking about 50 square feet. Curving the inside boundary will shave off a few square feet of planting, but this garden will be larger than the one at the lamppost, and that means more plants.

Invest most of your budget in a small tree or a few shrubs, if that's the look you like. Fill in with perennials of spreading habit to cover space cheaply and beautifully.

Depending on your plant choices, you can plant an 8-by-8-foot triangular corner for as little as $30, especially if you can take divisions of perennials or grasses from other beds. Buy the smallest pots you can find—4-inch perennials instead of gallon pots, young shrubs and trees instead of stately specimens. You'll save big money, and the plants will soon catch up to those pricier large plants.

Another trick: plant a small tree or a few shrubs, add a few rocks, and a single clump of flowers in one of your signature colors, and mulch the entire area. The bed will look satisfyingly solid, and then you can take your time filling it in with more plants.

EXISTING CORNERS

Your yard may already have sturdy corner "posts" in place. The corners of the property are a popular spot for builders to plop a Pfitzer juniper, forsythia, burning bush, or other inexpensive large shrub. And homeowners have a penchant for planting blue spruces or other trees at the corners, too. Those single specimens are a fine starting point for a bigger corner garden—a graceful one, instead of a lone plopped-in plant, and a garden that gets looked at, rather than overlooked.

Most of us can look right past a lone 30-foot-tall spruce or a big green blob of out-of-bloom forsythia without really seeing it. Our eye is seeking something more interesting. Something like color. Give that lonely spruce some interesting companions, and our attention will be tweaked. A threadleaf false cypress (*Chamaecyparis pisifera* 'Golden Mop' and others), a cool gray 'Blue Chip' creeping juniper, a spray of ferns, a bold white-streaked hosta—now that's a planting we will notice.

◁ Corners are the perfect place to plant a tree or shrub of eye-catching shape. This weeping Japanese maple has achieved the gnarled beauty of old age, evident especially in late winter. Fresh white snowdrops at its feet are a delicate, youthful contrast.

As for that big blob of a bush, imagine a dozen tulips and a silvery brunnera (*Brunnera macrophylla* 'Jack Frost'), with its sprays of sky-blue forget-me-not flowers and immense silver-splashed leaves, leading away from your Pfitzer or forsythia or burning bush. Instantly, your blah bush is transformed into a garden that hugs and encloses the corner. And that's what we want. A corner garden. Not just a corner post.

Driveway Decisions

When you come home from work or errands, you want an easy return. And you can't get much easier than having a garage attached to the house: tap a button, and you can get to or from the driveway in seconds. Front-yard driveways are practical and very convenient. But they can throw a monkey wrench into planting our corner gardens.

When you drive out, you need to be able to see the street clearly so you don't have to inch out. And you don't want to hinder your neighbors' view, either, when they're coming or going from their own driveways.

Shrubs, small trees, and tall perennials and grasses in corner gardens can make it hard to see who's coming and going. So go for safe low-growing choices that won't block your view. Play with a selection of groundcover sedums, woolly thyme, mat-forming junipers, and spice them up with bright petunias, hardy geraniums, veronicas, dwarf marigolds, and other low-growing flowers. Then, both driveway users and oncoming traffic will have clear passage.

When Not to Plant Corners

Corner gardens can be actually out of place in a few situations. Luckily, there are only two exceptions to the "plant a pair" guideline:

Isolated outposts If your lot is a big one, each corner garden could look lonely way out there, instead of appearing to be part of a pair. Following are two easy solutions, one that costs money and time, and one that doesn't:

1. Make the L-shapes longer and wider, until your eye says, "That's a good pair of corners." Yes, it'll cost more, because you'll need more plants to fill, say, 15-foot-long legs of the L. Keep the cost down by including rocks, fast-growing shrubs, and rapidly spreading perennials to fill in space.
2. Wait until you have other sections of your garden in place, such as flower beds or sitting spots, then add the corners as finishing touches instead of isolated outposts.

△ Opposites can be attractive. In this case, upright, graceful blue salvia with ground-hugging, hardy yellow ice plant (*Delosperma nubiginum*) are about as different as they can be, in color and plant shape.

▷ A riot of color, brightened even more by splashes of white: inexpensive annuals fill in fast to beautify a corner right through to frost.

Shade tree, small yard We've been talking about weight and balance, and a big shade tree in a smaller yard can throw off the balance. If you can check off all of the following points, skip the corner gardens:

1. Your front yard is small, say, no more than 50 feet across and 60 feet deep.
2. You have a big, mature tree in the front yard—and we're talking *big* tree, like an oak or maple, with a trunk at least 1 foot across.
3. That tree is in the lawn in front of the house, not next to the house.
4. You do not have a fence or wall along the front of your property.

If those four features prevail, you don't want corner gardens. The big tree is strong enough to draw the eye in its direction. It's the major focal point in the yard, and it's a feature no corner bed can balance. Competing with that tree can quickly make your yard look busy, because the eye doesn't know where to look.

Now, add a fence or wall to the front of your yard, in your mind's eye. Wow, what a difference! Now the corner gardens look great, because you have two weighty focal points—the tree and the fence or wall. Simply because of the fact that it is a human-made object, that fence or wall carries extra power as a focal point—enough strength to balance the big tree. Plus, the horizontal line of the wall or fence balances the height and vertical heft of the tree, so they complement each other instead of competing for attention.

Now, go ahead, paint a pair of corner gardens into that picture in your mind. See how good they look now? That's because they're an addition to the powerful fence or wall, not a pair of weaklings trying to compete with a big tree.

Finishing the Frame

Planting two corner gardens and then two more is easier on your wallet than planting all four at once. The total cost may be the same, but you'll only need to pay for one pair at a time. And if you plant your first corner now, the next one can be practically free. By waiting a few months or longer to start on the second corner bed after the first, you've given your plants time to grow. When you're ready to plant the next garden or pair, you'll be able to take starts of the perennials and seeds of the annuals in that first corner.

A Pretty Frame

AT THE CORNER

Vibrant 'Purple Wave' petunias add zing to the pastels in this pair of all-season corner gardens, each about 8 feet long and wide. The same plants, but in slightly different arrangements, fill both corners of the front yard, making the gardens more interesting as a pair but avoiding the matched look.

1. Two rocks, breadbasket size (about 2 feet long, 10 to 12 inches high, and 8 inches across) or bigger

2. Miscanthus 'Morning Light' (*Miscanthus sinensis* 'Morning Light'), 2 plants

3. Russian sage (*Perovskia* species and hybrids), 2 plants

4. 'Pink Knockout' or 'Double Pink Knockout' rose (*Rosa* 'Pink Knockout' or 'Double Pink Knockout'), 2 plants

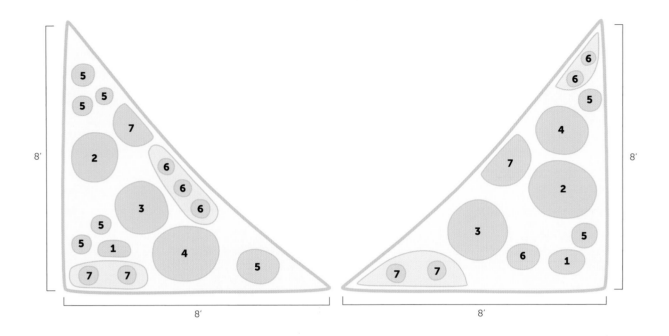

5. 'Monch' aster (*Aster ×frikartii* 'Monch'),
   8 plants

6. Lamb's-ears (*Stachys byzantina*),
   6 plants

7. 'Purple Wave' petunia (*Petunia ×hybrida* 'Purple Wave'),
   6 plants

Dress Up a Tree

SHADY SPOTS

△ A shade tree opens the door to a new world of plants and a new way of gardening, looking to leaves instead of flowers for color, and creating beauty with texture.

I f you have a shady place in your yard, you know it. It's where you hang your hammock or park your garden bench. It's where you plant hostas instead of petunias. You probably already have an idea, too, of just how deep and dark that shade is, and whether the sun slants into that area in late afternoon or in early morning. Shade is a matter of degree, giving us flexibility when it comes to playing with plants.

Gauging the Shade

As long as you have a spot that's sheltered from the hot sun, you can enjoy a shade garden. If your shady spot is in heavy, long-lasting shadow, such as under the wide canopy of a maple tree or along the north side of the house, that's full shade. If your shady spot is in shadow for most of the day, but in sun at times, that's part shade.

Plant sellers make it easy for us. Garden centers usually display shade plants in their own area, and labels help sort it out even more. Look at a label or a catalog, and you'll see symbols that clue you in. A picture of a sun or a circle, filled in with black = full shade. Half a black sun or circle = part shade.

Your plants will soon let you know whether they're happy in your shady spot, or whether they need to be transplanted to receive more or less sunlight. Too much sun, and they'll wilt. Too little sun, and they'll get leggy and not bloom as heavily or at all. Simply move them to a more fitting home, and plant something better suited to that spot.

▷ Ferns and hostas are traditional favorites for shade gardens, for good reason. In the shade, they're reliable, low-maintenance, live-forever plants, and their contrasting leaf shapes make them perfect partners.

△ Until they get their leaves, deciduous trees like these flowering cherries allow plenty of light to nourish early bloomers at their feet.

Seasonal Shade

The shade beneath a deciduous tree is temporary, depending on the season. In winter and early spring, when the branches are bare, it's a sunny area. And that opens the door to using a wonderful bunch of plants—spring ephemerals. These are the woodland wildflowers of deciduous forests, which take advantage of spring sun to quickly push up leaves and blooms. By the time the tree's canopy fills out with leaves, those plants are well on their way back to sleep until next year, having stored enough food in their roots to nourish a new batch of blooms next year.

Check a native plant nursery, online or in person, to find early-blooming beauties like those in the list (next page) for your seasonally shady spots. Most are truly ephemeral, leaving no trace aboveground once the flowers are finished. Some, like Solomon's seal, wild geranium, and wood poppy, however, retain their foliage to fill the shady spot from spring through fall.

EARLY BLOOMERS FOR SHADE

Native plants are some of the most dependable early-blooming plants for shade.

Bloodroot (*Sanguinaria canadensis*)

Dutchman's breeches
   (*Dicentra cucullaria*)

Dwarf larkspur (*Delphinium tricorne*)

Solomon's seal
   (*Polygonatum* species)

Spring beauty (*Claytonia* species)

Trillium (*Trillium* species)

Virginia bluebells (*Mertensia virginica*)

Wild geranium
   (*Geranium maculatum*)

Wood poppy (*Stylophorum diphyllum*)

Yellowbells, bellwort
   (*Uvularia* species)

Playing with Color

The shade-gardening scene has changed vastly since the days of hostas and more hostas. To satisfy our hunger for color in the shade, plant breeders have created every hue you can imagine in the shade garden. Purple, salmon, pink, red, orange, yellow, lime, chartreuse, copper, burgundy. And these are *foliage* colors. They'll last all season, not just for a few short weeks.

When it comes to shade gardening, foliage plants are the new flowers. Breakthroughs in perennial heucheras, the plants we called coral bells when they had plain green leaves, are the big news. Hot and spicy, light and bright, or dark and moody, these foliage perennials are irresistible.

Coleus has come a long way, too. New colors of those solid, streaked, or speckled leaves are arriving every year. Sold as inexpensive annuals, they splash lively color over shady beds or containers. Just pick your favorites. You'll find lots of other colored foliage plants, too, in both annuals and perennials, and even some shrubs.

And remember to take a look at the old reliables. Workhorse hostas and ferns are still as beautiful as ever, and a serene palette of green and white makes a shady spot feel cool and elegant.

So, you can enjoy hostas and ferns, but throw in an unexpected note of silvery purple Persian shield (*Strobilanthes dyerianus*), a dash of lime green or caramel-colored heuchera, and whatever other colors warm your heart.

Flowers for Shade

Impatiens is the top flowering performer in shade, but it's been hit by a debilitating disease in some regions. If the plants are available at your local nursery, the disease probably isn't a problem in your area. If you prefer not to take the risk, choose other flowering or foliage plants to brighten your shady spots.

Branch out with the following flowering plants, too, which like life in dim light. Just check the shade-gardening section at your garden center, where you'll find good candidates.

FLOWERING PLANTS FOR SHADE

Look for these shade-loving perennials and annuals:

Perennials

Astilbe (*Astilbe* species and hybrids)

Bear's breeches (*Acanthus spinosa*)

Bleeding heart (*Dicentra spectabilis*)

Bleeding heart, fernleaf
(*Dicentra eximia*)

Blue wood aster
(*Symphyotrichum cordifolium*)

Brunnera (*Brunnera macrophylla*)

Columbine
(*Aquilegia* species and hybrids)

Digiplexis (*Digitalis ×isoplexis* hybrid)

Fire pink (*Silene virginica*)

Foamflower
(*Tiarella* species and hybrids)

Foxglove
(*Digitalis* species and hybrids)

Goatsbeard (*Aruncus dioicus*)

Hardy cyclamen (*Cyclamen* species)

Hardy geranium 'Ballerina' and
'Brookside' (*Geranium* species
and hybrids)

Hellebore (*Helleborus* species
and hybrids)

Heuchera hybrids

Jacob's ladder (*Polemonium* species)

Lamium (*Lamium* species)

Ligularia (*Ligularia dentata*)

Lily-of-the-valley (*Convallaria majalis*)

Lungwort
(*Pulmonaria* species and hybrids)

Monkshood (*Aconitum* species)

Toad lily (*Tricyrtis* species and hybrids)

Woodland phlox
(*Phlox divaricata, P. stolonifera*)

Yellow corydalis (*Corydalis aurea*)

Annuals

Begonia (*Begonia* species)

Browallia (*Browallia* species)

Flowering tobacco, green
(*Nicotiana langsdorfii*)

Flowering tobacco, woodland
(*Nicotiana sylvestris*)

Fuchsia (*Fuchsia* species)

Impatiens (*Impatiens* species)

Monkeyflower (*Mimulus* species)

Torenia (*Torenia* species)

△ Spring bulbs, like these grape hyacinths, thrive under small flowering trees. By the time the tree leaves come in, the bulbs are well on their way to going back to sleep until next year.

▷ Old-fashioned bleeding heart, a charmer, is one of the most reliable flowers for shade. When the graceful stems of dangling hearts are finished, the plants go dormant, yielding the stage to hostas or other shade lovers.

PENNY-PINCHER TIP

Coleus Cuttings

See those square stems on your coleus? They're a big clue that these plants are super easy to propagate—they're in the mint family, Lamiaceae. And just about every member of that family roots swiftly from cuttings.

Before your first frost in fall—which will turn your coleus to mush—clip off several stems of your favorites. Strip off the lower leaves, and either poke the cuttings into a pot of moist soil, or put them into a jar of water. Keep them inside on a sunny windowsill. They may drop their remaining leaves and look limp for a while, but they'll soon start pushing out new growth, as well as a tangle of roots. And when planting time rolls around next year, you'll be ready with new plants at no cost.

Repetition

Repetition, the foundation of the building block garden method, is the reason your yard will look connected instead of like a bunch of unrelated beds. In different gardens, we've repeated some of the same plants. But now we're switching from sun to shade, and that means almost every plant will be different from those in other areas. So how do we make our shady spot look like it's part of the whole? Color.

Even though the shady bed holds different plants, you can repeat the standout colors in other parts of your yard. Just match the colored foliage of shade plants to sun-loving flowers in other areas. Pink or rosy purple foliage plants, including many varieties of coleus and heucheras, mirror the color of tall garden phlox, purple coneflowers, and many others. Golden-leaved hostas will echo yellow hues elsewhere. Partner them with dark foliage plants, such as reliable 'Purple Palace' heuchera, to make them pop.

Need a match for red? Try 'Fire Alarm' and other hot heucheras that repeat the hue of 'Hot Papaya' and 'Salsa Red' coneflower and other warm-colored sun-lovers. Even orange and apricot flowers meet their match in the warm shades of 'Southern Comfort' heuchera and 'Inferno' copperleaf plant (*Acalypha wilkesiana* 'Inferno').

If white is the color you want to repeat, go for variegated hostas, whose leaves have bold white centers or wide white edges, with white azaleas and

◁ Dwarf bleeding heart, with its delicate foliage, has a much longer blooming season than its tall cousin, and it doesn't go dormant. Pair it with colored heuchera to highlight its flowers.

⚠

MISTAKES NOT TO MAKE
Spread the Green

Bright colors near the tree trunk can distract attention from the tree itself, except when it's bare or in bloom. Plant peaceful green ground-covers 2 to 3 feet out from the trunk before adding color—except when you're planting under small flowering trees, such as Callery pears, flowering cherries, serviceberry (*Amelanchier arborea* and hybrids), dogwood, or flowering crabapples. For bright bloomers, you can go crazy with spring bulbs and other early flowers at the tree's feet, where they will become part of the display, not a distraction.

▷ Splashy colors, plain or fancy leaf shapes, and fast growth give coleus the Best in Shade award—and starter plants are as cheap as other annuals. This glowing beauty is 'Henna'.

later-blooming goatsbeard. Want silver? Look for splashy begonias, lungwort, or brunnera to echo the silver of sun-loving artemisia.

True blue is trickier, and if that's your signature color, you'll need shade flowers, since no one has figured out blue leaves just yet. Annual 'Summer Wave' torenia covers a gratifyingly large area—up to 3 feet in diameter—in a floriferous pool of blue.

You can repeat colors with shade-loving flowers, too. Azaleas and astilbes make a big impact, and so does annual impatiens, if it still flourishes in your area. But relatively few shade flowers bloom abundantly, and the selection of colors is more limited. Depend on colored foliage as your mainstay, and use flowers for reinforcement.

△ Variegated white-splashed ivy lightens up the deep shade beneath a pair of big Douglas firs in this simple, elegant bed.

▷ Turn your large shrubs into sculptures—and let in more light—by removing lower branches to show off their graceful "legs."

Under Trees

The good news about trees is that you can just let them stand alone in the lawn. A tree is perfectly beautiful on its own.

The bad news is that most of us can't keep our hands off the area under a tree. We circle the trunk with mulch, so that we don't hit the trunk with the lawnmower—but then we can't resist adding a ring of rocks. Or we put a shade garden under the tree, forgetting that the tree roots, big and little, are going to make digging a chore, and compete with our shade plants for water and nutrients. Or we try to grow plants under a dense, leafy canopy that blocks rain, making the soil beneath the tree much drier than anywhere else in the yard.

But by understanding our trees, we can work with them.

THREE TREE REALITIES

Take these to heart, and you're on your way to transforming your trees into kindly patriarchs instead of frustrating family members.

Trees drink through their leaves, as well as their roots And they drink a lot, to keep those thousands of leaves growing. When you plant in the "dry shade" beneath a maple, you are committing yourself to frequent watering. Plant outside the canopy of leaves, and you won't be always reaching for the hose.

Most trees have a surprisingly small root zone I'm always amazed at seeing the roots of a tree that's toppled in a windstorm. Yes, some roots do extend out to the edge of that leafy canopy or even farther. But the main root clump is often only 8 feet or so across, not the 20 feet you'd expect. The anchor roots and thinner feeder roots may extend much farther and deeper than the main tangle, but they are relatively few. Plant beyond the anchoring roots, and your shade garden will thrive.

Native trees have native companions that flourish next to them Look at wild places, and you'll find native shrubs, ferns, perennials, or wildflowers growing happily right next to their tree partners. Seedlings and young trees often shoulder right up to their big brothers. Plant these naturally harmonious companions as the basis of your shade garden, and limit non-native plants, which often need extra care, to accents.

△ Making a circle around a tree makes it look clunky, especially when it's accentuated with a ring of rocks. This impressive old Siberian elm was our starting point in Lou and Lila's front yard.

A WORD ON NATIVE PLANTS

Native plants are much easier to find these days than they once were, now that gardeners are quickly gaining an appreciation for these well-adapted, usually trouble-free annuals, perennials, and shrubs.

Start by asking at your independently owned nursery; often, a section is set aside just for native plants, where you can browse to choose your favorites.

Plant sales by local or regional native plant societies are often the least expensive option. Track down those in your area with an online search, so you know when sales are scheduled; many also maintain Facebook pages.

Shopping online, via nursery catalogs, is an easy way to go, too, and the selection is staggering. You'll meet hundreds of wonderful plants well suited to your climate and conditions. Just search online for "[your state] native plant nursery" to find those in your area.

RING-AROUND-THE-TREE SYNDROME

Why can't we resist making a ring of rocks around a tree? Well, because we want to beautify it. Some people even build a raised bed around the tree. In a circle, of course.

It may be common, but it isn't graceful. A ring-around-the-tree bed actually detracts from the beauty of the tree. It stops our eye at the circle, instead of encouraging our gaze to travel up the trunk and admire the tree. Take a look at a tree that rises right from the lawn, without any fussy circle at the bottom, and you'll instantly see the difference. That's grace.

Fix #1: Fast and (Almost) Free Grab your wheelbarrow, pile those rocks, bricks, or the lawn edging around your tree into it to cart away, and

◁ Stretching the bed outward to one side helps to balance the big tree, reducing its overwhelming command of the yard.

scatter grass seed on the bare spot. It's an instant fix, because a tree trunk rising from lawn looks perfectly natural. So natural, that we may barely notice the tree while our gaze travels to more colorful spots in the yard.

Fix #2: Winners' Circle Extend the bed under the tree to make a bigger circle, an oval, or an irregular shape—keeping the tree to one side, not in the middle. This arrangement is more appealing aesthetically, because the tree is balanced. The bigger size of the bed, and its extent to one side, puts it in proportion to the height of the tree and the heft of the trunk. It's the same kind of balance that a sweep of lawn gives to a tree with no bed at the bottom. And you can bet our subconscious sense of proportion registers the difference. We actually notice the tree now.

Groundcovers

Shade-loving groundcovers have shallow, fibrous roots that quickly spread out in all directions, and often their stems root as they go. All those roots mean that these plants are perfectly adapted to getting their share among tree roots.

DON'T PLANT A PROBLEM
Avoid Aggressives

Some shade groundcovers take their role a little too enthusiastically, escaping the bed and infiltrating lawn or wild areas, even with a metal edging. Once they're on the loose, they're tough to get back under control. English ivy, even variegated or fancy-leaf varieties, will eventually climb trees. Steer clear of the following notoriously aggressive growers:

Ajuga (*Ajuga reptans*)

English ivy (*Hedera helix*)

Goutweed
   (*Aegopodium podagraria*)

Ground ivy
   (*Glechoma hederacea*)

Sensitive fern
   (*Onoclea sensibilis*)

Vinca, periwinkle (*Vinca minor*)

GROUNDCOVERS FOR SHADE

These shade-loving groundcovers are some of my favorites:

Allegheny spurge
   (*Pachysandra procumbens*)

Fern (many species)

Lamium (*Lamium maculatum*)

Lily-of-the-valley (*Convallaria majalis*)

Liriope (*Liriope muscari*)

Mondo grass (*Ophiopogon japonicus*)

Moneywort (*Lysimachia nummularia*)

Violet (*Viola* species)

Wild ginger (*Asarum* species)

Yellow archangel
   (*Lamium galeobdolon*)

Reasoning with Roots

Digging and planting under trees is a matter of finesse, thanks to all those interfering roots. Use a narrow ditch-digger's shovel (also called a poacher's spade or a trenching spade) or hand tools, and when you hit a root, stop and assess the situation. If the root is a large one, move your intended plant hole to one side of it. If the root is less than ¼ inch in diameter, usually you can snip it with no harm done. A firm push on the shovel or a quick snip with pruners will sever it. An established tree will show no ill effects from the amputation, even for larger roots up to about 1½ inches in diameter. If your tree has been in the

Embrace Fallen Leaves

Fallen leaves are like a fluffy down quilt for plants in winter, and in early spring, they protect plants from the freeze and thaw cycles that can heave roots right out of the ground. Dead leaves break down fast—otherwise, we'd be up to our necks in leaves every time we take a walk in the woods—adding nutrients to the soil and improving its texture, thanks to the workings of an army of minuscule leaf-eating critters, fungi, and bacteria. That's why I always have to laugh, every time I see someone assiduously raking or blowing away their fall leaves, then buying compost and mulch in spring.

Fallen leaves naturally nestle around plants when the wind blows. If you can withstand the scornful looks from neighbors, wait to rake lawn areas until after the autumn winds have blown most of your leaves into garden beds. This natural, no-work mulch can save lots of time and money, because you won't have to haul in bags or bushels to cover your beds, come spring.

ground for less than five years, though, it needs every one of its roots. Move your planting hole elsewhere, and cover up the root.

And when roots are simply too difficult to deal with, such as under a maple tree, or you don't want to spend the time to work around them, you can fake it. Potted annual plants are one clever solution to root woes.

To take the easy road, get your perennials and shrubs planted, and mulch your shade garden. Then, cut out a 2-inch-wide strip across the bottom of the annuals' pots with a sturdy knife (carefully), scoop out a shallow hole in the mulch, and set your plants in, still in the pots. Scoop more mulch around the pots and over their roots, and no one will know that the plants aren't actually in the ground. Their roots will grow down into the soil. You'll have to water them more frequently, but for instant color without much work, a "planting" of flowering pots will keep the color coming right up until frost.

Let in the Light

Don't want quite so much shade in your yard? Limbing up the tree is a quick and simple solution. Use a pair of loppers or a pruning saw to remove the lower limbs from your tree, or the side branches from those lower limbs, to open up the heavy head of leaves. Take your time selecting branches to remove, aiming for a graceful overall shape. You won't harm the tree. And you'll end up with an artistic specimen. Removing twigs and small branches reveals the beauty of those big limbs.

This trick can work magic on flowering crabapple trees, turning what used to be a congested crowd of branches, beautiful only at bloom or berry time, into a small tree that's as elegant as bonsai in all seasons.

As the sun moves through the sky, those lower rays in morning and late afternoon will reach beneath your trees. Limb them up, and you can easily gain another hour or two of direct sun—and that means a wider selection of plants will thrive there.

A Rainbow for the Shade

Pity the poor gardener who has no shady spot to try out all the fabulous new colorful shade plants. Fast becoming must-haves are luscious foliage plants, new shades of torenia, new shapes of begonia leaves and flowers, and tall, exotic impatiens developed from African species that bear little resemblance to our old favorite shade flowers. Shade gardening is giving sunny gardens a run for the money. Get ready to fall in love.

▷ Shrubs and dwarf conifers are an easy solution for shady spots, and often less expensive than filling the space with perennials. Plant a mix of shapes and textures, just as you would with other plants.

△ It's easy to weave a tapestry of delicious texture and color with shade plants. Just mix plain and fancy leaf colors and shapes, like this froth of chartreuse-flowered lady's mantle and silvery lamium with dark heuchera and plain hostas.

▷ This tree has been "limbed up," by removing selected lower branches, which increases the amount of sunlight that can reach plants beneath the tree.

Dress Up a Tree

SHADY SPOTS

The gleaming leaves of spreading European wild ginger make a polished backdrop for variegated hostas and sweet-scented lilies-of-the-valley. A single rosy red–leaved heuchera, a sprawl of annual pink-flowered torenia, and silvery, spreading lamium will brighten the color mix and repeat pink tones of flowers in your sunnier gardens. The off-center tree in the wide oval bed makes this 4-by-6-foot planting much more appealing than if it were a circle around a centered tree.

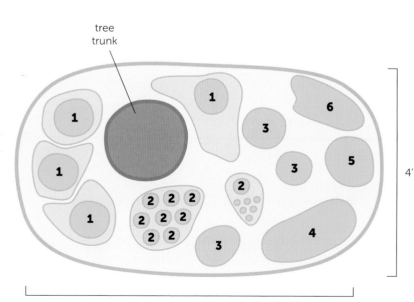

1. European wild ginger (*Asarum europaeum*), 4 plants

2. Lily-of-the-valley (*Convallaria majalis*), about 14 bulbs (also called pips); they will spread

3. Hosta (*Hosta* hybrids), 3 plants

4. 'Catalina Pink' torenia (*Torenia fournieri* 'Catalina Pink'), 1 plant

5. 'Sweet Princess' heuchera (*Heuchera* 'Sweet Princess'), 1 plant

6. 'Pink Pewter' lamium (*Lamium maculatum* 'Pink Pewter'), 1 plant

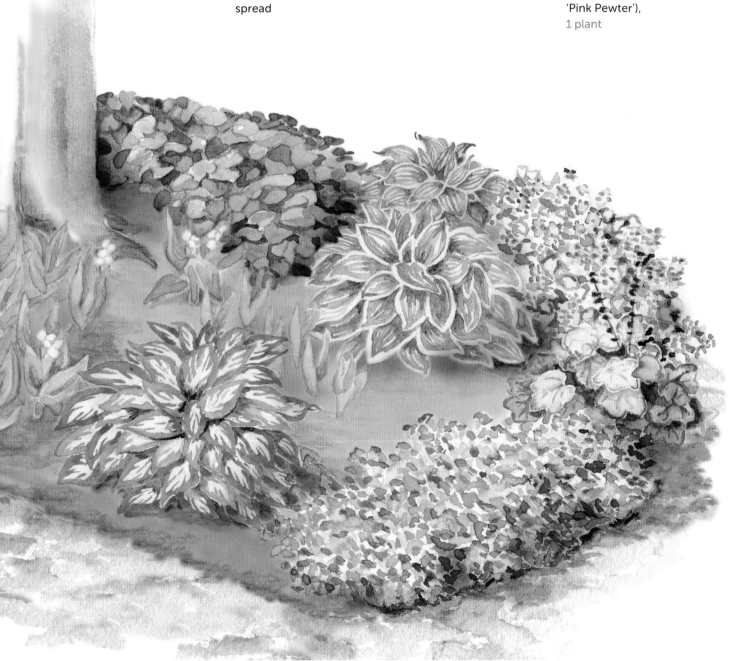

Between Neighbors

PRIVATE OR PRETTY?

△ Vivid roses soften what
could be a stern boundary,
delighting those on both sides
of the fence.

 When privacy isn't the issue, a flower bed of low-growing plants, like this fast-spreading Persian stonecress, makes a friendly way to mark the boundary.

Most people remember only one line from Robert Frost's poem, "Mending Wall":

"Good fences make good neighbors."

Would it surprise you to learn that the whole poem is about why walls are not a good idea? That memorable line is spoken by the neighbor, with whom Frost is disagreeing. Maybe Mr. Frost never had to deal with straying dogs or piles of junk or rowdy backyard parties next door. Maybe, since his own place was 150 acres, he didn't understand why we glommed onto that line and forgot the sentiments of the rest of the poem.

Good fences do make good neighbors, for many of us who live in spitting or binocular distance of our neighbors, instead of acres away. So do walls, and hedges, and even—my favorite way of marking the boundary line!—beautiful flower beds.

▷ Fast-growing coral honeysuckle (*Lonicera sempervirens* 'Blanche Sandman') will quickly spill over a tall fence, so that both you and your neighbor can thrill to the hummingbirds that come for its nectar.

High privacy fences invite tall plants, like these native prairie coneflowers (*Ratibida pinnata*). Repeating their sunny color at a lower height with black-eyed Susans draws the admiring gaze to the garden, not the fence.

Fence Me In

Most of our outdoor living goes on in our backyards, and that's where we put our serious fences.

Fences are designed to keep our pets in place, and to prevent our kids from wandering off. Fences at least partially block our view of the neighbors, and vice versa. Fences mark our property boundary lines.

High wooden fences quickly became the standard, beginning with the introduction of rustic, pointed stockade fences and morphing into today's more attractive versions, with flat tops or slightly friendlier "shadow slats" or fancified lattice crowning the vertical slats.

Some of us have split-rail, chain-link, picket, or other types of fences in the backyard, but privacy fences are most popular. Once called "spite fences," back in the days when housewives chatted across the picket fence or low clipped privet hedge, they're so common now that we accept them without a second thought. "Of course they want privacy," we think to ourselves, even if we may be curious about what's going on back there.

The only bone of contention these days, when it comes to privacy fences, is which side should be out, which side should be in. Answer: the ugly side—the side that shows the crosspieces—faces in, so that you, not your neighbor, sees it. We won't be looking at ugly for long, though. Because fences, no matter what material or style, are the ideal place to plant shrubs, vines, or a flower border.

Don't Fence Me Out

We're a lot friendlier when we're in the front yard than we are in the backyard. In the backyard, it's "I want my privacy." In the front yard, it's "Hi, neighbor!" or at least a cordial nod and smile when we're both outside at the same time.

A tall, solid fence seems out of place in the front yard, unless you have an overwhelming need for privacy. Luckily, we still have options for blocking out sights and sounds in the front yard, and for marking our territory. Lower, more open fences, for starters. Spaced pickets or post-and-rails can easily transition to tall, solid privacy fences once they get past the front yard.

To soften sounds as well as provide privacy, nothing beats a hedge. The dense foliage helps block out the sounds that filter through from next door, or from our own yapping dog to the neighbors' ears.

MISTAKES NOT TO MAKE

Background Player

Avoid alternating two types of shrubs in a regular pattern down the row. That unnatural look creates a focal point you don't want in this planting. Instead, plant, say, three forsythia, then one lilac, then six red-twig dogwoods—you get the idea. That way, each of the types is highlighted when it comes into its showy season, whether that's bloom time or winter color.

Hedges

The best hedge plants share two attributes: their branches are dense, and they knit together fast. Shrubs are the most popular plants for hedges. They're substantial in size, and they maintain their structure even in winter. Evergreens usually cost a bit more than deciduous types, but you may want to mix a few in to keep some green going in winter. You can plant all one kind of shrub, or a mix.

To calculate how many shrubs you need to fill the row, you can take a very detailed approach and calculate every one of your plants' mature widths, then subtract an amount for overlap, and space your planting holes accordingly. Or you can do it the fast and easy way, and just divide the length of your border by four. Most shrubs mature at about 5 feet wide, and that extra width will interweave to create the solid hedge you want. Intersperse perennials, ornamental grasses, or other plants (tall cannas, hollyhocks, and sunflowers are perfect) along the row between groups of shrubs to make the boundary planting more interesting, if you like.

◁ Stepping down the height of a front yard fence, whether it's on a slope or not, is a gentle way to maintain the division between neighbors

▽ A solid hedge, one neighbor's solution to defining the boundary, sets off the Impressionist mix of plants on the other neighbor's side.

FAST, GOOD, CHEAP—AND EASY!

Rely on the following workhorse shrubs for a hedge that grows like lightning, is easy to care for, and costs as little as $35 for a 50-foot length, if you buy young plants (which will grow rapidly). You can plant it along a fence, or all by itself to serve as a living fence.

A bonus: all of these plants, except for roses, are very easy to propagate. For lilacs and serviceberry, dig up and transplant the vertical shoots called suckers that arise from the roots. For all others (except roses), just break off a young branch 10 to 12 inches long, strip off the lower leaves, stick it about 6 inches deep into soil, and keep it moist. It'll root swiftly. Or bend a lower branch to the ground, mound soil over it, and anchor the soil with a flat rock, to root by what is called "layering."

DON'T PLANT A PROBLEM
Escapees from the Garden

Some old-favorite hedge plants have become pests in various areas, escaping to the wild as birds eat the berries and drop the seeds hither and yon. Pink- and white-flowered bush honeysuckles (especially *Lonicera morrowii* and *L. tatarica*) were once popular for hedges, but they've run rampant, infiltrating woods and other wildlands across a wide area of the country. Burning bush (*Euonymus alatus*) and barberry (*Berberis* species) are on the "no thanks" list in some areas, too; both are actually banned from sale in Connecticut. In the Southeast, all nine species of privet commonly used for hedges are invasive. If you can't find these plants at local garden centers, the reason may well be that they're not welcome in your area.

EASY SHRUBS TO GROW FROM CUTTINGS

Those plants marked with an asterisk are invasive in some areas.

*Barberry (*Berberis* species and hybrids)

Bayberry (*Myrica* species)

*Burning bush (*Euonymus alatus*)

*Butterfly bush (*Buddleja davidii*)

Cherry laurel (*Prunus caroliniana*)

Elderberry (*Sambucus* species and hybrids)

English laurel (*Prunus laurocerasus*)

'Flame' willow (*Salix alba* 'Flame')

Forsythia (*Forsythia* ×*intermedia*)

Golden privet (*Ligustrum* ×*vicaryi*)

Hibiscus (*Hibiscus* species and hybrids)

Hydrangea (*Hydrangea* species and hybrids)

Kerria (*Kerria japonica* 'Pleniflora')

*Privet (*Ligustrum* species and hybrids)

Red-tipped photinia (*Photinia* ×*fraseri*)

Red-twig dogwood (*Cornus alba*, sometimes listed as *Cornus sericea*)

Serviceberry (*Amelanchier* species)

Shrub roses, especially 'Knockout' and *Rosa rugosa* (*Rosa* species and hybrids)

Variegated Japanese willow (*Salix integra* 'Hakuro-nishiki')

Weigela (*Weigela florida*)

RAMBLING ALONG

A rose-covered fence is so beautiful that no one would ever mistake you for a curmudgeon who's trying to keep out the neighbors.

Ramblers are the traditional choice, but these heritage varieties, such as 'Paul's Himalayan Musk', tend to be prone to diseases. Go for climbers instead, which have a similar long-branched growth habit and aren't as finicky. Pale pink 'New Dawn' and its cousin 'White Dawn', yellow 'Golden Showers', red-and-orange 'Joseph's Coat', and red 'Blaze' tend to have stronger constitutions than true ramblers.

A split-rail or post-and-rail fence is ideal for climbing roses, because it shares the full beauty of the roses with your neighbor. But roses look beautiful on a picket fence, too, or on chain-link. You'll need to tie climbers in place, whatever fence you have. Green Velcro strips are a quick and easy method to securely hold the thorny stems; look for an inexpensive roll at any garden center.

Most climbing roses bloom for only a few weeks. To keep the color coming, add a trouble-free 'Knockout' shrub rose. It won't climb or ramble, and it has none of that swooning rose perfume, but it will keep blooming until frost.

▷ Bell-shaped clematis, like this 'Princess Diana', are a beautiful change of pace from their wide-open cousins. Their color complements the sprays of blousy roses, but their shape gives that satisfying zing of contrast.

△ Get together with your neighbor and make a boundary bed that's a joint project. It's more beauty for both of you, and less work because caretaking is shared.

A Border Along the Border

The border between neighbors, or along the front or back of your yard, is a long, narrow garden, about 3 feet deep. A border is a perfect place for flowers.

But that's a long row to hoe, and a lot of plants to buy. You can reduce the hoeing instantly by mulching it deeply after you're done planting. And to save money yet still have plenty of color, choose perennials that cover at least 2 feet of space with a single plant. Intersperse them with shrubs, small flowering trees, and ornamental grasses to vary the height and texture—and to fill the stretch rapidly.

If your border won't be backed by a fence, go for plants with good posture—tall annuals, perennials, and ornamental grasses that stand up straight without staking, if privacy is what you seek. Combine them with more relaxed mounds, clumps, or low plants that fill in quickly.

For a front border, stick to mid- and low-height plants, so they don't block the view of the rest of your lovely yard. Add annuals that are simple to grow from seed, too, for constant color. You'll get a 10-foot or better stretch of plants from one packet of seeds. Splurge on a few 'Wave' petunias from the garden center, too; it's hard to beat a 5-foot-diameter splash of concentrated color for just a few dollars.

Borderline gardens strongly reinforce the gardens in other areas of the yard, so be sure to use some of the same eye-catching colors, and some of the same plants you use elsewhere.

PLANTS FOR BORDERS

Some good plants for border gardens are:

Tall and Trouble-Free

Ornamental grasses
 (many species and hybrids)

Annual sunflowers
 (*Helianthus* species)

Bearded iris (*Iris* hybrids)

Canna (*Canna* species)

Dahlia (*Dahlia* species and hybrids)

Daylily
 (*Hemerocallis* species and hybrids)

New England aster
 (*Symphyotrichum novae-angliae*)

Hollyhock (*Alcea rosea*)

Maximilian sunflower
 (*Helianthus maximiliani*)

Red hot poker (*Kniphofia uvaria*)

Siberian iris (*Iris sibirica*)

Tree mallow (*Lavatera* species)

**Perennials That Cover
 at Least 2 Feet**

Bearded iris (*Iris* hybrids)

Beebalm (*Monarda* species and
 hybrids)

Creeping phlox (*Phlox subulata*)

Daylily
 (*Hemerocallis* species and hybrids)

Evergreen candytuft
 (*Iberis sempervirens*)

Gaura (*Gaura* species)

Persian stonecress (*Aethionema
 schistosum*)

Rockcress
 (*Arabis* species and hybrids)

Russian sage (*Perovksia atriplicifolia*)

Shasta daisy
 (*Leucanthemum* ×*superbum*)

Siberian iris (*Iris sibirica*)

Tall garden phlox
 (*Phlox maculata, P. paniculata*)

Veronica (*Veronica* species)

Winecup (*Callirhoe involucrata*)

Woodland phlox
 (*Phlox divaricata, P. stolonifera*)

Easy Annuals to Sow in Place

Bachelor's buttons (*Centaurea cyanus*)

Cleome (*Cleome hassleriana*)

Cosmos
 (*Cosmos bipinnatus, C. sulphureus*)

Marigold (*Tagetes* species and hybrids)

Sunflower
 (*Helianthus annuus, H. debilis*)

Zinnia (*Zinnia* species and hybrids)

▷ A lineup of fast-growing cannas gives plenty of head-high privacy in summer. In cold-winter climates, dig up the rapidly spreading tubers in the fall and store them inside until planting time the following spring.

△ Annual vines, grown in pots on the porch, will quickly cover this inventive privacy lattice between closely spaced houses in summer. But the lattice is attractive all by itself, in the off-season.

A Wall of Green

Want to save money? Plant some vines along your fence. A vine can easily cloak a 6- to 10-foot stretch of fence in greenery, or even more if you choose a particularly vigorous grower, such as a grapevine or small-flowered sweet autumn clematis (*Clematis paniculata*). Vines make a great backdrop for the flower border, too, adding height that stretches to the top and spills over the fence.

For quick and easy coverage—and cheap, of course—plant annual vines. Morning glories, cypress vine (*Ipomoea quamoclit*), scarlet runner beans, and super-vigorous hyacinth bean will quickly embrace your fence, with a bonus of lively flowers. Or try edible pole beans, including 'Kentucky Wonder' and many others. All are easy to grow from seed.

Long-lived grapes and other permanent vines have woody stems, unlike the tender green growth of annual vines. They climb by twining their stems or tendrils around a support, with some adding "sucker feet" disks that stick to the vertical surface for extra aid when growing upward.

Trouble-Making Vines

Think twice—no, make that, think many times—before you invite any of the following vines into your yard. All of the following but English ivy send up shoots from the roots, many feet away from the parent plant. Some are as strong as an octopus, breaking apart boards with their determined tentacles. And a few (climbing hydrangea, Virginia creeper, trumpet vine, and English ivy) have sucker feet that leave a lasting residue on wood or masonry surfaces.

English ivy (*Hedera helix*)

Hops (*Humulus lupulus*)

Passionflower (*Passiflora incarnata*)

Trumpet vine (*Campsis radicans*)

Virginia creeper (*Parthenocissus quinquefolia*)

Wisteria (*Wisteria* species and hybrids)

A Hand Up

You might think the boards of a privacy fence would make a happy home for vines, but that's usually not the case. The boards are too wide for many vines to get a good grip, and the fence lacks horizontal crosspieces for the tendrils of clematis or grapes to cling to. Even if a woody vine does get a grip, it may cause damage by forcing the boards apart as its stems grow thicker.

For a quick, cheap, good, and easy solution: hang a piece of sturdy wire livestock fencing on the wall of your privacy fence. Attach it to the upright posts with hooks, so that it's a few inches away from the boards. Now, any vine, from annual morning glories to clematis to grapes, can easily climb without struggling.

For a quick, good, easy solution, but not as cheap: erect a trellis about 2 inches away from the privacy fence. A decorative metal trellis about 2 feet wide costs $20 and more. Push the legs into the ground, and the trellis will be up in minutes, ready to support clematis, morning glories, or other lightweight vines. For extra stability, anchor it with screw-in hooks near the top.

Or attach premade lattice, either wood or plastic, to your solid privacy fence to give your vines a place to climb. Be sure to allow a bit of space behind it, so that the vines can easily make their way over and around the lattice.

◁ Draw the eye away from the fact that there's a firm fence between neighbors by planting eye-popping Oriental poppies and beautiful bearded iris along it.

VINES

Try your hand at vines. They are easy to grow, once you have given them something to climb on, and so rewarding.

Well-behaved vines

Annual morning glory (*Ipomoea* species)

Cardinal creeper (*Ipomoea horsfalliae*)

Clematis, large-flowered (*Clematis* hybrids)

Climbing rose (*Rosa* species and hybrids)

Coral honeysuckle (*Lonicera* species and hybrids)

Hyacinth bean (*Lablab purpureus*)

Moonflower vine (*Ipomoea alba*)

Scarlet runner bean (*Phaseolus coccineus*)

Very vigorous vines

Use with care; these enthusiastic growers require frequent pruning to keep in bounds.

Akebia (*Akebia quinata*)

Bignonia (*Bignonia capreolata*)

Boston ivy (*Parthenocissus tricuspidata*)

Clematis, small-flowered (*Clematis paniculata* and other species)

Dutchman's pipe (*Aristolochia* species)

Grape (*Vitis* species and hybrids)

Porcelainberry (*Ampelopsis brevipedunculata*)

Virginia creeper (*Parthenocissus quinquefolia*)

Woodbine (*Parthenocissus vitacea*)

If you cloak your chain-link fence or other support in annual vines, such as morning glories or scarlet runner beans, you will need to remove the dead stems at the end of the season. For easiest removal of all those twisting stems, do the job soon after frost kills the vines, before they dry out and become brittle.

Beautiful Boundaries

Whether we agree with Robert Frost's feelings on fences, beautiful plantings do make good neighbors. Planting the boundaries of your yard is a big step in beautification. And the best part? You can start with one side, and do the other boundaries later, using starts of your now-established plants to fill other borders. Connect them to the corner gardens, and your yard will be well defined.

Between Neighbors

PRIVATE OR PRETTY?

Make a hedge interesting by planting flowers and grasses between the shrubs. Mulch deeply to discourage weeds and to make it a cinch to pull those that do sneak in. This 5-by-30-foot boundary-line bed offers flowers in spring and summer, golden grasses and bright berries for autumn, and contrasting evergreen foliage in winter. Birds and butterflies will enjoy the plants as much as you do.

1. Bearded iris (*Iris* hybrids), 1 clump
2. Lilac (*Syringa vulgaris*), 1 plant
3. Purple coneflower (*Echinacea purpurea*), 3 plants
4. 'Morning Light' miscanthus (*Miscanthus sinensis* 'Morning Light'), 1 plant
5. Dahlia (*Dahlia* hybrid), 1 plant
6. 'Blue Arrow' juniper (*Juniperus* 'Blue Arrow'), 1 plant
7. Northern bayberry (*Morella pensylvanica* formerly *Myrica pensylvanica*), 1 plant
8. 'Elijah Blue' blue fescue (*Festuca glauca* 'Elijah Blue'), 1 plant
9. Winterberry 'Winter Red' (*Ilex verticillata* 'Winter Red'), 1 plant
10. Winterberry 'Southern Gentleman' (*Ilex verticillata* 'Southern Gentleman') (for a pollinator), 1 plant

Cheerful Color

IN THE LAWN

△ Light and sunny, and
accented with a dark
heuchera for that all-
important contrast, this
flower bed provides cheerful
color all summer.

△ A mix of colors, but in big solid sweeps—that's the secret to making a traffic-stopping garden. Here, the contrast of 'Burgundy Sun' and 'Electric Lime' coleus, both for sun, not shade, lend huge impact with blue and purple annual lobelia.

Making a flower bed in your yard sounds like the easiest thing in the world. Guess again! Slicing into your lawn is hard. Oh, it's easy, workwise. But it's the first garden that's not built around something else—a sidewalk, a property line, a lamppost. It's much easier to build on something that already exists than to start from scratch.

Take a look at your yard as a whole. And imagine yourself strolling around in it, meandering along a path that invites your feet to explore. If a path sounds more appealing, let's get to work. Let's make a flower bed that's worth its space in that lawn.

Bed or Border?

A bed stands alone, with space on all sides of it. It can be any shape: circle, square, rectangle, crescent, or freeform.

A border is a long bed that parallels a fence, walk, or boundary line, and so one side of it is fairly straight. The open edge of the border, the side that faces the lawn, may be straight, too, or it may curve in S-shapes.

▷ Stretch a flower bed along the front of your house to put it in easy reach for enjoying, every time you go in or out the front door. Reddish purple beebalm holds center court in this bed, tempting hummingbirds into easy view.

△ In this bed, we first notice the intriguing trunks of these 'Nellie Stevens' hollies. Their limbed-up shapes have a practical side: you'll have more plant choices for the part-shade bed beneath.

And then the distinction gets a little muddy. If we eventually dedicate a large part of our yard to plantings with paths leading through them, do we have beds or borders? Neither. We have a garden. And in that garden, we may have the sunny border, the shady fern and hosta bed beneath a tree, and the circular herb bed as a centerpiece. And to make it look all connected, use placement and paths.

If you wonder where the bed should go, just follow this rule of thumb: keep it close to the house. You can't go wrong with that location.

Paths

You already have a path to the front door. It may be a paved walk, or stepping-stones coming around the corner from the driveway. It's a path with purpose. A purposeful path is just what you want for everyday missions, such as carrying in groceries, connecting the hose to the faucet, or going to the mailbox.

When it comes to strolling around your yard for pleasure, though, we're talking about a path whose main purpose is the pleasure of admiring the gardens along it. Your flower bed needs a path to look and feel its best. So you'll be making both bed and path at the same time. At its simplest, the pleasurable "path" will be the lawn around your single flower bed.

Your flower bed in the lawn is a major factor in connecting the other gardens you've been creating. By itself, it has the power to pull everything together. It instantly bridges the distance to your other gardens. It also affects how you look at the whole yard. Up to this point, you've been working along the perimeter, filling in the edges, the corners, the doorstep. Now you're going to branch out. This garden is going to bring the eye into the yard. And it's going to shorten the distance among the other gardens.

▽ Do you want to build a garden around a single big rock, or a group of boulders? Modify the heavy strength of the rocks with soft plants and contrasting colors.

Each of your gardens is a steppingstone for the eye to light upon when you look at the yard. Soon, you'll have an appealing bridge across that gap of lawn.

Placing This Garden

Photographers and other artists use a simple guideline for composing their work: the rule of thirds. Our brains aesthetically prefer a composition that has the focal point offset, not smack dab in the middle. The spot a photographer wants us to look at first is either a third of the way from the left of the photo or a third of the way from the right, and a third of the way from the top or a third of the way from the bottom. But not in the center. That's the measurement you'll be using when you put in your new front yard flower bed. Every one of us can recognize one-third. Simple eyeballing is all you need.

And for gardeners, finding that line of one-third is only in one direction—from the house to the front boundary—so it's even simpler. From either viewpoint—from the street, or from the house—that bed will satisfy the rule of thirds.

Longer than Wide

Let's make this garden roughly parallel with the front of the house. It will be horizontally oriented. Overall, the bed will be longer from left to right than it is from top to bottom.

If your taste leans toward the formal style, make it a rectangle. Or if you want it to be more casual and graceful, go for a simple bean shape or a wide crescent.

Why parallel with the house? Because most of your other plantings aren't. Gardens along the front walk to the door are perpendicular to the house. Hedges or borders between neighbors are perpendicular. Corner gardens and lamppost plantings are triangular. A horizontal bed will contrast with those other shapes. And contrast intrigues the eye.

Longer than wide, that's our guideline, no matter what shape we use for the bed. Plan the bed to be one-half to two-thirds as deep (wide) as it is long. For a 6-foot-long bed, that's 3 to 4 feet deep. That's an overall size of 18 to 24 square feet, the perfect size to make in an afternoon, and to plant for a reasonable price. Later, you can easily extend the bed, if you wish.

If you're feeling more ambitious, and your yard is big enough to handle it, consider a bigger bed—say, a bed that's 12 to 15 feet across and 8 to 10 feet deep.

MISTAKES NOT TO MAKE
Bull's-Eye Beds

This lesson is short and sweet, but oh so important: do not put a flower bed in the very middle of the yard, unless you're going for strongly formal style. It will always look like a bull's-eye, because it's an unnatural arrangement.

▷ In this meadow garden, the flowers grow closely together, and hold each other up, thanks to the self-sowing habit of russet and gold rudbeckia and blue larkspur.

▽ There's a bearded iris for every garden, in any color under the sun. Here, the salvia spikes reinforce the purple tint of the iris petals, while adding contrasting shape.

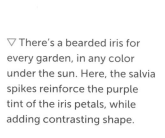

▷ A stone wall provides privacy from the street and highlights the pink tulips that brighten this flower bed in spring. Plant tulips in groups, not singly, to make impact.

Getting Around

Now that you have a rough idea of where your new flower bed is going to go, let's talk about how to approach it.

A simple flower bed is all one piece. To admire it, you walk around the outside of the bed. And when you maintain the planting, you do the same. That's fine for beds that are about 4 feet deep. Any wider, and you'll have trouble reaching into the middle without gingerly stepping between plants. This bed is simple and appealing. It would be even more welcoming if it has a concave curve along one of the longer sides. That curve is practically irresistible— we want to walk that way. The path, in this case, is the lawn around the bed.

For larger, deeper flower beds, guide the feet—and the eye—by making a path right through your new bed. A path invites you to come in, instead of peering from the edges. And a path makes maintenance much easier, for pulling a weed or picking a bouquet.

▽ Lawn is the simplest surface for a path through flower beds. Use edging strips or a manual edger tool to prevent the grass from growing into the beds.

△ Yarrow, a large plant, will cover at least 2 feet in its first season, and 3 feet or more thereafter. Fewer plants to fill the space = lower cost.

A bed 12 to 15 feet long and 8 to 10 feet deep is a good size for a front yard. But that's pushing the limit for an afternoon's work and a reasonable investment in plants. And, since it's too hard to reach the middle of an 8- to 10-foot-deep bed, unless you have arms like King Kong, you'll want to divide that bed into two smaller ones, with a path through them.

For now, keep the lawn grass as the surface of that path. It looks good, and will save you work and money. Later, you can pave it with bricks or lay in steppingstones, if you like.

Lay out the outline of your new bed, by marking it with a hose, a piece of rope, or twigs laid end to end. Stand back to eyeball it as you work, and adjust your markings until you're happy with the shape of the bed.

Next, figure out where you want the path to go. Start the new path not far from the doorstep of your house, so that it beckons you to walk that way every time you step outside. Branch the new path off your existing walk to that doorstep.

You'll have a stretch of lawn before the bed begins, but the path itself will show the way. To make the garden even more inviting, you can later add a garden ornament at the entrance, to say, "Right this way."

Your path will divide the garden, but it needn't be straight and narrow. Add curves, to make walking the path more of a leisurely stroll. We're not on a mission when we use the path, as we are on the purposeful paths in the yard. We want to take our time.

The end of the path will open out into lawn again. Plan a curve just before the end of the path, so the exit back into the lawn is slow, not hasty. The exit will double as an entrance, when you approach the garden from the other side.

Plan the width of your path to easily accommodate your lawn mower.

Lawn Versus Gardens

More and more homeowners are beginning to see a lawn as wasted space that eats up time, money, and water. Weekly mowing, fertilizing, dethatching, irrigating, dandelion digging, and related tasks now seem like chores we've been brainwashed into thinking we need to do to have that perfect patch of grass.

If your yard is small in size—say, 500 square feet or less—you may want to drop out of the perfect-lawn competition and turn the whole thing into a flower bed instead. For a larger lawn, you can start with one bed, and then extend the planting as time and money allow.

▽ A pool of lawn sets off the new flower beds in this ambitious project by providing a quiet, low contrast. Mulch gives this garden a finished look until more plants are added.

▷ Orange and gold butterflyweed (*Asclepias tuberosa*) lives up to its name, attracting nectar-seekers big and small. It's also a standout in a flower bed, thanks to its vivid color, here paired with 'Kent Beauty' ornamental oregano.

Tending a yard filled with plants requires more thought than mindlessly walking back and forth behind a lawnmower. You'll trade mowing chores for a weekly walk around your planted yard, nipping off spent blossoms, pulling a weed here or there, and thinking about which flowers you want to add or change.

Making this change will bring color and nature to your doorstep, too. The plants will attract and nurture butterflies, bumblebees, honeybees, and all sorts of other pollinators. Hummingbirds will visit for nectar, and songbirds for insects and seeds.

If you can't quite bring yourself to make such a dramatic change, keep a small patch of lawn to serve as contrast to a garden-filled yard. The smooth green will set off your new plantings beautifully, even if the lawn is now only a small patch 10 feet across.

It will take time to transform the entire lawn, or most of it, to plantings and paths. Start with one flower bed, and then extend the planting whenever you're inspired. You know—one building block after another.

Tidy Edges

Edging your flower bed serves two big purposes: it keeps lawn grass from creeping into the bed, and it makes mowing easier—as long as the edging is flat enough to allow your mower to glide over it. It also looks great, giving a clean and neat impression.

A manual edging tool, which costs about $25, is the cheapest and simplest solution. Use this step-on, half moon blade to slice out a shallow V-shaped trench between lawn and bed. That keeps grass roots from sneaking into the bed, and it's easy to mow right over it, with one wheel on the unplanted mulch and one wheel on the lawn. You can buy a gas-powered version for about $100.

You can expect to do your manual edging at least twice a year and possibly more often, depending on how aggressive your type of lawn grass is. Grass is designed to spread, and spread it will. The work is worth the effort, and the results are so satisfying—look at that nice clean edge!—that you may find yourself doing the job just for the fun of it.

If that hasn't lured you into going the manual labor route, you'll need a different solution to keep your grass and flowers separated: an edging strip.

Metal edging isn't cheap ($2 to $4 per linear foot), and installing it takes time. But it is permanent, unlike that tempting inexpensive plastic edging, which often works itself out of the ground.

△ A flower bed with a sense of fun, this simple garden of easy marigolds and sharply contrasting vertical 'Karl Foerster' grass includes whimsical iridescent balls.

▷ A half-moon shape adds to the interest of this flower bed, which includes spiky sprays of grass and iris leaves that offer lively counterpoints to the mostly mounded shapes.

Transforming a Specimen Shrub

Not so long ago, it seemed like every yard had a flowering shrub stuck right in the middle of the front lawn. One forsythia. One lilac. One spirea. In spring or summer, when the shrub was in bloom, it was pretty. But during the rest of the year? It was a shapeless green blob, and in winter, a bunch of bare sticks.

If you have a single specimen shrub you want to highlight, build a garden around it. Not in a circle, but in an oval or a crescent—or, for a more formal look, a rectangle. If you have two or more shrubs dotted here and there on the same side of the lawn, link them together into a large bed, giving those lonely shrubs a whole new aesthetic impact.

And you'll have a whole new beautiful garden to enjoy, once you start adding bearded irises next to that lilac, or lavender among the roses. Tall plants, such as hollyhocks, cannas, or sunflowers, will compete with the shrubs for attention. So keep the companion plants at less than about a third of the height of the shrubs, and include stretches of ground-covers to balance out the tall shrubs.

Backyard Flower Beds

Most of us do a lot of living in our backyards, and already have areas dedicated to those activities: a swing set, a deck, a patio, a vegetable garden, a bird-feeding station, a garden bench, a stretch of lawn for kids and pets to play, maybe even a swimming pool. Planting the perimeter and corners of the yard, and creating gardens around that patio, bench, or hummingbird feeder, are more likely to suit your needs in the backyard than a standalone flower bed, which can get in the way of socializing or roughhousing with the family dog.

But if your backyard is big enough, or if romping kids aren't a consideration, you may want to add a freestanding flower bed in the lawn. It can go anywhere you like, as long as it allows access to your activity areas. Plan a path through the bed so it leads to other enticing areas, such as the hammock under a shade tree.

Practicality and personal pleasure are the only goals here. If you've been hankering to try raised beds, this is the perfect place. Stack pavers or timbers into rectangles or invest in prefabricated kits, and line them up to fill with soil and flowers and food plants.

Decorate your backyard beds with all those ornaments you've collected, too, if you like the artsy touch. Your backyard is for you, not for passersby, so give it all the personal touches you like.

The Changing Scene

Wanting to change the size and shape of your flower bed is a natural impulse, as you add other plantings to the yard or just plain run out of space to plant all your favorites. When you get those urges, keep paths in mind. Instead of enlarging or reshaping the bed, why not tack on another one?

If you started modestly, with, say, a single bean-shaped bed, consider laying out an addition above or below it. Do you already have a bisected two-in-one bed? Maybe there's room to add a third bed at one end of it, with a path meandering between the old and new.

Try out the layout by outlining the new area. Like the look? Get digging!

Cheerful Color

IN THE LAWN

You can't go wrong with primary colors—red, yellow, and blue—as a color scheme, especially with a highlight of lacy, silvery 'Powis Castle' artemisia. Red barberry adds a deeper note in this bean-shaped 4-by-8-foot bed. If barberries aren't sold in your area because they've become invasive in the wild, use a dark-leaved weigela instead, such as 'Wine and Roses'. To calm any clash with the pink weigela flowers and red geraniums, shift the blue fescue to sit between them.

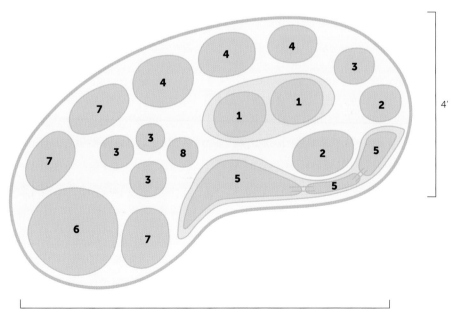

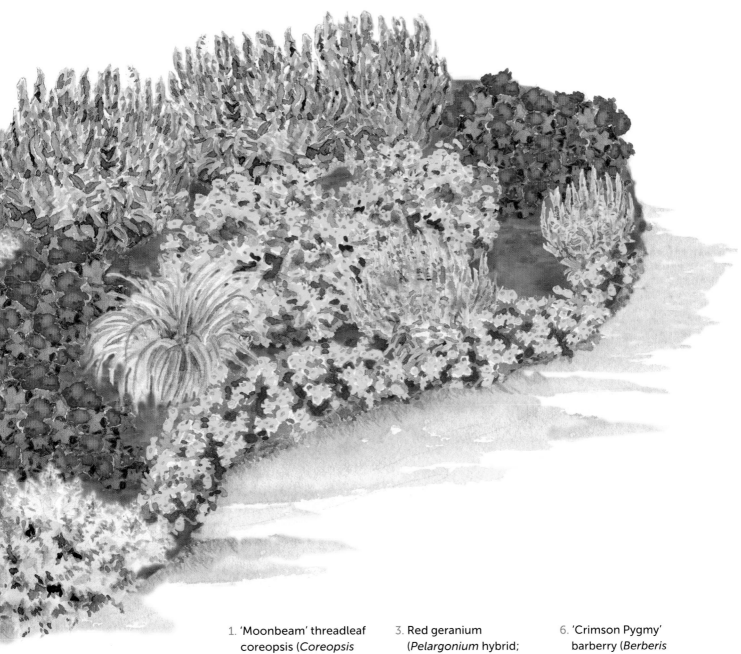

1. 'Moonbeam' threadleaf coreopsis (*Coreopsis verticillata* 'Moonbeam'), 3 plants
2. 'Sunny Border Blue' veronica (*Veronica* 'Sunny Border Blue'), 2 plants
3. Red geranium (*Pelargonium* hybrid; any red cultivar), 3 plants
4. 'May Night' salvia (*Salvia ×sylvestris* 'May Night'), 3 plants
5. 'Safari Yellow' marigold (*Tagetes patula* 'Safari Yellow'), sow 1 packet of seed
6. 'Crimson Pygmy' barberry (*Berberis thunbergii* 'Crimson Pygmy'), 1 plant
7. 'Powis Castle' artemisia (*Artemisia* 'Powis Castle'), 3 plants
8. 'Elijah Blue' blue fescue (*Festuca glauca* 'Elijah Blue'), 1 plant

An Ever-Expanding Garden

EXTENDING THE EDGES

△ Dramatic dark reds, in both the garden and the house trim, are the anchoring elements in this divided, extended entrance garden.

▷ A mosaic of separate groundcovers, each quickly enrobing an area with solid color, shows off against the green backdrop of a dwarf mugo pine.

Afinished garden is no fun. And fun is the reason we garden in the first place—the fun of planning, of putting plants together, of finding just the right shapes for that once-unloved corner, the fun of exulting in the payoff of pretty flowers. Declaring "Ahh, done," and lolling on the chaise the rest of your life sounds good at first, but soon you'll be itching to get your hands back in the soil.

We love adding new plants ("Oh—yarrow! I need some ferny yarrow, right here!") and new colors ("How'd I forget to plant *copper* bearded iris?"). We can't resist snatching up impulse buys at the garden center (those stunning green-edged purple 'Pretty Much Picasso' petunias), and squeezing in spring bulbs (more tulips!).

And we love to change things around, whenever we see a spot that would look better if we did a little rearranging or adjusted the color scheme. We're never done, for long. And, the building block method keeps it quick, easy, cheap, and beautiful.

Building on a Strong Foundation

Expanding a garden is a cinch, because you're connecting to an existing planting, not starting from scratch. What design should you use? That's simple: just go longer, wider, and maybe throw in a curve or two.

▽ Extend the doorstep garden along the front walk, and you have a perfect place to plant a cheerful greeting of plants.

PENNY-PINCHER TIP
Blocks of Color

To bolster the "beautiful" part of this quick, cheap, easy method, and save even more money, think big when it comes to plants. Not big in stature, but big in coverage. Include plants in your extended areas that cover a large stretch, about 3 feet across, with one significant splash of color.

Silver 'Powis Castle' artemisia, blue 'Six Hills Giant' catmint, beebalm, a dozen marigolds, a 'Wave' petunia, blue-gray 'Heavy Metal' switchgrass or other ornamental grasses—all will fill in fast to make your expanded garden come alive. Or consider long-blooming shrub roses or shrubs with colored foliage, to fill a lot of space with color.

You can see at a glance the areas that make sense to extend: stretching that lamppost garden out along the front edge of the yard. Linking the doorstep garden to the lamppost by planting all along the walk. Deepening and lengthening the curve of that flower bed or fence border into a bigger sweep—with more room for more plants. Making space for an edging of lavender in front of the roses. Expanding the shade garden with new plants you've discovered, like luscious water-spangled lady's mantle and silver-splashed lungwort (*Pulmonaria* species).

Plus, you can do this for very little money. By now, your finished gardens are ready to provide starter plants for those extended edges. Dividing plants is the quickest way of multiplying, so slice off a small chunk of the blue fescue grass, lift up some lamb's-ears, and separate some rhizomes from the dramatic black bearded iris.

If your wallet happens to be fat at the moment, here's your excuse to indulge in whatever catches your eye. You already have a great foundation in place in your gardens, with repeated plants and repeated colors, so adding new friends to your reliable companions will only make your yard look better.

The simplest way to extend the edges is to do exactly that: enlarge your existing gardens by making them wider and longer. Extend the garden by 1 foot along one of its sides, and you'll have space for an edging of honey-scented sweet alyssum, tidy coral bells, or lacy dwarf 'Gem' marigolds. Widen it by 2 feet, and you can squeeze in more perennials. Got enough energy to expand by 3 feet? That's like adding a whole new flower bed!

◁ Shrubs and ornamental grasses are a great low-budget foundation when you're switching from lawn in a large area. They anchor the area in all seasons, allowing you to take your time adding bright flowers as accents in the open spots.

▷ Removing only 8 inches or so of lawn grass from existing beds opens up enough room to plant an edging of coral bells, annual sweet alyssum, dwarf 'Gem' marigolds, or whatever you choose, to brighten the beds.

MISTAKES NOT TO MAKE

Reach Deep

When extending existing flower beds, keep access for maintenance in mind. If your bed approaches the 4-foot-deep mark, you may want to include a path before pulling the edges outward any farther. You'll have a new route to stroll as you admire your yard, and it'll be easy to reach into the plantings on either side of the path, to deadhead flowering shrubs or give that catmint a haircut.

Where to Start

Keep your expansion plan to easily doable pieces. Extend that lamppost garden 10 feet along the sidewalk, for instance, instead of doing the entire 50-foot-long front edge at once. Sweep the corners of your doorstep garden down along the front walk by just 6 feet on each side and see how you like it, instead of planting the whole walkway at once. You're not starting from scratch in a new area—you're connecting to an existing planting, and that makes it look good immediately, even if you tackle only a few extra feet at first.

And that's the goal! You want to pat yourself on the back after a few hours of work, not feel overwhelmed by how much you still have to do.

Consider your time, budget, and energy level, and then dig in wherever you'd most like to see more beauty. For most of us, an area of no more than 20 square feet is easily manageable in one afternoon, start to finish.

Two-Step Trick

Let's say you're not totally happy with that narrow, straight border along the front of your yard. You'd much rather have wide, sinuous curves that continue around the corners. But that's a lot of area to clear and plant in one day. And doing it piecemeal would look odd, with part of the bed straight and the rest swooping. Here's a simple solution: do the two-step trick!

Step 1 Lay out the new outline for the entire bed, and remove the lawn grass. Then blanket the new edge of the bed with the same kind of mulch you used in the rest of the garden. Set in a few rocks, scooping away the mulch beneath them so that they're nestled in naturally, not perched on top.

Step 2 Now you can take your time acquiring, arranging, and adding plants. The mulch gives the expanded bed a finished look immediately, even if plants are sparse or completely lacking, and the rocks top it off with interesting accents.

The same two-step trick works for straight beds, too, when you want to widen or extend while keeping the straight lines. And the mulch—without plants—makes the garden look bigger instantly, without making it seem raw and new. It simply becomes part of the existing mulched garden, to our easily fooled eye.

Perimeter Plantings

Outlining your property with plants is a popular impulse. No need to wrestle with how to design those beds; straight and simple works great. Later, you'll have plenty of time to add variety with curves or height, if you like, to make it more interesting than a lineup of plants. Take it slow, though, should you decide to outline the edges of your property.

▷ Self-sowing Corsican violets (*Viola corsica*), a little-known but beautiful perennial that's generous with its progeny, add completely free color to extend this rocks and gravel bed.

△ Look deeper, and there's a lot going on in this extended perimeter planting of colorful dwarf roses, bedding geraniums, and blue veronica. Emphatic cones of Alberta spruce mark the corner, shrubs of varying height make it feel substantial, and a single pop of yellow in the pot adds exciting contrast and draws your eye to the front porch.

Put the anchors in place first—the corners, the entrance to the front walk, the steppingstone path from the garage or driveway to the front door—and then build on those by extending them in manageable chunks. What's "manageable"? Anything you can start and finish in a single day, or if you're inspired, a weekend.

Vary the Line

Straight beds are plain and simple. But to make your extended gardens more interesting, vary the width by adding curves. Keep the outer side of the bed straight, along the property line, walkway, or fence, but snake the other edge of the bed in loose, graceful S-curves.

Vary the depth of the curves, and keep them wide, to prevent the bed from looking too regimented. Curves are informal, and a looser shape keeps the guiding hand of the gardener from being too obvious.

Plan out the curves before you begin removing lawn. Lay out a garden hose or rope, and adjust it until you're happy with the shape. Then scribe the line with a hoe or hand tool so you know where to dig.

Vary the Height

Our eyes love a surprise, so make some "Wow!" moments in your extended beds. Instead of using plants that are all roughly the same height, bring in some highs and lows. Step up the height in reasonable increments, not leaps.

△ Ground-hugging foamy white snow-in-summer (*Cerastium tomentosum*) looks its best next to a taller plant of strong color, like this upright salvia.

Towering annual sunflowers next to a patch of ground-hugging petunias is too big a step. Our eyes don't see them as a connected pair, and the tall guys stick out awkwardly.

Then again, the "stick out awkwardly" effect may be just what you want. Extra-tall plants are a powerful way to pull the eye, and then the feet, to a garden gate or entrance to a path. But for most beds, like perimeter plantings and flower beds in the lawn, step up the height in appealing increments.

A quick rule of thumb: keep the height difference to no more than 4 feet, and your eye will probably be satisfied with the surprise. Shoulder those sunflowers or a clump of cannas with mid-height lantana instead of groundcover petunias, and you'll get a smooth sense of surprise instead of a jarring jump.

Taking a step down is a delightful change of pace, too, and flowering groundcovers are great for that. A patch of creeping phlox sets off tulips and other taller spring bloomers like an area rug does a couch. A sweep of ground-hugging dianthus or zingy 'Fire Spinner' ice plant (*Delosperma* hybrid) creates a satisfying change of scene among bearded iris, yarrow, Shasta daisies, or purple coneflowers. Creeping thyme or groundcover sedums work wonders around a yucca; lamb's-ears make purple or hot-colored coneflowers stand out; and annual sweet alyssum makes a lovely lace collar for bold Oriental poppies.

As your plantings lengthen and expand, changes in height keep the eye moving—and enjoying the view.

◁ Showy milkweed (*Asclepias speciosa*), the western counterpart of common milkweed (*A. syriaca*), also spreads by roots, a good trait to fill space fast—and entice more butterflies, like this western tiger swallowtail.

CHANGE THE TERRAIN

I've always yearned for a mini-bulldozer, so I could push dirt around and make hills and valleys in the flat parts of my yard. But since Santa Claus is as tardy about fulfilling that wish as he was about the pony I wanted every year as a kid, I've learned to make changes to the terrain in other ways.

Varying the height of the yard itself is a big undertaking that requires a hefty budget or heavy labor. But even small changes in the terrain can make a big difference in the overall look of a flat yard. If you have a sloped section on your property, you're way ahead of the game. No slope? Then, unless you have the time and money to order a truckload of topsoil and the means to move it around, you're stuck with faking it.

Here's the quickest, easiest, cheapest, and prettiest way to alter the terrain of your yard: set in a hefty rock, pile soil behind it, and plant a bright and beautiful sprawling plant, such as a deep pink 'Brilliant' dianthus or shocking chartreuse 'Angelina' sedum, above the rock. You'll have an instant mini slope!

Repeat the Chorus

Extending the garden is a great time to try out new plants and new combinations. But before you get carried away with exciting newcomers, remember: repetition is important. As you expand, repeat the colors, and repeat some of the same plants already in your existing gardens. Repetition is the trick that makes your yard look tied together—one big whole instead of a bunch of unrelated gardens.

Bloom Time

Every garden looks fantastic in May and June, when perennials of almost every kind are blooming happily. Whatever you've planted, your garden is guaranteed to look great at peak season. But it is not so simple planning for flowers outside of that high blooming point. There aren't nearly as many early blooming perennials or late-season beauties.

You've solved part of that problem already, by depending on workhorse perennials that bloom much longer than the vast majority—for months, not just a couple of weeks—and you've added annuals that don't quit until a killing frost. You've added colorful foliage, too, that carries on all growing season without stopping to take a breath.

And don't forget to carry the color—be it red, yellow, or any other stripe of the rainbow—throughout the garden by planting early, midseason, and late bloomers of a similar color close together. Want a patch of rich blue right there? Start the gardening year with small but mighty dwarf iris (*Iris reticulata* 'Harmony' is vivid bluebird-blue), segue into ground-hugging 'Georgia Blue' veronica, spike it up with blue bearded iris, lead into 'Black and Blue' salvia, and finish the year with the glow of 'Wood's Light Blue' aster.

Or maybe sunshine is more your style? Plant daffodils to kick it off, then yellow tulips, followed by yellow bearded iris, then 'Moonshine' yarrow, then 'Moonbeam' threadleaf coreopsis, and open autumn with a finale of 'Fireworks' goldenrod. You get the idea—just keep the same color coming, and you'll never notice the pause between bloomers. Figure on 6 to 10 square feet of space for a group of three to five consecutive bloomers, depending on the mature size of the plants you pick. Then enjoy the show.

▽ A rosy pink hardy geranium, silver lamb's-ears, and self-sowing orange California poppies quickly cover a slope. Most hardy geranium plants rapidly blanket a 3-foot area of ground.

The Magnificent Seven

A perennial garden that's in bloom throughout the growing season may seem like wishful thinking, but we can do it with just seven plants. Use these perennials as the foundation of your garden, and you'll have continuous color throughout the growing season. Their bloom times overlap or follow quickly on each other's heels, and all of them bloom for at least several weeks.

The "magnificent seven," in order from April through August, are:

Creeping phlox (*Phlox subulata*)

Gold alyssum (*Aurinia saxatilis*)

Blue catmint (*Nepeta ×faassenii*)

Shasta daisy
(*Leucanthemum ×superbum*)

'Monch' aster (*Aster ×frikartii* 'Monch')

Tall garden phlox
(*Phlox maculata, P. paniculata*)

Coneflower
(*Echinacea* species and hybrids)

Consecutive Color

April through September is the growing season in most regions, and the blooming season, and most perennials bloom for only about two weeks of that time.

So many gardeners pore over bloom-time charts, or depend on years of experience, to fill their beds with continual color. Two weeks of bloom, and a twenty-four-week blooming season—that's a lot of plants! We'd need a dozen different two-week bloomers for each color! Then we'd need a dozen more perennials for another color, and another.

Relax. There's a much easier way to enjoy continual color:

→ Include annuals, to provide months of continuous, nonstop color.
→ Depend on long-blooming perennials. Add two-week bloomers, too (who wouldn't want Oriental poppies, even if they are brief beauties?), but select long bloomers for lasting color.
→ Add early and late-flowering plants, to stretch the bloom season on both ends.

Extend the Season, Forward and Back

A simple solution for keeping color in the perennial beds is to add annuals. Their mission is to bloom prolifically to set lots of seed, so they will offer flowers for a long period of time. And some perennials will put out a second round of buds and blooms if you deadhead the flowers (snip them off as soon as they

▷ 'Fire Spinner', a cold-hardy variety of ice plant (*Delosperma* hybrid), is accented with an equally cold-hardy brooch of burgundy hens-and-chicks and a spray of sedum.

▽ Tall garden phlox is a long bloomer with a sweet scent. Snip off finished flower clusters, and each plant will oblige with a fresh round of blossoms.

PUNCH IT UP

Plain and Fancy

Soft shapes, small leaves, and pastel flowers are all lovely, but too much delicacy in the garden makes us crave a dash of bold. Beds need stronger characters for that balancing contrast.

The simplest solution is to put plain next to fancy. Think smooth, simple leaves among busy textures, emphatic upright shapes to punctuate mounds and soft clumps, and a solid stretch of single color between a mix of hues. You'll recognize plants that will fulfill these three functions by just noting their leaves, habits, and colors. Think hostas for shade, and cannas or dahlias for sun, for big, plain leaves that contrast with finer foliage nearby; pick staunchly upright bearded iris and ornamental grasses for emphasis; and select ground-hugging 'Wave' petunias or vivid ice plant (*Delosperma* species) for a big area of solid color. Ice plant was formerly only for mild-winter climates, but newer cold-hardy varieties allow many more gardeners to enjoy this vivid groundcover.

One power player is sometimes enough to balance many feet of a long bed filled with softer personalities. Let your eye be your guide. If your extended garden feels like it needs more zing, add a powerful punch of contrast.

PENNY-PINCHER TIP
Fill Space Fast

To fill space quickly, use these cheap tricks for accomplishing that goal at a bargain price: add a pedestal birdbath, put in a fast-growing rose, include a hefty rock, or insert a clump of ornamental grass. Each of these nifty space-fillers can take up 3 to 5 feet of a bed. Incorporate all four of them as you're expanding your gardens, and they can fill a stretch of about 18 feet long and 3 feet wide. That's close to 50 square feet of garden for as little as $20—and you'll dig only two planting holes! Cover the new area with the same mulch you have used in the already established part of the bed, and your expansion will be seamless.

△ This daylily and dwarf mugo pine, an unusual combination, achieve the goal of combining plants of different shapes, textures, and colors. Each plant covers a relatively large area, a good trick for pinching pennies.

fade). Cut back the plants by about a third, too, while you're at it, to encourage them to branch—more stems means more flowers. Try this trick on these perennials:

Agastache
   (*Agastache* species and hybrids)

Beebalm (*Monarda* species)

Catmint (*Nepeta* species and hybrids)

Delphinium
   (*Delphinium* species and hybrids)

Jupiter's beard (*Centranthus ruber*)

Shasta daisy
   (*Leucanthemum* ×*superbum*)

Sweet William (*Dianthus barbatus*)

Tall garden phlox
   (*Phlox maculata, P. paniculata*)

Threadleaf coreopsis
   (*Coreopsis verticillata*)

Extending Your Gardens

As you create gardens here and there, you'll soon be getting rid of much of the lawn. And as you lengthen and widen your beds, the lawn disappears gradually with barely any notice. Extend the edges of corner gardens, add perimeter plantings and a bed around the tree, and before you know it, it's just a reasonable step to turning the whole yard into a garden.

Then you'll want to put in more paths. Paths make it easy to maintain a big garden. They allow you to maneuver a wheelbarrow through when it's time to renew the mulch, or to cut back plants after frost. But the biggest benefit of paths is the ease of daily maintenance—otherwise known as walking around and admiring.

Paths give us access to every part of the garden, so we can keep an eye out for problems as well as admire our creation.

The surface of the path is up to you. Lawn grass is lovely, with or without stepping stones laid in at intervals, but most kinds of turf will creep into the beds. Wood chips, gravel, or pavers eliminate the need for edging, once the sod is removed.

The layout of the paths is up to you, too. A simple way to start: pay attention to the way your eye travels around your yard, and follow that line with a path. Or lay out loose S-curves that traverse the entire area.

Never Finished—That's the Fun

Gardens have a habit of expanding. Every year, you'll fall in love with new plants you must have. Every year, the flower beds can get a little bigger, as plants fill in and the space that's available for new plants shrinks. Every

PENNY-PINCHER TIP

Buy Wholesale

Are you planning to extend gardens by more than a few feet, or to go whole-hog at turning your lawn into gardens? Check into buying plants in quantity.

Garden centers often sell entire flats of annuals or perennials at a lower cost per plant than individual pots. Wholesale growers have even cheaper prices—as little as 50 cents a plant for perennials, groundcovers, or ornamental grasses; $25 for 100 daffodils; and pennies for annuals. If buying wholesale, you'll need to add shipping costs to that price, but you'll still come out way ahead. Can't use a flat of seventy-two of the same perennial? Share with friends and neighbors!

year—or every month, or every week—you'll see new areas of the yard where you can plant flowers.

The garden is never finished, and that's why it's a lifelong joy. Whether you extend your beds by inches or cover your whole yard with gardens, there's always room for more beauty—at a bargain price.

▷ Extending your gardens to replace your lawn isn't as daunting as it may seem at first. Do one building block at a time, including wide paths for easy walking and appreciation, and soon your whole yard can be a showpiece.

A Beckoning Bench

GATHERING PLACES AND SITTING SPOTS

△ This appealing garden offers a sense of separation from the street—privacy, in other words—and lively color from objects as well as plants.

We live outside a lot in the warm months. And those spaces keep getting bigger, and more like outdoor rooms. Whether in the front yard or backyard, we enjoy our garden areas for gathering with friends or spending quiet time on our own.

Fire up the grill, and have a seat to enjoy a perfect summer day or the cool of the evening. Head for the garden bench for a peaceful hour of reading or daydreaming or a one-on-one chat. Share a pitcher of lemonade with a best friend at the bistro table. Watch the hummingbirds, the butterflies, the busy bees.

Getting Connected

We're gathering outside, but we still want to feel connected to the house. On the practical side, gathering near the house makes it easy to carry food and drinks and other supplies for our gathering—even if it's a gathering of two, or for one, for that matter. We can quickly wash our hands, stick a Band-aid on a scraped knee, or otherwise have quick access to all the comforts home provides.

Being near the house, yet outside, is an easy step for our minds to make, too. We like feeling sheltered, and we're reassured by having our familiar home nearby. A porch or deck, or a patio right outside the back door, provide that feeling instantly. A patio that's thirty steps across the lawn, not right outside the door? Even that little stretch of lawn grass we have to cross can be a formidable psychological obstacle. Oh sure, we'll gather around the grill out there, eventually. But until a "herd leader" guides us to the waterhole, we're likely to stand around outside the back door with our beverages, rather than be the first to make a break for the comfortable seating on the patio. As for that garden bench, fancy gazebo, or sweet little tea table sitting way out there in the yard? They may as well be in Siberia.

What's lacking? Connection. Even if that sitting spot is just a short stroll from the house, it's not connected, and there's a river of lawn or garden to cross. It can be daunting, on a subconscious level—unless that destination looks so inviting, we can't resist.

Fortunately, there's a simple solution to creating connection to a sitting spot that's separated from the house. Just make a path.

Like a trail through a forest, a path across a wide stretch of open lawn— even across only 10 or 20 feet of open lawn—clearly directs us. It first guides our eyes, loudly proclaiming "This way!" And our feet obey.

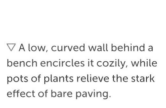 A pair of pots create the impression of sheltering arms around a bench, making it more inviting.

▽ A low, curved wall behind a bench encircles it cozily, while pots of plants relieve the stark effect of bare paving.

▽ Wide, spaced, vertical slats of wood and metal can offer a unique solution to the problem of privacy on a busy street. The staggered height of the slats makes the wall-like solution much less forbidding, both looking in and looking out.

◁ Two corner posts and a crosspiece, combined with an existing back wall, are all it takes to create the sheltering effect of an outdoor room, even in this front yard.

PENNY-PINCHER TIPS
Call It Art

For nearly instant corners, start with sticks.

Round up some dead branches with interesting shapes, about 6 feet tall. "Plant" them in the soil at the corners of your sitting spot, deep enough so that they're solidly supported. These sticks can be perfect support for fast-growing annual climbers, such as scarlet runner beans, edible pole beans, morning glories, or sweet peas.

You can use any material as the surface for this path—wood chips, gravel, crushed oyster shells, pavers, or separated steppingstones. Just make sure the path is strongly defined, so the eye makes a beeline along it. Make the path a generous width of 3 feet or more, which invites sauntering rather than hurrying, and add curves if you like.

The garden bench, bistro table and chairs, or gazebo at the end of that path? That's our reward for following the signs. And it's lovely to sit and gaze back at the way we've come!

Now we have the all-important connection. But we also want to make it the most comfortable, most popular gathering place on the block.

Creating a "Room"

You've saved your pennies for a classic wooden garden bench. You've found the perfect retro metal chairs or wicker set at a garage sale. You've invested serious money in some patio furniture. Whatever your budget and your style, you're happy with the furnishings you're chosen for your outdoor gathering place.

Let's make a "room" to put them in. We crave the feeling of being sheltered, so we want to create a space that feels welcoming. A paved patio or lawn is a fine start. But that's only the floor. We'll need the impression of walls, and perhaps a roof, to make it inviting. And then we'll need some plants in that outdoor living room to strengthen the invitation even more.

SHELTER

We humans like to feel cozy, sheltered and shielded from curious onlookers. Maybe this urge harks back to ancient times, when humans sat with their backs to the wall of the cave to watch for saber-toothed tigers at the entrance. Maybe it's simply an innate human trait to want to keep a lookout, while being protected.

Whatever the reason, a sitting area out in the open makes us subconsciously feel less comfortable than a sitting spot that's sheltered by walls or a roof. In the garden, those walls and roof can be human-made: a patio umbrella, a stone or stucco wall, a wooden arbor or pergola overhead. They can be created with plants, too: the canopy of a shade tree, a trellised rose, a container garden, a border of flowers or shrubs. Or they can be a combination of the two, depending on your taste, your time, and your budget.

Keep in mind that the walls and roof over and around a gathering place should be only a suggestion of enclosure, not a full-scale construction or planting project.

CORNERS

The simplest, quickest way to create a sitting spot that will gladly get used is to put it in a corner. A corner of a fence, a corner of a garden, a corner of the walls of the house.

Place the bench or chairs facing outward, and you've achieved the feeling of "cozy with a view." The magic happens because the "arms" (or "walls") of that corner, whether they're planted or not, enclose the sitting area.

A corner subtly but powerfully puts your sitting area within a space—the key to making it cozy. Use the corner trick to make any sitting spot feel sheltered in an open area of lawn, or on a bare patio. There's no need to build a continuous wall of plants. A "dotted line" of plants or containers, with gaps between them, is just as powerful. Our eyes and brain respond to even a slight hint of a corner. How cozy!

Room with a View

We want to be able to see out when we're resting in that sitting spot—out to the street, or across to the woods, fields, or neighboring yards. If the view for your resting place ends in a tall privacy fence, a high masonry wall, or a high green hedge, that's a sudden stop that is off-putting, not inviting.

To resolve that issue, position the sitting spot so that your line of sight includes an existing garden before your gaze hits the wall. No gardens in sight? Hang a hummingbird feeder or a hanging basket from a tall shepherd's hook a few feet before the fence, or set a pedestal birdbath there for an eye-catcher that wards off that walled-in feeling. Anything will work that stops the eye from zooming straight to that high wall of greenery or fence.

Creating Shade

Walls aren't always enough to make us feel sheltered. We want a roof, a ceiling, for shade. Many of us already have a roof of sorts: the patio umbrella over the table. Many yards already have another roof just waiting to be used: the sheltering branches of a shade tree.

△ Shelter a front yard bench with gardens to make it feel protected, instead of on display.

▷ Put in pollinator-attracting plants like this swamp milkweed (*Asclepias incarnata*) near backyard sitting spots, so you can watch hard-working honeybees and other insects while you relax.

△ Vertical 'Karl Foerster' grass provides a privacy border of simple, clean lines in front of this modern house.

Structures create a welcoming shady spot, too. Pergolas, arbors, gazebos—they're all popular places to set outdoor furniture, thanks to that sheltering roof that says, "Come on in, it's cool inside!"

The pergola is a popular outdoor living feature. It's a wide, deep structure with upright corner posts and a flat roof of spaced crosspieces. Attached to the house or freestanding, it can be made of any material. A pergola is room-sized, big enough to put a large dining set or full-fledged outdoor sofa and chairs beneath. A pergola hits all the must-haves of an inviting outdoor space—except for low price. Quickly growing in popularity as we move our living spaces outdoors, pergolas range from about $400 for a simple DIY job to exorbitant constructions.

An arbor is not nearly as deep as a pergola from front to back. It's not an outdoor room, but an outdoor resting spot. A bench or a pair of small chairs beneath an arbor is irresistible. Rose-covered or not, an arbor gives us a small spot of privacy, with roof and walls built in. It's a nook for sitting and contemplating, or for stepping away from the party on the patio for a moment of privacy.

A trellis can add privacy or pretty up other structures. It's a two-dimensional (flat) support for climbing plants that can go against a house or be erected in any garden.

DON'T PLANT A PROBLEM
Weighty Matters

When considering planting a vine or climbing plant to run up the support posts of your outdoor living space, match the habit of the plant's vines to the supports. Large-flowered clematis vines, for instance, remain lightweight, so any trellis will hold them, whereas small-flowered autumn clematis (*Clematis paniculata*) grows huge and heavy and can topple a flimsy structure. Annual vines are usually the lightest in weight and the lowest in maintenance—no pruning needed, although you will need to remove frost-killed vines. Woody vines and climbers, such as wisteria, grape, and climbing roses, need much sturdier supports and occasional pruning to keep them in bounds.

A gazebo is a small stand-alone outdoor room, open to the air, with corners and a roof. A gazebo is a destination, usually built of wood in an appealing, romantic style. When creating a gazebo for an outdoor gathering spot in your yard, use the following simple tricks to tie it to its surroundings, so that it doesn't feel isolated:

→ Lead guests to the gazebo with a path.
→ Flank the entrance with large pots of flowers outside, to instantly improve the appeal and entice visitors.
→ Add a pair of curved corner gardens at the entrance, sweeping the plantings down along the path to the structure.
→ Set a bench or pair of chairs outside the structure. They'll create a step-at-a-time approach to entering the gazebo.

Soon, you'll see an overflow of family or friends standing outside the entrance of the gazebo, as well as filling the space within. A gathering space is a valuable asset; we just have to make it inviting.

▷ This pergola, designed by Jeffrey Van Maren for a California garden, uses a sun sail shade cloth as the roof of the Asian-influenced structure.

△ Bring the garden right onto the porch or patio with pots of flowers or foliage. Place petunias in a sunny corner for an easy and rewarding enhancement.

DON'T PLANT A PROBLEM

Keep the Vineyard Away

Grapevines are super fast growing and give great shade if planted to grow up and over a pergola, but they can cause problems at a gathering place in your yard. The ripe grapes attract birds, and the fruit also lures raccoons, opossums, skunks, and even foxes. Fallen fruit makes a mess and can stain pavers. Worst of all, the ripe or overripe grapes, both on the vine and dropped on the ground, attract stinging yellow jackets and other wasps, not exactly the sort of guests we want at our outdoor gatherings. Keep your grapevines away from gathering places to avoid potential problems.

Plant Pleasures

Like a philodendron or Boston fern in the living room, plants on and around the porch, patio, or deck soften the scene by adding living greenery. This is your opportunity to indulge in hanging baskets and create container gardens to bring color and beauty to your gathering place.

Speaking of those houseplants, a shaded deck or patio is an ideal destination for a summer vacation for your indoor plants. A few months outdoors will reinvigorate them, so that you have lush beauties to bring back inside for winter.

Houseplants are a start, and a definite budget-saver, but you'll want other plants, too. Climbers, containers, and edging plants bring a sitting spot alive.

Keep containers and gardens limited to areas where they won't block traffic in and out of the patio or other gathering spot. Group smaller containers together, to reduce tripping hazards. Watch the placement of hanging baskets, too, so no one bonks their head, and don't put tall plants too close to chairs, where tickling foliage can be annoying.

Group potted plants to make a bigger splash in your gathering place. Tie them to the rest of the yard by repeating your signature colors and including some of the same plants. Annuals are a standby for container gardens, but you can use perennials, shrubs, and ornamental grasses, too, to add more flair.

Patio Privacy

When planning how to arrange your patio plants, go minimalist. Accent plants show off better than planting all around the edges. So, emphasize the corners with large containers or by growing plants up the posts. Add a few pots around the patio, too, for extra color and warmth.

Mark the patio entrance, too, with a pot or planting of colorful flowers, so that it's clear where to enter the space. Plant a bed along one side, if you like, to add fragrance to the patio pleasures, and to bring in delightful butterflies and hummingbirds.

If your yard is wide open to the neighbors' line of sight, and lacking a fence or hedge, you'll want to put "privacy" at the top of your priority list for that gathering place. Try the following tricks for screening the view of your patio from the neighbors' yard:

→ Install a single section of fence on one or two sides of the patio. Part of the activity will still be in full sight, but that 8-foot stretch will make you and your friends and family feel comfortably sheltered from full view. Decorate

▷ A big-leaved philodendron houseplant and its indoor friends enjoy a summer vacation outdoors while adding generous spots of greenery to this shady sitting place.

▷ Old-fashioned hollyhocks are tall enough to provide privacy, and they bloom at peak outdoor-living season. They'll stand straight without staking, another plus.

PUNCH IT UP

Trellises and Vines

Flat, tall metal trellises are cheap ($20 to $25), quick to poke into the ground, and lend privacy even before vines cover them. They're also focal points that add eye-pleasing height to gathering-place gardens. Set a container at the base or between a pair of trellises for instant color, while you wait for vines to climb.

△ "Can you add a sitting spot?" asked Lou and Lila, in the middle of the front yard makeover we were doing for them. A niche between tree and house provided the necessary cozy feeling, while gardens and a birdbath offer an interesting view.

the inside of the fence with a mirror, plaque, or other artwork that can stand up to the weather. Park a group of pots in front of it to soften the starkness of the barrier.

→ Put up a wall of readymade lattice on the offending wide-open side. To save money, buy a narrow piece of lattice, about 2 feet wide, and mount it horizontally at about head-to-shoulders height. Block your own view with a barrier at head height, and you'll forget that your legs are visible. Frame the lattice to give it a finished look, and grow annual vines on it to soften the woodwork.

→ Attach a length of cheap chicken wire fencing to the corner posts of your patio, mounting it at about head height, as with the lattice. Plant fast-growing seeds of hyacinth bean, pole beans, or annual morning glories to cloak it in greenery and flowers.

→ Insert three inexpensive metal trellises along one side, spacing them about a foot apart. They'll provide a screen just as is, but they'll be even prettier with morning glories or other annual vines covering them.

→ Plant a screen of tall ornamental grasses, such as miscanthus. They'll grow fast, with each plant covering 3 to 4 feet.

→ Grow a row of annual sunflowers, for screening and sunny summer cheer.

A Moonlight Garden

For the ultimate romantic touch, plant a summer garden that waits until sundown to show off. An all-white garden is elegant and serene, but there are plenty of colorful characters, too, that will bring after-dark attractions to your gathering place.

Plant flowers that open in the evening, to enchant friends and family when the blossoms unfurl like a slow-motion film. Perfect patio partners include evening primrose (*Oenothera* species and hybrids), moonflower vine (*Ipomoea alba*), and night-flowering tobacco (*Nicotiana sylvestris*).

Some flowers wait until dark to release their fragrance, or bump up their scent when the sun goes down. They're hoping to attract moths and other nighttime pollinators with their heady aroma, but what a treat for our noses, too. Include white and pale flowers that are visible even in the dim glow of patio lighting, because against their pale petals, it's easier to see the fascinating moths that come seeking nectar at night.

Fragrant Plants

Fragrant plants are better than any indoor air freshener at sending delightful scents wafting through a gathering place in summer. Include superfragrant tropical tuberose (*Polianthes tuberosa*) and angel's trumpet (*Datura* and *Brugmansia* species and hybrids) in your pots, and sweet-scented annuals and perennials in your plantings. And don't forget scented foliage, which will release its aroma whenever anyone brushes against it or idly rubs a leaf.

MISTAKES NOT TO MAKE

Fragrance Duds

Flowering tobacco (*Nicotiana* species and hybrids) is famed for being sweet-scented, but many modern varieties are lacking in fragrance. White or pale colors are usually much more strongly scented, but do the sniff test before you buy, so you don't get a fragrance dud. White-flowered *Nicotiana sylvestris* and *N. alata* 'Jasmine' are reliably fragrant.

FRAGRANT FLOWERS

Angel's trumpet (*Datura* and *Brugmansia* species and hybrids)

Annual sweet alyssum (*Lobularia maritima*)

Four-o'clock (*Mirabilis jalapa*)

Freesia (*Freesia* species)

Heliotrope (*Heliotropium arborescens*)

Moonflower vine (*Ipomoea alba*)

Petunia (*Petunia* hybrids)

Rose (*Rosa* species and hybrids)

Tall garden phlox (*Phlox maculata, P. paniculata*)

Tuberose (*Polianthes tuberosa*)

FRAGRANT FOLIAGE

Anise hyssop, hummingbird mint (*Agastache* species and hybrids)

Beebalm (*Monarda* species)

Lavender (*Lavandula* species and hybrids)

Lemon balm (*Melissa officinalis*)

Lemongrass (*Cymbopogon citratus*)

Lemon verbena (*Aloysia citrodora*)

Rosemary (*Rosmarinus* species and hybrids)

Scented geranium (*Pelargonium* species and hybrids)

EXOTIC PERFUMES

Jasmine. Gardenia. Tuberose. Freesia. These legendary floral fragrances for perfumes are equally welcome in the night garden. In the steamy South, jasmine and gardenia are right at home in the warm temperatures and abundant rain. Elsewhere, they're a challenge. But tuberose (pronounced "tube rose," and a dreadful name for a lovely spire of sweet white flowers) is as easy to grow as daffodils, and surprisingly inexpensive—about a dollar per bulb, if you buy from home growers on eBay or local ads—for weeks' worth of heady perfume at your patio. The bulbs multiply quickly, doubling or tripling your supply every year. Freesia is equally easy to grow, and even cheaper, at about 25 to 50 cents a bulb from commercial sellers. If your winters dip below freezing, you'll need to dig up the bulbs in fall to store over winter in a cool, dry place protected from the cold. If you plant the bulbs in a pot, not in the ground, it'll be a cinch to lift them for winter storage.

△ Even a small balcony has room for a cook's garden of herbs and greens in simple but ample containers.

Herbs at Hand

Every outdoor chef appreciates having fresh herbs near at hand. Lemon thyme to crumble over the chicken, fennel for the fish, stems of rosemary stripped of their leaves to use as mini-skewers for cherry tomatoes—my mouth is watering already, and we haven't even gotten to mint for the mojitos. Indeed, it's a cook's delight to have summer seasonings just a few steps from grill or table, so you can experiment to your heart's content.

Keep your herbs grouped together so that plucking them takes only a few seconds. Make a grouping of pots filled with your culinary favorites. Or fill a few inexpensive plastic or wooden boxes with the herbs you reach for most often, and place the containers as a pretty edging along the patio.

Edible flowers like nasturtiums, pansies, calendulas, and chives are nice to have nearby, too, to scatter atop a potato salad at the last minute, toss into a green salad, or decorate a platter of grilled chicken. The flowers add a splash of color, too, to brighten the varied textures of culinary herbs in your containers.

More Life at the Party

Hummingbirds, butterflies, honeybees, and other entertaining party guests appreciate flowers as much as we do. Just add some of their favorite nectar flowers to the pots and plantings of your gathering place garden, and you'll be enjoying more life at your party all summer long.

Plant these easy and cheap attractions (beautiful, too!), which are guaranteed to boost the guest list:

→ Poke seeds of red-flowered cypress vine (*Ipomoea quamoclit*) or scarlet runner bean (*Phaseolus coccineus*) into a pot. Use a trio of dead sticks to make a tepee for the vines to climb, attracting hummingbirds.

→ Plant annual moonflower vine (*Ipomoea alba*) on a trellis or arbor at your favorite sitting spot, to thrill to hummingbirdlike sphinx moths at dusk.

→ Bring in butterflies with purple coneflowers (*Echinacea purpurea*) and blue anise hyssop (*Agastache foeniculum*). Both of these perennials bloom for months and are irresistible to butterflies and pollinators of all sorts.

→ Grow a fiesta of zinnias (*Zinnia* species) along the patio for nectar-seeking hummingbirds and butterflies.

→ Add 'Autumn Joy' sedum (*Sedum* 'Autumn Joy') to give bees and other pollinators a late-summer feast as patio season winds to a close.

△ A welcoming entrance, a sheltering wall, a shady roof of trees, and this country gathering place has everything it needs to be a popular destination in summer.

The Joys of Summer

Spending time in the garden with family and friends, or simply enjoying the solitude in a favorite sitting spot among the flowers, can be a summer treat that's even better than homemade ice cream. And it's available to all of us, at any time, no matter how short we are on time or money. Make your gathering place a destination for months of pleasure by adding paths and privacy the building block way. Make it cozy with corners, and double its delights with fragrant flowers and fresh herbs at hand. Then sit back and enjoy your summer vacation, just a few steps outside the door.

A Beckoning Bench
GATHERING PLACES AND SITTING SPOTS

A corner garden (with 6-foot sides and a 5-foot depth) creates a cozy place for a garden bench. Reinforce the feeling of enclosure with pots on either side of the bench that echo the plants and colors of the corner garden.

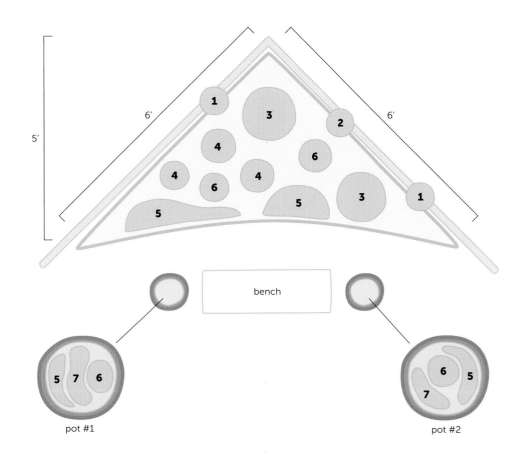

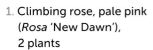

1. Climbing rose, pale pink (*Rosa* 'New Dawn'), 2 plants
2. Variegated miscanthus grass (*Miscanthus sinensis* 'Cosmopolitan'), 1 plant

3. Pale yellow Shasta daisy (*Leucanthemum ×superbum* 'Banana Cream'), 2 plants
4. Veronica, bright cool-pink (*Veronica spicata* 'Red Fox'), 3 plants
5. Dwarf yellow 'Gem' marigold (*Tagetes tenuifolia* 'Lemon Gem'), sow 2 packets of seed

6. Deep pink bedding geranium (*Pelargonium* hybrid, many cultivars; 'Boldly Hot Pink' is a widely available Proven Winners selection), 4 plants
7. Variegated licorice plant (*Helichrysum petiolare* 'Licorice Splash'), 2 plants

Sidewalk Strip

CREATING CURB APPEAL

△ A garden along the curb
calls for plants that can take
tough conditions of heat and
dryness and still look good.

▷ Strolling the sidewalk beside this garden is a pleasure, with so many flowers to admire along the way. Sweeps of bearded iris stand proudly above self-sowing blue catmint that has found new homes in the smallest cracks.

O bsessed gardeners like I am will soon start eyeing that strip between street and sidewalk and considering the possibilities. It's garden-sized already, a long, neatly defined bed that's just begging for plants. But other folks make these gardens for less selfish reasons. They create them to share something beautiful with the world.

You have no strip between the street and the sidewalk? The border of the yard works just as well to delight sidewalk strollers. The sidewalk strip isn't a private place. It's seen by everyone who passes by. When thoughtfully planted, this garden is a generous gift that pretties up the whole block.

This spot requires more careful plant choices, too, because life can be hard for the plants in that confined area, being far from sprinkler systems or the garden hose. It calls for dedicated maintenance to keep it in tip-top shape, worthy of being admired instead of becoming a weedy eyesore. It's also the ultimate show-off garden, simply because it is so public. It gets noticed first, so let's make it as beautiful as can be.

Repetition

We've repeated colors and plant shapes throughout the yard to make it look all of a whole, like pieces of a quilt. And the sidewalk strip is no different. Repetition is still the name of the game. The sidewalk strip reflects your style

△ The intricate foliage of partridge feather (*Tanacetum densum*) differs in shape, not color, from the plainer lamb's-ears, and the contrasting texture is a nice addition to a sidewalk strip, where the combination will be seen up close.

MISTAKES NOT TO MAKE

Forewarned Is Forearmed

Sewer lines, gas lines, buried utility cables, fiber optics—it can be a Pandora's box beneath that ground you want to turn into a garden. Make a phone call to the "Call Before You Dig" number before you get started, so that they can mark the potential hazards. In the United States, just dial 811—it's the same number all across the country.

and your sense of beauty just as surely as any other planting around your home.

If your yard is a festival of color—bright hues—or accented with powerful plant architecture—bold shapes—you'll want to keep that theme when you make a splash streetside. Going bold is one sure way to get attention. But if you lean toward a more romantic look in the rest of your yard, a curbside strip of pale colors and gentle shapes will have great appeal. This tone instantly softens the hard surfaces around it—the curb and paving of street and sidewalk. A touch of romance in the neighborhood is always welcome.

If your next-door neighbor already has a sidewalk strip garden, you may want to make your own strip a gradual transition rather than an abrupt change of style. For example, repeat some of the neighbor's choices of colors and plants, along with your own, and the adjoining strips will complement each other instead of competing.

And there's an even bigger consideration: if a neighborhood or city group has laid down the law about what you can and can't do with that strip of real estate. A homeowners' association (HOA) may dictate what's allowed to be planted in that space. A town may want to do a whole street of flowering cherry trees, say, with nothing at their feet. Since that strip is technically part of the roadside right-of-way in many areas, it's a good idea to check with your local government, and especially your HOA, before you start digging.

Clear Passage

Take some time to think about how others use the street and sidewalk when you plan your streetside garden. Folks on foot, drivers on the street, bicyclists, delivery people, dog walkers, and those who park on the street or turn into nearby driveways all need clear access. Some considerations:

→ Plants that block their access will soon be trampled flat.
→ Plants with thorns or spines, placed near the edges, may land you in a lawsuit.
→ Plants that block the line of sight for drivers or pedestrians may cause an accident.
→ Support stakes or pointy sticks, as my mother always warned me, can poke an eye out, should someone lose their balance and stumble into the garden.
→ If your street is popular for parking, make sure passengers can open vehicle doors and step out without difficulty.

△ Set a fence well back from the sidewalk, not up against it, so a billow of clematis and roses (as here) don't get in the way of passersby.

If all those warnings make you apprehensive, take heart. Common sense and the following tips will keep this planting trouble-free:

Clear access Allow a clear way of access from street to sidewalk every 6 feet or so along the curb. Openings need to be convenient, just a few steps away, or your plants are likely to get stomped. Denote the pathways with mulch, bricks, or steppingstones so that they're instantly noticeable. Keep plants trimmed back along the paths.

Gentle to the touch Don't plant sharp-pointed, saw-edged, or spiny plants in this space. A straying bicyclist, kid, or dog may end up in the garden. Ouch!

Stay in bounds Avoid tall plants that can topple over, or arching plants that can sprawl into the way of passersby. Some spillover on the curb side is charming, but keep the garden within bounds on the sidewalk side. Clip back groundcovers and other plants that stray more than a couple of inches onto the sidewalk paving, so they don't trip passersby.

Save special treasures for other gardens, and stick to plants you won't mind too much seeing damaged. Tromped and snapped stems are everyday events in a curbside garden. Romping dogs, swerving bikes, and other missteps will take their toll. Entire plants may be flattened by an errant driver. The risk goes with this garden, so use tough plants here.

Flowers can be mighty tempting for passersby to pick, so don't be surprised if you see your curbside flowers disappearing down the street, clutched in a little fist. Instead of glaring and fuming, put in plants that are attractive but without lush blooms or are covered with blooms so you'll feel like you can spare a few.

Consider the Commitment

It's all too tempting to let a curbside garden take care of itself. The plants are tough customers by nature, needing no coddling and no extra water once they settle in. If you've done your job of mulching deeply and have planted closely, you won't even do much weeding.

Sounds good on paper. "Looks good," we think. And maybe it does, from a distance. But the perspective is different to others on the street—the dog walkers, the bike riders, the parkers, the mail carriers, the evening strollers, and especially the neighbors. They see this garden close up.

While you're out back, tending your tomatoes after dinner or playing with the puppy, they're standing on the sidewalk, wondering why you don't pull the weeds they can so clearly see, or prune back that hollyhock that snapped off when someone opened the car door right into it . . . last week.

How much extra commitment does this garden need? Not much in terms of time, but definitely more in terms of frequency. Can you handle 10 minutes a week? That's all you probably need to do to keep up with snipping, weeding, and tidying up. But you can't put it off.

For this garden, weeks of maintenance deferred to one marathon 3- to 4-hour session won't do the trick. What this garden demands is regular attention, so it doesn't become a wild thing. Cut plants back to keep them compact, clip off fading foliage and flowers, and add a dustpan and brush to your tool kit so you can sweep up mulch or gravel that's been knocked out of the bed.

Mulch goes a long way to conserve moisture and keep down weeds, both big factors in a curbside garden. But in this location, we have another consideration, too. The mulch can reflect sunlight to help keep the soil cool. Try gravel in this spot instead of wood chips or other organic materials, even if your other gardens use a different material. Light-colored gravel will reflect the sunlight as

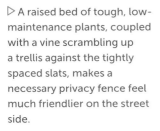 △ Because so many passersby see and enjoy the sidewalk garden, it needs small, frequent doses of care throughout the year.

▷ A raised bed of tough, low-maintenance plants, coupled with a vine scrambling up a trellis against the tightly spaced slats, makes a necessary privacy fence feel much friendlier on the street side.

well as slow evaporation. And it won't absorb precious moisture from the soil like organic mulch.

Gravel also makes a great seedbed for the progeny of xeric plants, giving them the superfast drainage they prefer. It may seem like the most inhospitable of conditions in which to start life, but your drought-tolerant plants will love it.

Curbside Color

One sure way to draw in onlookers to your curbside garden is with color: impossible to overlook color—of any hue, but in a splash that's big enough to make people wonder, "What's that blue-blossomed plant?" and cross the street to investigate.

One or two continuous stretches of bright color, 12 to 36 inches in diameter, are enough to accent the whole strip. Combine them with quieter hues or with perennials that go in and out of bloom, and you've painted a pleasing picture in just a few strokes. You can plan the garden to include a succession of perennials for good-sized patches of color through the year. Or you can take the easier route, and depend on annuals to fill the role for months. Or you can mix and match, according to your taste and space.

You already know which colors grab attention. They're the ones that catch your eye across the yard. A splash of hot pink, fuchsia, red, orange, or bright yellow livens up a garden in a hurry, and we definitely want some of those eye-catchers in the curbside garden, especially if they're already in other places in the yard.

Go full blast, if that's your style, and fill your sidewalk strip with traffic-stopping color. Or limit those eye-popping colors to accents, interspersing them among quieter colors and neutrals. The contrast will make them stand out even more strongly. Since most go-with-anything plants are large ones, using the brights as accents is a sneaky way to save money, too.

Supporting Cast

Billows of blue catmint (*Nepeta ×faassenii*) and fountains of blue Russian sage (*Perovskia atriplicifolia*) are standards in sidewalk strips. A single plant of either of these sturdy customers fills a 3-foot space, blooms for months, and is handsome even without flowers. The deep blue-purple of catmint and lighter blue of Russian sage look great with any other color, boosting the impact of brighter characters.

▷ Starry yellow summer flowers are almost an afterthought with 'Angelina' sedum. The foliage wins hearts—rich tints of red and orange in winter that brighten to glowing lime-yellow in spring and summer.

▽ Little combinations are a big part of the pleasure of sidewalk gardens, where they're easy to notice. Here, ever-versatile bearded iris accents a spread of irresistibly charming hens-and-chicks.

But it's not only the lovely blue flower color that makes neighboring plants look better—it's also the silvery leaves and stems of the Russian sage and the grayed green of the catmint's foliage that furnish a foil for other colors. Gray plants go with everything, and they come in a whole spectrum of shades, from whitish silver lamb's-ears to blue-gray fescue, and every hue in between—blue-grays, green-grays, pewter, metallic silver, near white, as well as combinations. Silver shades are spotlights; they're more noticeable from a distance and to those driving by. Gray-greens and blue-grays are more neutral colors that take a background role.

You can't go wrong with grays, no matter which shade you choose. Plant a wide-branching clump of feathery 'Powis Castle' or curlicue 'Lambrook Silver' artemisia in the sidewalk strip, and its color will gently brighten the garden while providing contrast for any other color. Track down the nonflowering lamb's-ears 'Helen von Stein', and give it a good-sized area to cover with its pewter-colored foliage. Add mounds of cool blue-gray fescue as fine-textured accents, or spiky blue-gray 'Heavy Metal' switchgrass or bearded iris leaves for an emphatic contrast to softer textures and shapes. Neutral colors give the eye a rest, something every garden can use.

And don't be concerned about gaps in bloom times. Green foliage is a resting place for the eyes, just like gray foliage is, and is a natural, neutral contrast to flowers around it. Ornamental grasses serve that purpose, as well, providing restful green, but with the bonus of contrasting texture and shape.

White and deep burgundy work as neutrals, too, as well as contrasts. In fact, every neutral goes with every other neutral, but that's not the case with bright colors. Different shades of pink, yellow, or blue can clash horribly. Plant a neutral between them to instantly make peace between warring colors.

Grow Low

A curbside strip filled with 3- to 4-foot-tall perennials can be exciting, but save some space for low growers, too. Dianthus, ice plant, and other flowering groundcovers add significant color, but they also create a refreshing change of pace from their exuberant taller friends. Out of bloom, their low forms offer a sense of calm to the riot around them. Many remain green in winter, keeping the strip interesting even in the sleeping season.

Ground-hugging plants require much less maintenance than tall ones. In most cases, there's no clipping back needed to keep them compact, because

△ Cool pink veronicas are planted parallel with warm pink yarrow—and a river of white between them defuses the potential color clash.

▷ Blue catmint, purple- and white-flowered silvery lamium, and golden 'Angelina' sedum—one plant of each of these groundcovers will quickly fill a 10- to 12-foot strip. Clip back the edges of each clump once or twice a year, to keep them from intermingling.

they're born that way. A once-a-year shearing to remove dead flower stems, on some, like creeping sedums (*Sedum spurium* and other species) is the extent of maintenance.

LOW GROWERS FOR A SUNNY SIDEWALK STRIP

Following are some low-growing plant suggestions:

Blue fescue (*Festuca glauca*)

Creeping phlox (*Phlox subulata*)

Creeping thyme (*Thymus serpyllum, T. praecox*)

Dianthus (*Dianthus* species and hybrids)

Dwarf basket-of-gold, dwarf gold alyssum (*Aurinia saxatilis* 'Compacta')

Evergreen candytuft (*Iberis sempervirens*)

Ice plant (*Delosperma* species and hybrids)

Lamium (*Lamium species*)

Perky Sue (*Hymenoxys scaposa*)

Petunia (*Petunia* hybrids)

Red monardella (*Monardella macrantha*)

Sedum, groundcover types (*Sedum* species and hybrids)

A Desert in Disguise

Hot and thirsty. That's the state of affairs in curbside strips that aren't shaded by trees or buildings. Full sun, reflected by pavement. Concrete or blacktop soaking up heat, which then transfers through the soil and keeps even the air warmer. Heat from traffic, too, and exhaust fumes. Dust stirred up by passing cars. Soil that doesn't stay moist, even if you water it, because the extra heat and sun make moisture evaporate faster than anywhere else in your yard. No wonder some people call them "inferno strips." That length of soil that looks like such an inviting place to put a garden can be more like a desert, even if the rest of the yard is a lush temperate oasis.

If your region gets reliable rain in summer, you have a wide plant palette to pick from. But regular water from the sky can't be counted on, especially in today's changing climate. Rather than regarding this situation as a drawback, I like to think of it as a golden opportunity. Here's a place to play with xeric plants that thrive in hot, dry conditions. These plants are naturally adapted to punishing conditions because they began as wildflowers in places of similar climate—hot, dry summers and cool, rainy winters—including the Mediterranean, the Middle East, and our own desert Southwest. They're also

DON'T PLANT A PROBLEM

Elbow Room

Most plants labeled as groundcovers spread fast and indefinitely. And so do many ground-hugging annuals and perennials. Read the label to see how much space you need to give each plant, so they don't intermingle. Be ruthless about trimming back and yanking out rooted stems to keep them within their boundaries. A mosaic of individual colors and textures is more appealing than a hodgepodge of groundcovers that have grown into each other's territory.

△ In mild-winter climates, cascading rosemary is first choice for spilling over a raised sidewalk bed. Its small but prolific pale blue flowers make bees extra happy, and its clean, sharp scent does the same to human passersby who pinch off a sprig to sniff.

surprisingly cold hardy, and can take snow, ice, and winter wind. And if a summer should happen to be unusually rainy? As long as the soil in that strip is fast draining, most of them will be fine.

You already know and probably grow many xeric plants, but new ones are coming on the market every year as gardeners plan for drought. Have fun paging through catalogs and strolling nurseries to discover new favorites. The following plants are not just survivors, but thrive when water is scarce—and do even better when rain falls from the sky:

Artemisia (*Artemisia* species and hybrids)

Bearded iris (*Iris* hybrids)

California poppy (*Eschscholzia californica*)

Catmint (*Nepeta* species and hybrids)

Hens-and-chicks (*Sempervivum* species and hybrids)

Lamb's-ears (*Stachys byzantina*)

Lavender (*Lavandula* species and hybrids)

Penstemon (*Penstemon* species and hybrids)

Rosemary (*Rosmarinus* species)

Russian sage (*Perovskia atriplicifolia*)

Salvia (*Salvia* species and hybrids)

Santolina (*Santolina chamaecyparissus*)

Sedum (*Sedum* species and hybrids)

Sunrose, rock rose (*Helianthemum* species and hybrids)

Shrubs for Structure

In spring and summer, a sidewalk strip garden needs no shrubs to make it look beautiful—the flowers and grasses will take care of the pretty part of things. But in winter, the branches of shrubs lend structure and beauty to what would otherwise be a mostly bare garden. Stick to shrubs that won't outgrow the space, keeping maintenance to a minimum. Consider width even more than height, and read the tag carefully to get an idea of mature size so you won't be taken by surprise.

Since shrubs will be the winter stars, choose those that add color with late fall berries or bright winter bark, or those that have interesting shapes, such as Japanese maple or Harry Lauder's walking stick (*Corylus avellana* 'Contorta'). Dwarf red-twig dogwood (*Cornus sericea* 'Kelsey's Dwarf'), purple-fruited beautyberry (*Callicarpa americana*), and dwarf winterberry (*Ilex verticillata* 'Nana' or 'Berry Poppins') are adaptable choices that won't make a big dent in the budget.

▷ Variegated sweet iris (*Iris pallida* 'Variegata') is striking all by itself, but let it poke up through a tangle of California poppies, and you have a traffic-stopper along the sidewalk.

▽ Shrubs don't get much respect, except in winter, when the warm orange of sprawling heather, or heath, and the purple fruit of American beautyberry (*Callicarpa americana*) take over for still-sleeping flowers.

▷ Include sweeps of easy, inexpensive creeping phlox in your sidewalk strip to welcome spring with a blast of color.

Bright Color, No Watering

If it's a challenge to get water to your curbside strip, turn to annuals that are drought-tolerant. Concentrated color is what we're after, and nothing fills the bill better than California poppies (*Eschscholzia californica*). Classic pure orange, blended orange and yellow, creamy white, or less common shades of orange-red and rose-pink will supply enough choices of color for any garden. Scatter the seeds in fall, even in cold-winter climates, to get a head start on next spring, and enjoy them wherever they spring up. They don't transplant happily.

There's no need to go for evergreens. In this small space, bare branches are more appealing to the low-key winter picture than a big blob of green, and they're easier to navigate between than branches of prickly needles.

What About Winter?

The timing of maintenance for a curbside strip is different from the rest of your yard. Besides needing frequent maintenance throughout the growing season, when cold weather comes, they can use an immediate cleanup. Your neighbors and visitors will appreciate a tended garden.

Instead of letting dead stems and seed heads stand in winter to catch snow and feed birds, like we might for other areas of the yard, tidy up plants when they are finished growing. Pull out annuals as soon as frost lays them low, and cut back perennials. Rake up dead leaves and other debris. Ornamental grasses can stay, as long as their bleached leaves and seed heads don't shatter and blow away in winter winds. Let evergreen shrubs and silver-leaved plants stay until their foliage looks shabby, then tidy them up, too. Then add a fresh layer of mulch as the finishing touch while the garden waits for spring.

A Gift to the Neighborhood

If the thought of weekly tidying up and then winter cleanup doesn't scare you off, make the neighborhood beautiful by creating a sidewalk strip garden. Fill it with a bounty of well-suited plants. Remember to keep clear access paths through the strip every few feet, for visitors, delivery folks, and playing children.

Sidewalk Strip
CREATING CURB APPEAL

Splash your neighborhood with traffic-stopping color in a sidewalk strip. The cool gray theme of perennials, groundcovers, and ornamental grass makes the stunning 'Wave' petunias stand out from a block away. Substitute any other color of reliable, fast-spreading 'Wave' petunias, if you prefer; the neutral grays go with everything.

This design fills a 5-by-20-foot space.

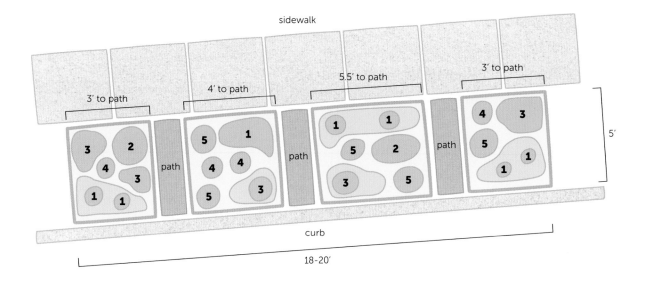

1. Magenta petunia (*Petunia ×hybrida* 'Purple Wave'), 7 plants
2. Blue catmint (*Nepeta ×faassenii* 'Walker's Low'), 2 plants
3. Nonflowering lamb's-ears (*Stachys byzantina* 'Helen von Stein'), 5 plants
4. Bluebird-blue bearded iris (*Iris* hybrid, many cultivars), 4 plants
5. Blue fescue (*Festuca glauca*), 4 plants

Lots of Pots

A CAN'T-MISS CONTAINER GARDEN

△ A lively container garden of nasturtiums and scarlet runner beans in lightweight plastic pots, splashed with bluest-of-the-blue California bluebells (*Phacelia campanularia*), brightens the author's rustic deck in the high Rockies, bringing a constant buzz of hummingbirds.

Containers aren't the finishing touch of a building block garden; they're major players, right from the start. Pots add a welcome sign at the lamppost and the doorstep, punch up beds and borders with concentrated color, make gathering places feel homey, and make beautiful garden ornaments wherever you put them.

Notice the use of plural? Like a handful of potato chips, it's impossible to stop at just one pretty pot. More patio pots. A whole row of hanging baskets. Planters on the deck and clipped to the rail. With so many beautiful containers and so many perfect plants to play with, one more will always make a contribution.

▽ Every plant in this container plays off its companions, with colors echoed throughout the variety of plant and leaf shapes.

Love at First Sight

It's instant gratification that makes hanging baskets and already-planted containers so irresistible. And plant growers have surely recognized our weakness! In a few short years, the offerings have gone way beyond an 8-inch plastic pot of geraniums ready for the doorstep, to a full-size garden of a dozen different plants spilling over a gigantic container.

Another huge part of the appeal is that the DIY feature makes us all feel like artists, as we decide on just the right combination of colors and just the right plant shapes. We also get almost instant payoff from newly planted containers, because these fast growers fill in in just a couple of weeks.

Tables and racks of container plants now fill a good portion of the garden center, rating their own section. Cool blues and purples this year? A hot-sauce mix of spicy orange and red? An edgy lime green and burgundy mix? Maybe you'd better add another pot.

Choosing a Container

Every gardener soon has a collection of containers, whether you bring them home with inexpensive annuals, pick them up at garage sales, or break the budget with a big new beauty. Plain, simple pots in medium to dark natural colors of green, brown, or terra-cotta are the backbone of a collection. They may not be very exciting to look at, but they're the most versatile. They go with

▷ Save your pennies to buy
the biggest pot in the color
that's most dear to your heart.
The container is just as much
a part of the composition as
the plants you put in it.

△ A simple, single shrub lets this decorated Asian pot hold the spotlight year-round. Pink flowers by the doorstep pick up one of the main colors of the container.

MISTAKES NOT TO MAKE
Think Big

Too dinky. That's the main pitfall to avoid with pots. A single small- to medium-size pot isn't strong enough to serve as a stand-alone accent all by itself, even if it's bright purple or overflowing with pretty flowers. Make a group of pots instead—a group that varies in height. Use smaller containers around a large one, or set a couple of the smaller pots atop a support to stagger their heights. An upside-down empty pot is an instant height booster, and it allows for closer spacing than bricks or blocks.

everything—every color of flower, every color of house or trim, every style of garden. And they're the cheapest.

But you'll also want a few showpiece containers—pots that catch the eye even before you add plants. Buy the biggest, most beautiful pot(s) you can afford, because there simply is no substitute. A single container has to be of hefty proportion to look balanced against the bulk of a house, the sweep of a garden, the size of outdoor furniture, or the open space of a patio.

Big pots have other big benefits, too. With more soil, you can plant shrubs, vines, or good-sized grasses, as well as perennials and annuals. Watering chores are reduced, too, because the ample potting soil is slower to dry out from evaporation.

Plastic pots are much less expensive than clay pottery, and they're catching up rapidly to the natural look of their high-priced cousins. From a few feet away, it's hard to tell the difference between a pot made of real terra-cotta or glazed clay and a plastic pot that mimics the size, style, and finish of the real thing.

Brace yourself for sticker shock, though, even with plastic versions. Plastic pots can easily reach $100, and actual pottery or terra-cotta can triple or quadruple that amount.

What's a gardener on a budget to do? Save our pennies, for starters, but also look for bargains to make that piggybank stretch. Here are some tips:

→ **Hunt for used pots** Garage sales are a container gardener's best friend. So are thrift stores, Habitat for Humanity and other resale shops, and local ads, including online Craigslist or Freecycle, as well as printed classifieds.

→ **Buy an unplanted pot** The selection of pots at a well-stocked nursery is staggering, a rainbow of beautiful colors and shapes. And the cost of a DIY container garden is usually much lower than paying for the privilege of buying one already planted.

→ **Buy a planted pot** Sometimes, a preplanted container can be a better buy than putting together your own. The savings on potting soil and plants, plus the head start the plants got in a greenhouse, can save several dollars and several weeks of waiting for your DIY garden to fill in.

→ **Compare prices** Similar or even identical pots can vary hugely in price, depending on the retailer. Invest a day in comparison-shopping and visit several outlets, to get an idea of whose prices are lowest.

△ Raising a pot on a pillar or post multiples its impact so powerfully that a single licorice plant (*Helichrysum petiolare*) is enough to make a significant splash.

▷ It'd be hard to replicate these lush arrangements for a lower price: figure $25 retail for the pot, $10 for the potting soil, and $30 or more for at least six color spot–size annuals. And, because they were already started in a greenhouse, you can enjoy full-blown beauty for months longer than you could a DIY version.

MISTAKES NOT TO MAKE

Contrast the Color

Even a huge pot can vanish before your eyes if you place it against a wall that's similar in color. Go for contrasting color instead, so your investment doesn't disappear. Light-colored wall, dark-colored pot, and vice versa. Brick wall? No terra-cotta, please. You spent a good chunk of change on that pot, so place it where it shows off.

MISTAKES NOT TO MAKE

Off-Center Focus

Forget that spike of strappy leaves, usually dracaena, in the center of the pot that we see so often. For a more appealing look, place your tallest plant, or your spiky accent plant, off-center. It's the rule of thirds again: place the focal point to one side rather than in the middle.

→ **Watch for a sale** Some garden centers and nurseries run sales on pots at the start of the season, so sign up to be added to online mailing lists for advance notice, and watch the ads. Nearly all retailers slash prices near the end of the summer, to reduce the inventory they'll have to store over the winter. That half-price pot can sit in your garage all winter, ready to go come spring.

→ **Shop the damaged pot corner** Accidents happen, and container sellers seem to always have markdowns on pots with a chipped rim or a crack. Sometimes those imperfect pots are mixed in with regular stock; often, they're relegated to a separate section. The discounts can be significant—a reduction of 50 percent is not uncommon. The cost of a tube of transparent caulk to repair a crack is barely a blip when we're getting a high-priced pot at a bargain price.

Sometimes we have objects around the house that might be useful for container gardens. Consider these: old work boots or cowboy boots; galvanized washtubs and wicker laundry baskets; a hanging three-tier wire fruit basket; wheelbarrows and little red wagons; an old bike with a basket on its handlebars.

A crafty container must be able to drain freely or it'll soon be a soggy mess. Punch holes in the bottom of those objects, and add a layer of stones or gravel before you add the potting mix. Containers that drain too quickly are just as bad for plants as those that are slow to drain. Line wire or wicker baskets with coco fiber, moss, or a black plastic trash bag (with drainage holes) to slow down the outflow.

Plants for Containers

The small size of a container garden is both a relief and a frustration: a relief, because we only have to pick out a few plants that look good together; a frustration, because we have to limit ourselves. Narrowing down the choices is the hard part of container gardens—and the glory of them.

PLEASING PROPORTION

It's hard to go too tall or too wide with container plants, but too short is common. A collection of low growers is perfect in a wide, shallow pot or in a container that's no more than 12 inches tall. But a collection of low growers in a larger pot that's taller than it is wide is a composition that's badly off-balance.

Choose plants that reach at least a third of the height of the container, for any pot taller than about 12 inches.

The "too tall" problem is a stumbling block with tall, skinny pots, such as a classic urn. To balance that narrow height, choose wide plants that extend to at least twice the width of the pot. Tall, stiffly upright plants will make the pot look poorly proportioned. We need the strong contrast of a wide or arching plant to balance that skinny pot.

PLAY WITH COLOR

Containers let you play with color in a different way than other gardens in your yard. Pots contain concentrated plantings, and we can use them to play off the color scheme we have elsewhere. Here's the place to highlight those small dabs of red or orange scattered around the yard, and bring them together in a big way. Here's the place to go simple and serene, skipping the brights and filling the container garden with restful silver, white, or greens.

The container presents a garden in itself, so you'll want to include a variety of plant shapes, sizes, and textures, as well as a great combination of colors. This garden rewards us many times over, but it also depends on us, not nature, to supply food and water. And because the plants are on display at a closer view than in the garden, we may need to tend it during the season to keep it looking tip-top.

PLANTING POTS WITHIN A POT

Container gardens take a while to reach their peak, as young annuals fill in and trailing plants lengthen into lovely drapery. The sad truth is that many don't stay at that level for long. As temperatures climb, plants run out of energy and get leggy or stop blooming, or if, perish the thought, we forget to water, container plants begin to look worse for wear.

To stave off the summertime blues of tired plants past their peak, don't spare the pruners. Cut back any plants that are beginning to look spindly by about one-third to one-half, to encourage a rush of fresh growth and new flowers.

And try a new approach, to keep containers looking fresh—planting pots within the pot.

Did you know that plants can make do with surprisingly little soil, as long as they have regular food and enough water? A 4- to 6-inch pot is plenty of

△ Use interesting pots, with or without plants, to accent flower beds. Imperfections, such as the flaking blue paint on this pocket pot, are part of the charm.

▷ Permanent plants, such as the Oregon grape holly (*Mahonia* species), dwarf red shrub, and arching grass in this pot, keep containers beautiful year-round. This pot holds a pansy yet to bloom, but it's not even missed.

space for the roots of any annual, and a 1-gallon pot will suffice for most perennials, as long as you keep the nutrients and water coming.

You can simply leave the plants in the pots they came in, and plant them in your container, pots and all. Transplant small multipack annuals into larger plastic pots of at least 4 inches in diameter, put them in the container, and they'll flourish, too.

If a potted-within-the-pot plant begins to look spent, simply lift out the pot and pop in a fresh one. Plant the tired plant in a garden bed—out of its pot—if the season still has at least four weeks to go, prune it back a bit, and it's likely to recover.

This trick is a great one to use seasonally, too. I can't resist pansies in my pots, but as soon as the parade of summer annuals calls to me from garden centers, I want to use them instead. It's so easy to lift out my still-potted pansies and move them to an appropriate spot for summer. And I just replace them with bright annuals like petunias or marigolds.

I do the same with herbs, burying them in their pots in larger containers, so that I can bring them in for winter without causing a setback from transplanting. Pop out the pot of lemongrass or basil when frost threatens, and you have the fresh fixings for lemony chicken soup or a quick pesto all winter. Lift the flashy coleus, and you won't have to buy new plants next year. This nifty trick can save you lots of money!

SHOP AROUND

Annuals for containers vary hugely in price, from as little as $1 for a 4-inch pot to $8 for the same plant at a different retailer. Shop around, and watch for sales anytime during the season. Most sellers receive new shipments frequently during the growing season. Ask when deliveries are expected to get the best selection. This is one time when shopping the "orphan corner" of the garden center doesn't usually pay off—neglected annuals may take a month to recover, if they ever do.

Permanent Potted Plants

A single perennial or small shrub can command a large container all by itself. Partner it with annuals, especially trailing types, and you can paint a plant masterpiece for less than the price of using all annuals. If a potted perennial plant looks healthy at the nursery, there's no reason you can't keep it looking good in a container with regular watering and fertilizer.

▷ A dollar a pot is a great price for 4-inch annuals. Five miles away, at a tony nursery, these same grocery store selections, identical in size and variety, were selling for $4.99.

△ Compelling colors of coleus and ornamental sweet potato take the place of flowers in this large planter. Overwinter cuttings of these frost-tender foliage plants on a windowsill, and you won't have to buy new plants next year.

▷ The equal spacing of a trio of pots strongly invokes a formal attitude in this setting, despite the casual spill of petunias planted in them.

Remember, though, that most perennials bloom for only about two weeks. So look for long bloomers, such as warm-colored hummingbird mints (*Agastache* species and hybrids) or cool blue catmint (*Nepeta* ×*faassenii*). Or plant perennials with beautiful foliage, such as colored heucheras, New Zealand flax (*Phormium* species), or hostas, or with striking form, such as yucca. Ornamental grasses thrive in pots, too, and look good all season, no matter what you combine with them. Planting perennials or shrubs in a container can be risky business, because the roots or crown can fatally freeze over winter. Super-size containers are usually safe, and that's a good thing, because they're too big to move. Still, pile a layer of fall leaves over the top to insulate the growing point of the plant. Protect perennials in smaller containers by moving them into an unheated garage for the coldest months, after frost has killed the top growth.

Plant in Place

When situating large pots, think ahead. You'll want to avoid having to move those containers once they're planted. Start by putting the empty pot in place before you fill it. Stand back to check its location. Adjust its position as needed, until it's just right. Make sure you can open nearby doors, fire up the grill, and otherwise have clear access around the container.

Caring for Container Gardens

Life in a pot isn't easy for plants. The soil soaks up the heat of the sun, getting much warmer than soil in the garden. Moisture evaporates quickly, and roots on the outside or near the top may be much drier than roots in the interior soil. Sunlight reflects off house walls or patio paving, instead of being absorbed by the neighboring greenery in a garden. And with plants crammed in cheek-by-jowl, there's strong competition for water and nutrients.

What we have, essentially, is a crowded bunch of hot, thirsty, starving plants. So you need to pay close attention to nurturing the plants in that unnatural setting.

Frequent watering—daily, in most regions—is the first task. Regular feeding is the second task. Plus, you'll need to give extra attention to cutting back or replacing plants that are past their prime.

The good news is there is no weeding with a container garden. Commercial potting soil, the kind you buy in bags at garden centers, is sterilized to kill weed seeds. So until the wind blows in dandelion seeds, or a squirrel or jay

▷ A simple combination, like this trio of color-changing 'Coral Reef' petunias, 'Golden Goddess' *Bidens* daisies, and a dash of dark coleus contrast, is stronger than a confetti of colors.

buries nuts or sunflower seeds in your container, you won't see a weed in your pretty garden.

Compost, on the other hand, can be full of weed seeds, depending what you or the supplier put in the pile. Still, weeding is a simple matter in a container. The dense planting blocks many weed seeds from sprouting, and the few that do manage to outgrow the desirable plants can be uprooted.

FEEDING

Container plants are crammed into a small space, tighter than planting space in a garden, and potting soil drains faster than garden soil. So potted plants need a lot more feeding than a garden in the ground.

Keep them well fed with water-soluble fertilizer. A weak manure tea, made by adding aged manure to a bucket of water, is ideal for a weekly watering. Commercial fertilizers work well, too, but be sure to follow the instructions to the letter—too much fertilizer is worse than too little; the nitrogen can burn or stunt plants.

△ A bouquet of *Aeonium* rosettes—a frost-tender relative of hardy hens-and-chicks—makes an elegant topper for this gleaming pot. Their red-tinged leaves subtly echo the color of the door and a nearby shrub.

WATERING WISDOM

Watering is by far the biggest chore of container gardening, because it's usually a daily duty. Moisture evaporates quickly from a container. Porous unglazed pots are the worst offenders, because the water is wicked into and away through the walls. But even glazed pots and plastic containers take their toll on soil moisture. They heat up, warming and drying out the soil inside.

And all containers lose precious water through evaporation, from the top of the potting soil and from the plants themselves. It sounds like an inefficient system, but plants use only about 1 percent of the water their roots take up; the rest of the moisture is released into the air through the leaves, and often the stems and flowers as well. This transpiration isn't wasteful, because it is vital to the plant's health. Evaporation cools the plant, just like the cooling effect of the drying perspiration in your summertime T-shirt. And the minerals the plant is taking in via its roots, along with the water, keep it well fed.

On a hot day, or in low humidity, the rate of transpiration increases because more water is needed to cool the plant. So on those days, you may need to increase the water supply. Smart plant selection can go a long way toward minimizing your watering chores. Choosing plants that make the most of limited moisture can make watering a once-every-few-days chore instead of as often as twice daily.

Discover how much water a plant needs by reading the label. Some pointers:

→ **Choose plants with small or needlelike leaves.** The bigger the leaves, the more water is lost, and therefore the more water is needed. Plants with small leaves lose much less water. Ornamental grasses fall into this category, too. Some, such as Mexican feather grass (*Nasella* species), are widely famed for drought tolerance. Nearly all ornamental grasses shrug off dry soil better than broad-leaved plants.

→ **Fuzzy and waxy leaves.** You can tell with one quick touch whether a plant is a water miser. If the leaves are fuzzy, like those of lamb's-ears (*Stachys byzantina*), or waxy, like the spears of agave or yucca, that texture is a clue that the leaf is protected from rapid evaporation.

→ **Built-in water balloons.** The plump leaves of sedums, hens-and-chicks, aeonium, echevaria, dudleya, and other succulents look almost inflated—and they are. They're filled up like balloons with extra reserves of water. When water is scarce in the soil, these plants pull moisture from their leaves instead of through their roots. Usually, that can get them through many weeks of drought. But if the leaves go too long without a refill, they will wither and eventually dry up and die.

Choosing plants with low water needs is still the best way to minimize container watering chores, but these tricks conserve water:

→ Invest in big containers, which dry out more slowly than smaller ones. Glazed and thick-walled pots preserve moisture better than thin plastic or unglazed pots.

→ Group containers to minimize the amount of surface area that's exposed to the air. Push the pots as closely together as you can, to further reduce air flow among them.

→ Shelter container gardens from prevailing winds, which increase evaporation exponentially.

→ Eke out a few hours of shade a day by positioning your pots in the shadow of the house, a fence, tree, or patio umbrella, rather than in full sun all day.

→ Potting mixes are light and water runs through them quickly. Use a saucer to catch water that drains through, so that the plant roots can absorb it at leisure. Do empty any water that remains after a few hours, so the roots don't drown in the puddle.

→ Investigate self-watering pots, which have a built-in reservoir for thirsty roots to draw upon. The larger the reservoir, the longer between waterings.

→ Mulch, mulch, mulch! Just as in a garden, a layer of mulch preserves soil moisture by slowing evaporation from the surface of the soil. The dense planting in a container provides a living "mulch," shielding the soil from direct sun, but a layer of gravel or wood chips will slow down evaporation even further.

→ Add water-holding hydrogel granules to your potting soil, following the directions on the package. (Don't overdo it. These granules puff up to many times their size when they're full of water, so much that they can push out plants and soil.) Like the material in disposable diapers, these additives absorb water when it's plentiful, and release it to the plant roots as the soil dries out. This isn't a miracle solution, unfortunately, because of the fast-draining nature of potting soil, which runs through before the granules can replenish their supply. But they are a terrific backup.

→ If you have an irrigation system, add emitters in your pots, and include them on your automatic watering schedule.

Too little water, or forgetting to water, can ruin a container garden faster than anything. Don't wait until wilting plants remind you to haul out the hose. Days after they've recovered from wilting, the leaves and buds may suddenly yellow and drop as the plant sheds top growth to put its energy into root recovery.

Until you gauge how fast or slow your container garden dries out, give your pots a good drink at least once a day, every morning. If you notice the soil pulling inward from the pot, and it feels dry when you poke your thumb in about

△ A few dollars' worth of annuals in and around a pair of inexpensive pots becomes a priceless garden of happy colors.

▷ Add a pot of flowers to a garden for an instant burst of color. Raising the pot— here, it's done with stacked pavers—gives it even more presence.

2 inches deep, water again, later in the day. Twice a day is not unusual for a container garden in a sunny spot.

Room for One More

Container gardens are habit-forming, but it's a great habit—making small gardens that set us free to play with plants and color. Container gardens are both a finishing touch and a starting point for inspiration.

Pots are artistic accents and powerful focal points—a way to put a bouquet of concentrated color in any area that needs a boost. They bring the garden right up onto a patio, porch, or deck, where there's not an ounce of soil for a roothold. They're a self-contained place to experiment with plant combinations, to discover new partners for color, texture, and shape that we can incorporate in other, bigger beds. And they let us spotlight special plants by raising them closer to eye level.

Artist's Canvas

GARDENING ON SLOPES

△ Groundcovers and rocks
are your biggest erosion
prevention allies on a slope.

▷ Spring bulbs nestle into the spaces among slope-holding rocks, repaying an hour or two of work in autumn with heartwarming color in spring.

A slope may seem like a liability when you're lugging a lawnmower up and down it or mowing sideways on a slant. But that slanting part of your yard can be a real asset when you transform it from hard-to-mow lawn to an area of garden beauty. It can also be even more of a frustration, once you turn it into a garden. Maintenance can be tricky on a slope, because it's challenging to keep your balance, and often difficult to reach into the garden. But plant a slope right, by following the tips in this chapter, and you'll have a showpiece garden.

Paths Make Maintenance Easy

Easy, inviting access is the main trick to keeping up a sloped garden. If you have to clamber around on a hill, you're not going to want to spend much time strolling this garden. And that means you'll have a weedy mess, rather than the showpiece you want. On a small slope—one that doesn't cover more than about 4 feet top to bottom—it's no big stretch to reach into the garden from below to pull a weed or snip off a stem. In fact, it's even easier to work on a small sloping garden than in a garden that's on the level, because you don't have to bend as much. Plants are above your feet or higher, giving your back a break.

But slopes that are wider than you can easily reach call for a different approach. You'll want to establish paths—wide, level paths that invite your feet in.

▷ A retaining wall is a big investment, but the security of a well-built wall is worth it if you have a space that requires it. You can help the budget by choosing perennials that cover at least 3 feet apiece, and filling in with quick-spreading groundcovers like this creeping sedum.

Tame your sloping garden by adding a path. Use the path as your base for maintenance, to stand securely to nab weeds or tidy up plants at any point, or to bring in a wheelbarrow.

Plan the placement of the path after you remove existing lawn or weeds, and before you start planting. The position depends on the size and steepness of the slope. Assess your own physical ability, of course, but also consider visitors and ease of maintenance. Some pointers:

→ For a slope deeper than 4 feet, say 6 to 10 from bottom to top, a single path that leads gradually upward at an angle across the garden is perfect. Simply bisect the garden area on a diagonal, and you've got it covered. Make the path 2½ to 3 feet wide, so that both sides of the garden are no more than 4 feet deep at the widest point.

→ For larger, steeper, or deeper slopes, plan more than one path. A horizontal path across the garden, plus an angled path (or steps) for when you're going up or down, is a simple arrangement that allows safe, secure access.

Cover the path with a thin layer of wood chips or bark mulch, which will blend in among the plantings. This material will offer secure footing, wet or dry, and it soaks up water, helping to prevent mud puddles, especially in spring when plants are still sleeping.

▷ The quickly draining soil on a slope makes it an ideal place to start a rock garden of moisture-sensitive treasures, like this glorious gentian. Gravel mulch mimics the stony soil of an alpine slope, the natural home of this plant.

◁ A river of self-sowing Shasta daisies shoulders a river of rocks in this casual hillside garden.

Minimize Weeds

The very worst weed of all? Grass.

Grass with running roots—and that describes nearly every type of lawn grass—requires a lot of work to eradicate. Leave a few bits of roots in the soil, and before you know it, it's back. Ignore it for a few weeks, and the roots will rapidly take hold.

Grass is the only weed that's ever tempted me to reach for a chemical cure-all. I resisted the urge, because I like the insects and birds and the natural world too much to add more poison to the mix. Still, grass with running roots can be an enormous vexation. Get rid of it thoroughly, by whatever method your conscience allows you, before you plant any garden. But especially before you plant a slope, where maintenance is especially tricky.

If you think weeding out grass from an open space is hard, wait till you try disentangling it from the stems and roots of a beloved perennial.

When planning your sloped garden, my advice is to first strip the sod, as you would when preparing for any other garden. Then, wait. After about a week, examine the area for grass shoots poking up. Dig them out, making sure not to break the roots—get it all—and wait another week or so. By this time, other weeds are probably popping up, too. Hoe them off, if you like, or simply ignore them. They'll soon be suffocated under mulch. It's the grass we're after. Soon, (nearly) all of it should be gone.

Then plant and mulch. A deep layer of mulch, at least 4 inches thick, is the final line of defense against weeds.

Plants are important allies here, too, in fighting grass and weeds, so use lots of groundcovers. Their coverage works as a living mulch, providing the benefits of less watering and fewer weeds, while shielding the soil from washing away. Weeds will be back, as seeds blow in or are dropped by birds or carried in by ants. Keep your eyes open for them, every time you wander in the garden.

A Sloped Masterpiece

A garden on a slope is held up for better viewing. Like a painting set on an easel, instead of lying flat on the floor, it's angled for appreciation. The entire composition can be seen at a glance. And so, a sloped garden requires extra thought in painting those brushstrokes of color, texture, and shape.

△ Whether you call it rock rose or sunrose, a single plant of *Helianthemum* 'Hartswood Ruby' is a star. Place rocks just below it at planting time, to keep soil from washing away from its roots.

No need to fret, though. Just paint this picture in broad, bold strokes. You, and others, will be viewing it from a distance, so go for bold. And follow the same guidelines of planting a variety of colors, shapes, and textures that you've been using for the rest of your gardens. Soon, it'll be a masterpiece.

EROSION

Gravity's a mighty strong force, and soil has a habit of sliding down slopes. A driving rain makes matters worse, sweeping mulch downhill, carving out gullies, and baring plant roots when soil washes away. Rocks, blocks, and roots—that's what you'll use to stop the slide and keep that slope from giving way to gravity.

▷ Sometimes a slope is just too big or too steep to do it yourself. Know your limitations, and call in the pros if the job is way beyond a weekend's work.

MISTAKES NOT TO MAKE
Call for Help

Big slopes—anything more than about 25 feet across and 15 feet from top to bottom, or whatever size or steepness makes you think, "Hmm, can I really do this?"—are a major undertaking that usually requires professional help to move materials and soil. If your yard includes a large or steep slope, try tackling it bit by bit, if your budget doesn't allow for a backhoe. Limit yourself to creating one walled bed—at the foot of the slope. In years to come, you can then build the second tier, and so on, until the whole hillside is covered in terraced gardens. Meanwhile, your finished bed near the bottom will pretty up the place and add some support to the slope.

ROCKS AND BLOCKS

To keep plants and soil in place in this sloped garden, you'll want to use hefty rocks that stay where they're put. On a short or gentle slope, set the rocks here and there, at staggered levels and positions, wedging their base into the soil. On a steep slope, terraces are the only way to go. The terraces can go all the way across the slope, creating a tiered effect of defined layers. Or you can make shorter terraces, only part of the way across the slope, to stagger the terrain for a less regimented effect.

Both rocks and concrete landscaping blocks serve as hard-working materials for holding back erosion on a slope. Choose whichever you like best, depending on your budget and sense of taste.

Today's wide assortment of landscaping blocks gives us plenty of choices in color and style. Go for neutral, natural colors of blocks for building walls or terraces; they shift the focus to the plants in this garden, instead of spotlighting the terrace walls themselves. Red-tinted concrete looks unnatural unless you live in the red rock desert. Soft tan is much less obtrusive. Standard gray will do, too, if you hide parts of it with creepers and sprawlers. The "tumbled" blocks and pavers now on the market make your gardens look even better, because they create the impression of age instead of raw newness.

SETTING IN SLOPE HOLDERS

I've made gardens on some pretty intimidating slopes. I started at the bottom. Working above, with my feet planted solidly, felt a lot more secure than bending to work below. Working from the bottom up is effective at stopping soil from sliding immediately, too. Soil that gets dislodged as you work on upper levels will go only as far as the rocks or blocks you've placed below.

Set rocks here and there, paying attention to their shapes and colors. Many of them will be hidden by plants, at least partly, but get the arrangement to your liking anyway—winter will lay most of the garden bare. Then, working on one rock at a time, set it aside and scrape out about 2 inches of soil beneath it. Put the rock back in place, and it will look as though it's been there forever, partly buried in the soil instead of just perched on top.

To start a terrace, scrape out a trench about 3 inches deep at the bottom of the slope for the first course of rocks or blocks. Set the soil aside. Lay the rocks or blocks in solidly, and add a second or third row on top. Fill in behind the rock course with the soil you removed, and pull additional soil from above to create a bed that's at least 2 feet wide from front to back. Make another trench, lay another course, and so on, all the way up the slope.

It looks beautiful already, doesn't it? And you haven't even started planting!

Planting this Masterpiece

In this garden, roots are most important when selecting foundation plants. You'll continue the colors of your other gardens, but some specific plants may need to be different. You want spreading roots, or deep roots—roots that will anchor themselves solidly in the soil, no matter how intense future rain will be.

Here, you have a place for those plants you've previously steered clear of in your other gardens—the super-fast spreaders that quickly overtake less pushy plants. Now, the aggressive habits of that 'Silver King' artemisia, bright red beebalm, arching goldenrod, 'Goldsturm' rudbeckia, and overenthusiastic yarrow are just the ticket. Ground-hugging sedums that seem to spread before your very eyes? Perfect!

Paint this garden in broad splashes of color, giving the spreading plants plenty of room to stake out a big piece of ground. Figure on an area of about 4 feet in diameter for each of them, and let them interweave when they reach their neighbors.

These spreading plants are soft in shape and texture, so you will need the contrast of stronger shapes, too. Turn to deep-rooted plants that can cling to a slope. That list starts with daylilies, which are easy to grow, handsome when

▷ Practically neon, especially against a mass of budding dwarf 'Sweety' goldenrod, 'Meteor Red' coneflower (*Echinacea*) is fascinating to watch as its fluffy centers develop from flat disks.

▽ In a sloping garden, as long as you have hefty rocks scattered about and set solidly into the soil, you can leave bare stretches of mulch among your plants without fearing a slide. The empty space highlights the plants, even if they're sparse.

MISTAKES NOT TO MAKE

Prairie Possibilities

Native prairie plants from the North American grasslands are renowned for their deep roots, but they may not be good candidates for this garden. Those deep roots are usually topped by equally tall top growth.

In a tallgrass prairie, plants grow closely together, standing up straight, raising flowers and seed heads above the surrounding grasses. In a hillside garden, where gravity is in play, these plants tend to topple or splay outward unless they're staked. The ultimate effect can be messy with bare spots.

Explore the world of short-grass prairie plants instead, for flowers that hold their heads up without a support-ing cast of tall neighbors. Try purple coneflower and its warm-colored hybrids, bright orange butterflyweed, black-eyed Susan, eye-popping magenta winecups (*Callirhoe* species) and gayfeather (*Liatris* species)—all native plants whose deep roots settle easily into a slope.

not in bloom, and have big, luscious blossoms in every shade and every com-bination of yellow, red, orange, cream, and purple you can imagine. They're at the top of the list of deep-rooted plants that will keep a slope in shape, and their strappy, arching leaves provide satisfying contrast to softer plants.

For additional attention-grabbing contrast, include bearded iris, which will quickly get a grip. So will spiky yucca, red hot poker, and hesperaloe; and New Zealand flax and agave in mild climates. Unlike many daylilies, all of these will persist into winter, keeping the slope from looking barren.

Once the spreading and deep-rooted anchoring plants are in place, you can add any other plants you like, tucking them into niches. The stouter perennials and rocks will stop the slide of soil, helping to keep the shallow-rooted plants safe from erosion.

LOW-MAINTENANCE PLANTS

You will want to keep this garden as low maintenance as possible, to avoid climbing around on the slope to care for plants. Considerations include:

→ Stick to low- and medium-height perennials and ornamental grasses about 2 ½ feet tall or less. They'll be less apt to keel over than tall plants.

→ Choose densely branched, compact perennials, such as gold alyssum and white evergreen candytuft, that maintain their shape throughout the seasons.

→ Look for plants with stiff, sturdy stems, including beebalm, goldenrod, and mounding marigolds.

→ Choose tidy mounds of ornamental grass, such as fountain grass (*Pennisetum* species) or blue fescues, for accents. They will keep upright, and they won't block the view of plants behind them.

→ Avoid tall, willowy plants, such as cosmos or delphiniums, or large clumps of mums, perennial sunflowers, asters, and other perennials that tend to spill open, revealing a center that's empty of flowers.

Neat and tidy plants are the way to go in this sloped garden. Vary the tex-tures, sizes, and shapes, and this area will be just as lush and beautiful as any other planting.

MEDITERRANEAN PLANTS

A sunny slope, studded with rocks or terraced with walls? Fast draining, and dry in summer? This kind of garden sounds like one in the Mediterranean

▷ Old-fashioned pinks (*Dianthus* species) usually grow into an expanded mat, with the roots remaining in a central group. Their foliage, often evergreen, prevents the soil below from eroding.

region, and that's another source for plants that thrive in this garden. Fortunately, many Mediterranean plants are available at nurseries and garden centers, and some may already be in your other gardens.

Imagine an entire hillside planted in nothing but types of lavender, including traditional English and French types as well as the bigger, looser Spanish lavender. This garden will be breathtaking at bloom time, but handsome in winter, too, when the silvery-green foliage fills the slope.

Also consider the cooking herbs. Some of the herbs most familiar to you got their start as plants on the sunny slopes of the Mediterranean. Add rosemary, if your winters allow (most grow best in warmer areas). Upright varieties grow to shrub size, and recumbent types will drape gracefully over walls or rocks. Culinary sage and its colored-leaf cousins are sturdy plants, too. Like lavender, these herbs are actually subshrubs, which maintain their structure in winter instead of dying back to the ground. Trim them back by about one-third in late winter, and they'll sprout new growth from their woody stems.

Oregano, marjoram, and mats of creeping thyme aren't shrubby, but they do persist into winter as groundcovers to hold the soil. The familiar pink-flowered oregano is pretty and a huge draw for butterflies. And check out the newer ornamental varieties, laden with clusters of scaled flowers that look like hops. Give these perennial herbs plenty of room to stretch out. They root quickly along the stems.

The delightful aromas of all these plants tickle our noses, but those same scents deter deer and rabbits from munching away. If Bambi's been chomping on your garden, give aromatic Mediterranean plants a try on your sunny slope.

And don't forget sedums—the Mediterranean is the home base of many species, including *Sedum rupestre*, the parent of popular golden 'Angelina', as well as species of hens-and-chicks (*Sempervivum*), another great plant for slopes.

▷ Low-growing sedum (*Sedum spurium*) and surprisingly deep-rooted hens-and-chicks quickly spread over and among rocks, helping hold walls in place. The charming rosettes of hens-and-chicks occasionally produce tall bloom stems that some call "roosters."

▽ Low terraces planted with carefree shrubs, grasses, and a burst of bright pink creeping phlox boost the privacy of this cottage.

INSTANT STABILITY

It takes several months to a full year for perennials and shrubs to grow strongly anchored new roots, so help them stay in place by using modest rocks as anchors at planting time. Dig the planting hole, set in the plant, and then make a mini-terrace on the downslope side by wedging a rock or two a few inches below it. Any eroding soil or mulch will pile up against the rock, instead of washing away downhill.

A medium-sized rock, about 6 inches long by 3 or more inches high, will serve the purpose. I carry along a bucket of rocks that size when I'm planting a slope, so I can park one or two beneath each new plant in just a few seconds. You don't need to remove the rocks later, since the growing plants will quickly hide them.

▷ The peeling bark of a river birch highlights this hillside, but it's worth taking a closer look at the collection of shrubs. That's a bird's-nest spruce (*Picea abies* 'Nidiformis') tucked beside the versatile mugo pine.

Grow Low

Many perennials tend to be about the same height, roughly 3 feet, and that sameness can make a garden look ho-hum, except for the time they're in bloom. Yuccas, ornamental grasses, red hot poker, bearded iris leaves, and other plants with striking architecture will add some pizazz, but to really punch it up, grow low. Save some space for ground-hugging plants among your taller perennials. Reserve areas of about 3 feet in diameter for a patch of spreading petunias, a soft gray-green stretch of creeping thyme, a bright glow of golden 'Angelina' sedum, or other low growers. The change in plant height makes a garden more interesting.

SHRUBS AND GRASSES

We want our slope to look good in winter, too, so be sure to include some shrubs and grasses. Both provide contrasting texture and shape to softer perennials during the growing season. And in fall and winter, after perennials are cut back, shrubs and grasses will hold center stage all by themselves.

Creeping junipers are a natural choice, but this is also a great spot to show off specimen conifers with unusual shapes or colors, such as threadleaf golden cypress. Dwarf hollies and upright columnar junipers and other evergreens are elegant accents. Heaths and heathers spread well to cover ground with all-year color.

Include a shrub rose for summer beauty, and add shrubs with bright winter bark, such as red-twig and yellow-twig dogwoods. Go for ever-silvers, too, like artemisia, santolina, culinary sage, and lavenders, which will hold their foliage through much of winter for a different dash of color.

Admire Your Artwork

You can admire every plant in your sloping garden. Each contributes to your own personal art show. And whoever else views this garden artwork will be appreciating your composition, too. Keep it a masterpiece by being vigilant about weeds. Pay special attention to any weeds that sprout in groundcovers. They'll interrupt the rhythmic flow of those low growers.

Artist's Canvas

GARDENING ON SLOPES

Give an elegant composition of silver, burgundy, and blue
a modern twist with a dash of golden yellow, a shock of
chartreuse, and a dramatic dark accent from reblooming black
bearded iris. The 30- to 40-degree slant of this 8-by-12-foot
sloped garden makes all of these low-care plants a living art
gallery, on display for full admiration.

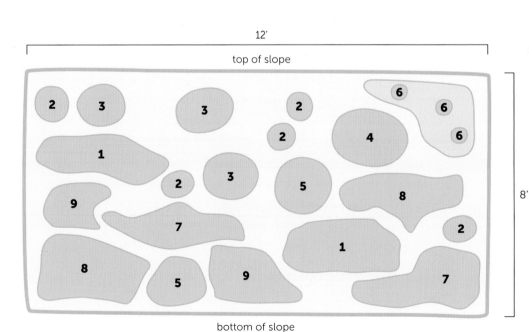

12'

top of slope

8'

bottom of slope

1. 'Powis Castle' artemisia (*Artemisia* 'Powis Castle'), 2 plants
2. 'Hello Darkness' reblooming bearded iris (*Iris* 'Hello Darkness'), 5 plants
3. Lanceleaf coreopsis (*Coreopsis lanceolata*), 3 plants
4. Culinary sage (*Salvia officinalis*), 1 plant
5. 'May Night' salvia (*Salvia ×sylvestris* 'May Night'), 1 plant
6. Snow-in-summer (*Cerastium tomentosum*), 3 plants
7. 'Dragon's Blood' sedum (*Sedum spurium* 'Dragon's Blood'), 2 plants
8. 'Angelina' sedum (*Sedum rupestre* 'Angelina'), 2 plants
9. Lamb's-ears (*Stachys byzantina*), 2 plants

Now You See It, Now You Don't

DEALING WITH EYESORES

△ Use soft-textured plants,
such as grasses and Russian
sage (*Perovskia* species),
to offset the strong lines of
eyesores.

△ Workers may be lifting that manhole cover or tinkering at that utility box, so keep your treasured plants well away, where they won't get trampled.

Many of us have eyesores in our gardens, like utility poles, electrical boxes, manholes, or propane tanks. In most cases, we quickly stop seeing these mundane objects. Even bright yellow fire hydrants seem to vanish mentally, when we admire our gardens. The wrong kind of garden near an eyesore, though, can actually draw attention to the object, instead of away from it. A ring of annuals around a fire hydrant, for instance, instantly turns that hydrant into a focal point. And that's not the effect you want.

Practicality Is Paramount

The eyesore objects we think of as basic utilitarian necessities are useful elements of our way of life. They control underground electrical or phone lines, they hold informational signs, such as speed limit or stop signs, and they provide the water that may be needed for fires. But look around on your next drive, and you'll see examples of people purposely trying to hide them from view or making the mistake of planting trees or shrubs that make it difficult to see them.

Gardening around an eyesore requires a different perspective than plantings in other parts of the yard. In this garden, the practicality of the object is most important. We need to keep these eyesores both visible and accessible, yet still improve their presence as a necessary feature on our property.

INSTANT VISIBILITY

Each of the utilitarian objects in our yards must be instantly visible to workers. While our own eyes may quickly dismiss them, the workers who use them are attuned to spotting them from a distance—all the way down the block. That's why they're placed near the edge of the yard, or between sidewalk and street.

Don't hide them among plants, even though that may be your first instinct. If you can't see them clearly from down the street, neither can the crews whose work is so vital. Use only groundcovers beside the object, so that workers who need to access these "eyesores" can easily find them.

And keep the access open. That's the main guideline for choosing plants and figuring out where to put them. Your best choice for what to put around one of these eyesores is mulch, in a wide enough area to allow people to work around the object. Then put in plants 2 to 3 feet away. Your utility workers will bless you.

For detailed guidelines, check with your local fire department or utility. Most have informational pamphlets or other guidelines on local planting.

DISTRACT TO DISAPPEAR

We want to pull the eye away from that utilitarian feature in the yard or along the street, not guide the gaze straight to it. Here are two ways:

1. Put the garden completely away from the object, leaving the utility box or hydrant surrounded by nothing but lawn grass or mulch. A bright planting in a corner of the yard or along part of the perimeter or in the lawn will distract attention.
2. Include the object in the garden.

If you want to help an eyesore disappear, keep the object off-center. Don't plant a tight circle around it. Don't plant a big circle, either, with the eyesore neatly centered in the middle. Both options announce, "Focal point, right here!"

△ If the box in your yard is crooked, call the utility company to see if you can give it a wiggle or shim it up to set it straight. An object that's askew, even slightly, keeps our attention focused on it.

▷ A stout oakleaf hydrangea shrub, which is super-fast growing, distracts the gaze from ugly but necessary objects. Even in winter, it keeps at least some of its russet-red leaves.

DON'T PLANT A PROBLEM
Clear Access

A utility pole, stop sign, or other street sign may seem like the perfect support for a climbing vine. Honeysuckle, Virginia creeper, trumpet vine, and other vigorous growers will quickly grab on and climb for the sky. But we must resist that idea, because work crews need to easily access the pole. They may also need to climb it. And once the vine grows beyond the top of the pole and out onto the wires, it might cause a power outage. So keep vines off poles.

MISTAKES NOT TO MAKE
Protect Yourself

Utility companies don't always do an accurate job of marking the locations of their lines, and homeowners have been billed for damage when they hit a line that wasn't marked. Save the number of the work order that you receive when you "call before you dig," and take photos of the markings so that you have proof in your defense, should you happen to hit a line that wasn't marked.

Instead, position the object at one side of the bed. Plan to make one side of the garden longer than the other. Or extend the garden out behind it so that the eyesore is in the front. With all the pretty plants in the garden, the focus will be diffused. Our attention is transferred to the plants almost immediately after taking a quick mental note: "There's a fire hydrant. Oh, look at that gorgeous rose!"

Call Before You Dig

"Call before you dig." We all know this advice, but do we follow it? It's such an important first step for any gardening project, but absolutely crucial when you're working around underground lines.

Years ago, water, sewer, and gas lines were the only community lines we had to be concerned about, and the big, sturdy pipes gave us a good warning when our shovel clunked against one. Nowadays, delicate fiber optics and electricity lines run underground, too, in many places—lines that are all too easy to slice through. If you think the sickening crunch of slicing through a tulip bulb is bad, wait till you hit an underground cable.

The Call Before You Dig utility service is completely free, so take advantage of it instead of playing guessing games when you have shovel in hand. At least two full business days before you plan to dig, dial 811—it's the same number, all over the country. The phone is answered 24 hours a day, 7 days a week. A representative will come out and mark your property with bright temporary paint that shows the location of all underground utility lines and pipes.

If you haven't had the lines marked and happen to sever one, you're liable for the cost of fixing it, and that can run into the thousands of dollars. Most lines are about 2 feet beneath the soil, but the depth can vary, depending on your utility company. Be safe, and find out for sure from the utility itself.

Get information from the utilities on how near to their lines you can plant. Companies have different policies on planting, so check the specifics before you begin. Often, you'll receive a handout on those rules when the company comes to mark their lines.

Now that you know where you can dig, you can get planting!

Color and Contrast

A garden around a utility box or hydrant will be relatively small. An area of about 4 by 10 feet will properly encompass most eyesores, and not all of that will be planted. (Mulch for easy access, remember?) To draw the eye away

△ And where are the roots of that old-fashioned shrub rose? The long, arching branches nearly reach the sign, but the roots are at least 10 feet away from the line, where they won't cause problems.

from the item, you'll want to use plants that garner attention. That calls for color and contrast.

COLOR CHOICE

Cure your eyesore by using colorful companions. Repeat the main colors that you've used elsewhere, but keep the color of the human-made object in mind, too. Go for a high degree of contrast in the colors that are nearest to the eyesore. Use blue veronica or salvia beside a yellow fire hydrant, for instance, instead of golden coreopsis next to the yellow hydrant. Plant silver or white around a dark green utility box; place deep purple or red beside a pale green box.

Utility crews will instantly spot the object against the contrasting colors of its planted companions. But, curiously, the contrast will also help the object disappear to our own eyes. We'll notice the flowers most of all, and overlook the eyesore.

△ The stop sign isn't hidden at all by the low- to mid-height plants that beautify this street corner, nor is the attention of drivers diverted from the stop sign. But passersby may linger a second or two to admire the garden.

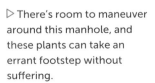 ▷ There's room to maneuver around this manhole, and these plants can take an errant footstep without suffering.

Choose annuals and perennials that stay in their allotted space for this garden. Enthusiastic spreaders, such as beebalm, yarrow, or threadleaf coreopsis (*Coreopsis verticillata*), will multiply your maintenance time, because you'll need to cut them back or uproot new shoots when they get too close to the box or hydrant. Save yourself the effort, and choose well-behaved plants instead—those that stay in a clump or mound, expanding in size only gradually.

Plant for fall and winter color, too, by including ornamental grasses and shrubs with bright bark or berries. Be extra careful in spacing those permanent plants. The planting hole may be far enough away from the lines, but the eventual spread of the plant may encroach on access. Take the time to read the fine print on the plant label, and then add an extra 12 inches for insurance.

SOFTEN THE SHAPE

Utilitarian eyesores in the yard or along the curb are often emphatically geometric in shape. They're rectangles, or squares, or upright cylindrical objects, usually made of metal. All those traits say "hard." Stiffly upright plants have a similar personality. Put them next to that utility box, and you're reinforcing the effect, not minimizing it.

Calling all graceful plants! You'll need some curves to soften those emphatic edges. Plant soft shapes, arching form, fountains of grass beside the utility box; put vertical accents farther away.

▷ Gravel mulch highlights this utility box, but who even notices it when there's a waterfall of Russian sage (*Perovskia* species) and a bright green carpet of groundcover nearby?

A TOUCH OF GRACE

Aster (especially *Aster ×frikartii* 'Monch' and billowing native asters)

Beauty bush (*Kolkwitzia amabilis*)

Blue fescue (*Festuca glauca*)

Boltonia (*Boltonia* species)

Bowles's golden grass (*Carex elata* 'Aurea')

Chrysanthemum (*Dendranthema* species and hybrids)

Cotoneaster (*Cotoneaster* species)

Daylily (*Hemerocallis* species and hybrids)

Dwarf Japanese maple (*Acer palmatum*, including *A. palmatum* var. *dissectum* 'Atropurpureum' and other cultivars)

Miscanthus grass (*Miscanthus* 'Morning Light', 'Gracilimus', 'Purpurascens')

Forsythia (*Forsythia ×intermedia*)

Fountain grass (*Pennisetum* species and hybrids)

New Zealand flax (*Phormium* species and hybrids)

Rose (*Rosa* species)

Russian sage (*Perovskia atriplicifolia*)

'Silver Mound' artemisia (*Artemisia schmidtiana* 'Silver Mound')

'Snowmound' spirea (*Spiraea nipponica* 'Snowmound')

▽ A major streetlight pole barely rates a glance in an enchanting corner garden that brings our eye down to earth.

Spheres or tightly domed plants offer good contrast to square or rectangular geometric objects. But they can work against the "I don't see you" effect we're going for, because their form is so regularly geometric itself. To counteract creating a collection of geometric shapes, use a fountain or arching plant first, and save the sphere-shaped plants for more distant neighbors. They're focal points, so they'll work well, at a distance, to draw the eye in their direction, away from the eyesore.

'Purple Dome' aster keeps its compact domed shape; so do globe-shaped conifers, such as 'Compacta' holly (*Ilex glabra* 'Compacta'), 'Winter Gem' boxwood (*Buxus microphylla* 'Winter Gem'), dwarf barberry, and spirea 'Little Princess' (*Spiraea japonica* 'Little Princess').

EVERGREENS

Green is a color that delights the eyes in a barren gray or snowy winter landscape. Adding evergreens to this garden is a good idea, because eyesores don't go away in winter.

Follow the same guidelines as with other plants: keep the utilitarian object visible and accessible. Don't make the object the center of attention, by flanking it with a plant on each side. Instead, plant one evergreen behind and slightly to one side of the eyesore, or make it a trio with two others, planted together, several feet away.

Ornamental grasses can add long-lasting color, too, because they'll hold their tan leaves all winter. Keep ever-silver plants in mind, as well. They make a good contrast to evergreens, by adding a bright spot.

Turning Necessary into Nice

Avoid the impulse to circle your utility pole or hydrant with flowers, and you'll instantly help the disappearing act of that eyesore. Yes, you can leave it alone completely, but why would you want to, when it's such an inviting spot to put a garden? Just repeat some of the main colors and same plants of your other gardens, and before you know it, you'll be thinking fondly of that fire hydrant. It's now an ornament that only you will notice. Other people will be looking at the garden.

Now You See It, Now You Don't

DEALING WITH EYESORES

Lighten up the heavy weight of a phone pole in this 4-by-8-foot area with an expansive garden of pale yellows and grays. Dots of bright red bedding geraniums provide further distraction from that utilitarian upright feature in the garden.

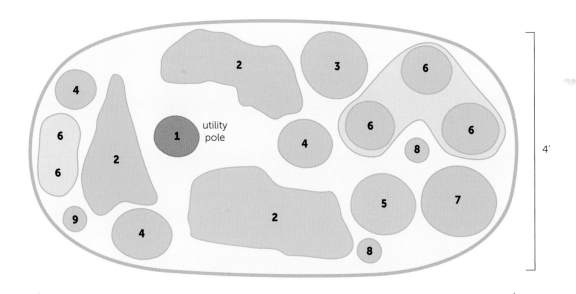

1. Standard wood
   telephone pole
2. 'Blue Rug' creeping
   juniper (*Juniperus
   horizontalis* 'Wiltonii'),
   3 plants
3. 'Variegatus' miscanthus
   grass (*Miscanthus
   sinensis* 'Variegatus'),
   1 plant

4. Lemon-yellow daylily
   (such as *Hemerocallis
   flava,* lemon lily,
   or any hybrid cultivar
   of the color),
   2 plants
5. 'Heavy Metal' switchgrass
   (*Panicum virgatum*
   'Heavy Metal'),
   1 plant

6. 'Moonbeam' threadleaf
   coreopsis (*Coreopsis
   verticillata* 'Moonbeam'),
   5 plants
7. 'Oso Easy Lemon Zest'
   rose (*Rosa* 'Oso Easy
   Lemon Zest'),
   1 plant

8. Red geranium
   (*Pelargonium* hybrid;
   any red cultivar),
   3 plants
9. 'Elijah Blue' blue fescue
   (*Festuca glauca*
   'Elijah Blue'),
   1 plant

Gardening Secrets

TOP TEN WAYS TO SAVE TIME AND MONEY

△ A gardener's best friends are a shovel of your choice, and a sturdy wheelbarrow to move mulch, rocks, containers, and plants around the yard.

△ If sumptuous color warms your heart, check out the spectacular shades of yarrow that go far beyond basic white. No green thumb is required—it grows like a weed.

I n this chapter, I'm going to share some gardening secrets that will save you time and money.

Gardening Secret #1: Plants Want to Grow

Seeds want to sprout. Young plants want to get bigger. Buds want to bloom. And, best of all, plants want to make more of themselves. They want to make seeds and drop them, or they want to send out running roots to grab a bigger piece of ground, or both. Plants want to grow. So start from that understanding: unless we ourselves put roadblocks in their way, our plants will flourish.

See how easy that makes gardening? You're starting from the idea that success is built in with plants, not from the view that success depends on the care you give your plants along the way. Oh sure, your care can make a difference in the final outcome—bigger plants, more flowers, a second round of bloom. But the vast majority of plants are perfectly able to take care of themselves.

So put plants where they belong, in the proper conditions, and they will flourish.

△ Self-sowing annuals,
like this blue larkspur, and
self-sowing perennials, like
quirky Mexican hat (*Ratibida
columnifera*) are a budget-
minded gardener's best friend.
More plants for free!

▷ Significant patches of the
same plant make a bigger
bang than intermingling
them. Plant in multiples—two
groups of three stalwart red
hot pokers, seven smaller
clumps of dianthus—to make
satisfying splashes.

△ Tropical plants aren't likely to thrive in Minnesota, but pushing the limits of hardiness zones just a bit can be tempting, especially when winters lately seem to be gradually warming up. Enjoy your risky plants while they last, but be prepared to lose some.

Gardening Secret #2: Most Garden Plants Aren't Finicky

Most garden plants adapt to all sorts of soils, and to variations in weather. They happily thrive in sun, but they'll do well in quite a bit of shade, too. Most plants also easily adapt to a wide range of regional differences in winter cold, summer heat, humidity, and rainfall.

Garden centers and catalogs make it easy for us to use common sense. Plants are clearly labeled as to what hardiness zones and conditions they'll do best in. Follow those guidelines, and your plants will flourish.

Yes, the climate is changing, and the world is warming up. But we still can't depend on one winter's unusually mild weather becoming the new normal. Sometimes a Zone 7 plant may survive a few years in a Zone 5 garden, if winters are warmer than usual. But if a "real" winter comes roaring back, it will be sayonara to that Cape fuchsia (*Phygelius* ×*rectus*) you'd hoped might make it. To minimize the risk of losing plants, choose those that fit your climate and conditions.

Gardening Secret #3: The Shadow of the Gardener

What makes a garden grow best? The answer isn't fertilizer. It isn't a bottle of Grow Bigger Better spray. It isn't extra nitrogen or phosphorus or potassium. It's you. Your shadow, cast upon the plants in your garden. You're out there, every day, or as often as you can. You're walking around, noticing things, tending to issues.

We can't resist strolling around in our gardens, seeing what's coming up, sniffing the irises, and taking in what's happening. Those daily strolls are vital to a good garden, and they keep maintenance manageable. Instead of an hours-long weeding session once a month, we can pull a weed here and there as we meander, taking stock.

Weeds are much easier to eradicate when they're young. The gardener's shadow is vital for keeping weeding at a manageable level. Do it little by little, pulling some weeds every time you stroll the yard, instead of saving the chore for a marathon session.

That shadow you're casting on your daily stroll notices other things, too. The troubles: the oddly curled leaves that say "something's not right here." The weak, spindly petunias that say "not enough sun." The first Japanese

▷ Spot a ladybug on your plants? Look around for aphids, the favorite food of both adult ladybugs and their larvae. The ladybug and its progeny will soon gobble them up.

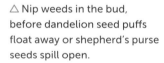

△ Nip weeds in the bud, before dandelion seed puffs float away or shepherd's purse seeds spill open.

beetles in the roses. Noticing problems early gives you a jump on stopping them in their tracks, before you have a big job on your hands.

Your plants will tell you when they're not happy. You'll notice yellowing leaves, or wilting flowers, or a stem coated with aphids—everything and anything that isn't the usual vigorous, healthy appearance of your plants. And as soon as you do spy something that's out of whack, take care of it.

Pesky insects are usually easy to deal with—or not. Often, I choose not to step in, such as with an outbreak of aphids. Instead, I let Nature takes its course, and soon, chickadees and ladybugs move in on the aphids. Japanese beetles and other bugs with big appetites? It's handwork: tap the eager eaters into a jar of soapy water in early morning, when they're slow to fly. Caterpillars of any kind are tolerated, nay welcomed, in my gardens, because birds come to consume the caterpillars and the moths or butterflies they turn into.

Maybe I'm a lazy gardener, but I'd much rather relocate an unhappy plant than test my soil, add amendments, apply fungicide, or spend hours poring over books on disease and deficiencies. So, instead of going the research-and-fix-it route, I depend on a quick, easy, all-purpose solution that works more often than not.

▷ Check the discount area of nurseries frequently. Plants that start to look shabby are moved there before they are tossed altogether, and you can find great bargains. With a little TLC, those plants will recover and be glorious in your garden.

First, I cut back the unhappy plant by about a third, or all the way to ground level if the whole thing is sickly. Then, I simply move the plant to a new spot. Cutting back makes it easier for roots to supply water and nutrients to the remaining growth. And it encourages a flush of new growth, which begins as soon as those roots settle in. Transplanting a plant that's failing to thrive to a different location gives it a fresh start, away from any possible soil-borne diseases or nutrient imbalances. Give it a try, and you're likely to be surprised by what a change of scene can do.

Gardening Secret #4: Count the Stems

You'll find a list of perennials that are easy to divide in this section. But you can keep it simple and just use your eyes to examine the stems. Hold the top of the plant aside, and peer at the stems that come out of the ground. Here's what to look for:

→ If you see only a single main stem, or a tight cluster of stems, going into the soil, don't divide. Chances are the plant has a thick, fleshy taproot; you'll slice into it with the shovel, damaging the plant. Columbines, lupines, and delphiniums all show this trait—and they're all tricky to almost impossible to divide.

→ If you have a plant with multiple stems—about a dozen or more—supporting top growth, sprouting up evenly in an area about 10 inches or more across, you have a perfect candidate for dividing. Multiple stems that sprout 1 inch or more away from each other say, "Hey, we each have roots!" Look at the bottom of a clump of asters, chrysanthemums, Shasta daisies, beebalm, 'Goldsturm' rudbeckia, or a huge number of other perennials, and you'll see that the expanding clump gets bigger because new stems are striking out on their own.

Perennials with multiple stems arising from the soil have either fibrous roots, which quickly reestablish when they're sliced apart, or running roots that sprout new plants as they travel. Some perennials even have stems that root where they touch the ground. All are easy to make more of, by simply slicing off a piece of the plant with a spade or sturdy hand trowel.

You'll quickly be able to tell which plant is which type just by using your eyes. To check for running roots, pull up on one of the outer stems to see whether it's attached to the main "mother" plant. Mat-forming plants, such as creeping phlox, sedums, creeping thyme, and ground-hugging dianthus, can be tricky. Before you dig, feel around beneath low-growing plants to establish where the roots are. A large clump may have only one point of roots and will not be a candidate for dividing.

SIMPLE DIVISION

All of the following perennials are gratifyingly easy to divide to extend your plantings. There's no need to uproot the entire donor plant; just slice off a fist-size or bigger piece, a minimum of about 3 inches in diameter, with a shovel or trowel, depending on the size of the plant.

Aster (*Symphyotrichum,* some of the formerly *Aster* species)

Beebalm (*Monarda* species)

Catmint (*Nepeta* species and hybrids)

Coneflower (*Echinacea* species and hybrids)

Creeping phlox (*Phlox subulata*)

Creeping thyme (*Thymus* species)

Daylily (*Hemerocallis* species)

Goldenrod (*Solidago* species)

Lamb's-ears (*Stachys byzantina*)

Mum (*Chrysanthemum* and *Dendranthema* species and hybrids)

Ornamental grass (*Miscanthus* species, *Panicum* species, and many other species)

Red hot poker (*Kniphofia* species)

Sedum, creeping types (*Sedum* species)

Sedum, upright types (*Sedum* species)

Shasta daisy (*Leucanthemum* ×*superbum*)

Siberian iris (*Iris sibirica*)

Threadleaf coreopsis (*Coreopsis verticillata*)

Yarrow (*Achillea* species)

△ An incredible display of ninety-eight flowers at one time appeared on this native Rocky Mountain columbine, but there was no chance of dividing the plant because of its single taproot. Luckily, it sows itself, providing a handful of new plants each year to spread the beauty.

▷ Unsure whether to divide a groundcover, like this 'Brilliant' dianthus? Lift the mass to see exactly where the roots are, and to discover whether there's a big enough bunch to slice apart.

△ Three months after planting divisions of Shasta daisies, Lou holds the top growth aside to see whether this plant is big enough to cut off another chunk, and it is.

Gardening Secret #5: Anytime Is the Right Time to Divide or Transplant

Perennials are easiest to divide in spring, when they're just waking up from a winter's sleep. Transplant them then, and they'll barely notice they've been moved. A quick slice with a spade, a move to a new planting hole, a generous drink of water, and they're good to grow.

Fall is the second season of choice for dividing, when bloom is finished and roots have months to settle in before the ground freezes. Cut back the plant to a few inches above ground level. There's no need to save the top growth, which will soon be frostbitten and fall off.

▷ Tall garden phlox is an especially generous garden plant—it grows fast from a small division, and it sows itself, too, although often in a different color than the parent, usually reverting to purple-pink.

I've been dividing plants for fifty years any time I get the urge. Spring, summer, fall, as long as the soil isn't frozen. First leaves, full growth, in bud, in bloom, gone to seed—all of them happily moved to new homes as sliced-off divisions, handfuls of rooted stems, or as entire plants. I've even lifted shovelfuls of daffodils and tulips in bloom and moved them elsewhere without missing a beat, as well as almost any perennial you can name. All it takes is one magic ingredient—water.

Plants in full leafy growth and in bud and bloom need water to sustain fresh leaves and upstanding stems. Lots of water. Not only does the water fill the cells of those leaves and stems and buds to keep them plump, but it's simultaneously evaporating from the foliage at a rapid clip because of the sun and breeze.

You've probably noticed the effect when a hot, sunny day follows a gray, rainy spell. Suddenly, leaves droop and curl, until their water reserves catch up to the evaporation rate. But as soon as the sun goes down, bam, like magic, they're back to normal. Roots keep the water coming.

Dividing a plant damages the roots. It's not fatal damage, and the plant will recover quickly, usually in a matter of a few days. But in the meantime, the unavoidable cutting of those roots when you take divisions or transplant an

△ The magic ingredient for transplanting in full bloom? Water, and plenty of it.

entire plant means the top growth will wilt, and many of its buds may never open—unless you "muddy it in."

Before you divide or transplant, decide on the plant's new home, and dig the hole for it. Fill the hole with water, let it drain, fill it with water again, and repeat, until the water takes several minutes to drain. That's usually three to four fillings, depending on how moist the soil was to start with and the soil's consistency. You are wetting the surrounding soil at root level, so that it doesn't instantly wick away the water in the plant hole.

When the hole holds only 1 inch of water, slice off your division of yarrow, beebalm, Shasta daisy (or dig a whole shovelful of tulips or other entire plant), and set the plant into the hole. Fill the hole about halfway with soil, and again fill it with water to the brim. Then, fill in the rest of the soil, patting gently as you go (your hands will get really muddy). The goal is to firm up the soil without patting all of the air out of it, which would suffocate the roots. Do not stomp down the super-wet soil with your foot so hard that your shoe sinks into the mud. Use a light to moderate patting touch with your foot or hands to firm it up a bit—just like when you were making those childhood mudpies.

Layer wood chips or other mulch over the wet soil around the plant, and give it a few days to recover. Set a lawn chair over the plant for temporary shade, to shield the plant from the sun and to slow down evaporation.

In the meantime, your muddy planting hole is like a vase for a bouquet of cut flowers—making sure that the leaves, buds, and blooms get the water they need to stay looking fresh.

Give the new plant a light watering about every two to four days, depending on the weather. Your newcomer may take a few weeks to become firmly rooted in its new home, but if you use the magic ingredient of water—a lot at planting time, and a little as it recovers—you won't lose a single blossom.

Gardening Secret #6: Gray Skies Mean "Go!"

I used to think my mother was off her rocker to be outside gardening in the rain. While I curled up inside with a book, she'd happily muck around in her muddy sneakers, digging and moving heavy clumps of plants. "It's the best time for gardening!" she'd exclaim, shaking the raindrops off her sweater before hanging it to dry.

As usual, Mom was right. When it's drizzling, the top growth of a plant isn't calling for extra water from the roots. The roots can recover without having

▷ Don't hide inside during a stretch of rainy weather. Watch the weather forecast, and think of a rainy spell as a golden opportunity to get outside and move plants around.

△ Start noticing square stems on plants, like on this blue 'Six Hills Giant' catmint, and you've found perfect candidates for taking cuttings—members of the mint family. They'll root like lightning in moist soil, boosting your plant collection by the dozens.

to deal with the extra demand of evaporation from bright sun. Move plants during a rainy stretch, and they won't even wilt. Move the same plants on a sunny day, and they'll look sad for a few days before they get back to growing.

Gardening Secret #7: Start with Square Stems

How would you like twenty new plants from one catmint plant? A dozen splashes of color from a single coleus? A whole border of dahlias from your single plant? A blazing bed of bright red cardinal flower from that lone specimen? Dividing plants is fun and easy, but it only gives you a few plants, at most, from each established parent. Rooting cuttings multiplies your plants exponentially.

Cuttings of perennials require patience. For most of them, it takes a full year for a cutting to grow to full size. Still, the allure of lots of free plants is hard to beat, especially when it's as simple as snipping off a stem, stripping the lower leaves, and poking it in the ground. There's no need for rooting hormone or a greenhouse or hours of tender loving care. Just do this the quick and easy way: snip, strip, poke. You'll have the beginnings of a dozen or a hundred new plants in just a few minutes. The selection of plants that easily root from cuttings is more limited than those that can be divided. But you'll find plenty of beauties that are a breeze to make more of with this couldn't-be-easier propagation method.

Spearmint, peppermint, and all their aromatic culinary kin are notorious for spreading beyond their allotted garden space. They gallop across the garden via creeping underground stems called stolons. Plants in the mint family are also super easy to start from cuttings, so easy that you can save the sprig of mint from your celebratory mojito, carry it home, and poke it into the garden for a sentimental reminder of that special occasion—or simply because you were charmed by its fancy white-and-green leaves.

Take a close look at a sprig of mint, and you'll notice it has a square stem. That's the signature of a plant that belongs to the mint family, Lamiaceae. This family includes many garden flowers, as well as culinary mints—all of them easy to start from cuttings.

Take "hummingbird mints," for instance, the blue-flowered or warm-colored *Agastache* clan. They are pretty pricey to invest in, as blooming perennials. But you can break off a stem and root it in a matter of weeks. Many mint family members don't include the word "mint" in their names, but a little detective work investigating the stems of plants in your garden will reveal their square-stemmed identity. Examples include: salvia, including ornamental golden or variegated culinary sage; lobelia, including red cardinal flower; catmint (*Nepeta*); beebalm; lamb's-ears and other *Stachys* species; lamium; Russian sage (*Perovskia*); coleus and plectranthus; and even some shrubs, including blue spirea (*Caryopteris*), and blue-flowered chaste tree (*Vitex*).

Lavender is one mint family member that belies the easy-rooting trait of its kin. Although it's part of the family, it's tricky to start from cuttings.

Three other biggies, beyond the mint family, are super easy to start from cuttings: dahlias, begonias, and fuchsias. In fact, you can take cuttings of any of these—with the buds and blooms—and root them without losing the flowers! How's that for an instant addition to the garden?

Try your hand at shrubs, too. Hydrangeas of any kind, forsythia, weigela, and butterfly bush are just as easy to root as garden flowers, although the cuttings will take a few weeks longer to grow roots, and a year or two to get to shrub size. Use the same technique for shrubs as you do for perennials: this year's growth, and snip, strip, stick. Start your shrub cuttings in a garden bed where you won't forget to water them, and transplant them to permanent homes the following year, after they're well rooted.

Taking cuttings is an early summer activity, because you'll need this year's new growth for suitable cuttings. That's "early summer" by the garden calendar, not by the date of the solstice, May to June in most places. Just snip a stem of this year's growth, about 6 inches long, strip off the leaves from the lower 3 to 4 inches, and stick the cutting into the soil. Keep the soil moist, and your cuttings will take off before you know it. Most will start pushing out new leaves—a sign that they've begun growing roots—in just a few weeks.

Gardening Secret #8: Separate Colors, Not a Mix

Seeds are another easy way to increase your plant wealth. And yes, that's wealth in dollars, as well as in beauty. If you can be patient for a few weeks, you can have fifty plants for the price of just a packet of seeds.

You can often find seed packets of a mix of one annual in different colors, so you get a nice variety of hues. But to make a big splash, plant swaths of single colors of annuals. Plant all blue bachelor's buttons, for instance. Or plant an area of only 'Rose Queen' cleome next to a patch of 'White Queen', or bright orange-red zinnias next to a stretch of lime green zinnias.

SUPER-EASY ANNUALS FROM SEED

Indian blanket (*Gaillardia pulchella*)

Annual sunflower
(*Helianthus annuus, H. debilis*)

Bachelor's buttons (*Centaurea cyanus*)

Breadseed poppy, lettuce poppy,
opium poppy (*Papaver somniferum*)

California poppy
(*Eschscholzia californica*)

Calliopsis (*Coreopsis tinctoria*)

Catchfly (*Silene armeria*)

Cerinthe, honeywort (*Cerinthe major*)

Cleome (*Cleome houtteana*)

Corn poppy, Flanders poppy,
Shirley poppy (*Papaver rhoeas*)

Cosmos (*Cosmos bipinnatus,
C. sulphureus*)

Larkspur (*Consolida ajacis*)

Marigold (*Tagetes* species and hybrids)

Peony poppy (*Papaver paeoniflorum,
P. laciniatum*)

Sunflower (*Helianthus* species)

Zinnia (*Zinnia* species and hybrids)

Gardening Secret #9: Save the Babies

Perennials and biennials aren't nearly as prolific with their progeny as annuals. But many of them will produce occasional offspring, and some are relatively generous. Perennial seedlings are tiny when they first crop up, but their relation to their big strong parent is apparent, if you look closely at second leaf shape. (First, the plant sends up seed leaves, which are generic looking, so look at the second leaves, which look very much like the parent plant leaves.) Keep a sharp eye out for the babies when you're working in the garden; each one has a good chance of growing into a fine plant.

All of these plants will produce a small crop of seedlings. Move them to new homes, and you'll have multiplied your holdings—for free!

Blue flax (*Linum perenne, L. lewisii*)

Columbine (*Aquilegia* species and hybrids)

Foxglove (*Digitalis purpurea*)

Gaillardia (*Gaillardia* ×*grandiflora*)

Hollyhock (*Alcea rosea*)

Lamb's-ears (*Stachys byzantina*)

Lanceleaf coreopsis (*Coreopsis lanceolata*)

Native asters (*Symphyotrichum* species, formerly *Aster* species)

Mexican hat (*Ratibida columnifera*)

Purple coneflower (*Echinacea purpurea*)

Red valerian, Jupiter's beard (*Centranthus ruber*)

Rose campion (*Lychnis coronaria*)

Sweet William (*Dianthus barbatus*)

Gardening Secret #10: Make Mulch a Mainstay

Mulch is a miracle, pure and simple. It's also the biggest time saver you could ever imagine. Half an hour of spreading mulch saves weeks of Saturday morning weeding duty. Mulch saves money as well as time when it comes to watering, too. It slows evaporation of moisture from the soil, so water needs are minimized.

Even if mulch weren't such a great way to save time and money, it'd still be worth spreading it around. It acts as the finishing touch to a garden. It makes a planting look like a completed piece of art, even if the plants themselves are sparse.

Mulch comes in many natural materials, colors, and textures. Choose a type of mulch that looks good with your house, your style of garden, and your color scheme:

△ Even if mulch didn't do such a good job of conserving moisture and blocking weeds, it'd be worth using for sheer beauty. For large areas, save money by buying a truckload instead of bags.

→ Wood chips soon mellow to a grayish tan color that fades into the background, letting the plants have the spotlight. Because it doesn't grab attention, wood chip mulch works with any style of architecture or planting, from xeric desert styles to an English border.

→ Bark mulch holds its fresh color longer than wood chips and has a less casual look. Dyed bark mulches often look unnaturally red or dark and steal attention from the plants, and sometimes the dye smells strange.

→ Shredded bark mulches have a finer texture that's ideal in semiformal gardens, but they decay faster than chunkier mulches.

→ Pebbles, marble chips, and crushed oyster shells or clamshells are a permanent mulch; they don't rot like bark or wood chips.

→ Grass clippings decay quickly, fading from green to tan in a matter of days. Keep this mulch material relatively shallow, no more than 1 or 2 inches, to prevent it from becoming compacted and odoriferous as it decays; the nitrogen-rich clippings produce ammonia as they deteriorate. A light layer, about ½ inch deep, is perfect for seedling beds; it'll decompose as the seedlings grow, but help block weeds until the seedlings are tall enough for coarser mulch.

△ Light-colored gravel mulch reinforces the desert effect, while preserving moisture. Larger rocks conserve water, too, by blocking evaporation by the sun.

▷ Take time to enjoy what you've created—and to notice all the wonderful visitors, like this red admiral butterfly, that come to see your beautiful new gardens.

→ Chopped fall leaves are free and fabulous. They decay relatively quickly, adding humus to the soil, and their color is unobtrusive. Use a lawnmower with attached bag to collect them in fall, instead of raking.

We all wish we had an unlimited budget and a garden filled with all the high-priced treasures we can haul home. But there's even more pride in the satisfaction of making beautiful gardens on the cheap—even if saving money isn't the main motivation.

We gain know-how with every plant we divide, every packet of seeds we sow, every load of chopped fall leaves we spread like the treasure it is. We get a deeper understanding of our gardens, and we enjoy passing that knowledge along. We feel proud of painting a prettier picture by transplanting our flowers to more appealing locations, even if that's only 6 inches to one side or the other. And our plants become lifelong friends that we care about and care for.

Look at all those salvias, all those dahlias, all those daisies, from a single clump! Look at that inviting sweep of new bed just waiting to be filled!

With each building block, we transform the yard into a place of beauty. Fast. Cheap. Good. Easy.

Resources

Finding Plants

The plants mentioned in this book are widely available at independently owned nurseries, garden centers, and from online sites or printed catalogs.

Prices vary hugely, depending on the seller, so compare the cost before you buy, unless you're immediately convinced it's a good buy. Keep the shipping cost in mind, if you're not buying in person, and sign up for e-mail alerts. Many sources run special promotions, including free shipping, at various times of the year.

An important issue: investigate the reputation of the seller if you're planning to buy online. Read reviews by actual customers on the fabulous website "Garden Watchdog" (davesgarden.com/gwd), which is like a Better Business Bureau for plant sellers, free of charge.

The Dave's Garden website (davesgarden.com) also contains profiles of particular plants, complete with detailed growing notes, photos, and comments by gardeners, plus forums, where you can ask a question or join conversations about everything in the gardening world. It's free to browse, as often as you like.

Catalog Shopping

My favorite catalogs, including those listed in this sampling, include more than glowing plant descriptions, and their content is reliable, not exaggerated to make you buy. They're packed with useful information, too, to help you make smart choices as well as learn about the plant. They're "a whole education," I often gush to friends who are looking for plants. You'll notice that none of the big mail-order catalogs are included in this list. That's because I've always been able to find the same plants they offer at much lower prices at local nurseries and garden centers.

DIGGING DOG NURSERY

PO Box 471
Albion, CA 95410

diggingdog.com
(707) 937-1130

Who doesn't love hummingbirds? You'll find page after page of beautiful temptations for our zippy friends, with all sorts of delightful perennials, including many mentioned in this book, as well as unusual treasures, native plants, and grasses. It specializes in plants for the Southwest, but most are adaptable enough to grow elsewhere, especially if you're looking to drought-proof your garden.

FORESTFARM

990 Tetherow Road
Williams, OR 97544

forestfarm.com
(541) 846-7269

Plant nuts, beware. One look at this catalog, chockfull of perennials, grasses, shrubs, and natives from across America, and you'll be hooked. Remember the starting-small mantra, "Buy small plants!" before you take out a second mortgage to cover your order. Go for the smallest size listed; it'll soon catch up to its bigger, pricier brothers.

HIGH COUNTRY GARDENS

2902 Rufina Street
Santa Fe, NM 87507

highcountrygardens.com
1-800-925-9387

The western gardener's wish book, but crammed with plants that will thrive across the country. Fabulous low-water and xeric choices to drought-proof your garden, plus dozens of other great perennials and grasses that go far beyond typical offerings. New mouthwatering introductions every year. Sign up for e-mail notices for their frequent sales.

PRAIRIE MOON NURSERY

prairiemoon.com
1-866-417-8156

32115 Prairie Lane
Winona, MN 55987

Don't be fooled by the name. Yes, you will find all manner of magnificent prairie plants, including coneflowers, liatris, and grasses, but you'll also uncover a tempting palette of woodland native plants, such as Virginia bluebells (*Mertensia virginica*), that are perfect for your shady spots.

EMERALD COAST GROWERS

ecgrowers.com
1-877-804-7277

PO Box 10886
Pensacola, FL 32524

Call your friends and neighbors, and get together on an order from this wholesale grower. Wait till you see the list of thousands of fantastic perennials and grasses at ultra-cheap prices. The catch? You have to buy in quantity, usually 48 or 72 of the same kind. But your bargain-loving heart will almost burst when you open that box of, say, 'Ruby Star' coneflower for 53 cents each, or blue 'Walker's Low' catmint for 57 cents apiece. Shipping costs are reasonable, too. The healthy, vigorous plants are in small, deep, flimsy plastic pots—the same size that greenhouse growers use to pot up into gallon containers and resell at 10 to 15 times the price a few months later. Let them do their growing in your garden instead. Most will bloom the first year in the ground.

BRENT AND BECKY'S BULBS

brentandbeckysbulbs.com
1-877-661-2852

7900 Daffodil Lane
Gloucester, VA 23061

Here's your secret weapon for filling your gardens with spring bulbs at a bargain price. Hundreds of kinds of daffodils, tulips, and other spring bloomers, plus a summer catalog for lilies, gladioli, dahlias, all at pocket-change prices. Buy in quantity to save even more. And remember—bigger flowers give you more garden bang for the buck, so skip the miniature daffodils and tulips and go for full-size types. Buy small bulbs, like crocus, in big quantities, to make a substantial splash of color.

Further Reading

You'll find plenty of useful nuts-and-bolts information in these books, as well as inspiration for creating your own garden masterpieces.

Armitage, Allen. *Armitage's Vines and Climbers: A Gardener's Guide to the Best Vertical Plants.* Portland, OR: Timber Press, 2010.

Blanchan, Neltje. *Nature's Garden.* Republished in 1901, as *Wild Flowers: An Aid to Knowledge of Our Wild Flowers and Their Insect Visitors.* New York: Doubleday, Page & Company, 1900.

Burrell, C. Colston. *Perennial Combinations: Stunning Combinations that Make Your Garden Look Fantastic Right from the Start.* Emmaus, PA: Rodale Books, 2008.

Clausen, Ruth Rodgers, and Thomas Christopher. *Essential Perennials: The Complete Reference to 2,700 Perennials for the Home Garden.* Portland, OR: Timber Press, 2015.

Cohen, Stephanie, and Jennifer Benner. *The Nonstop Garden: A Step-by-Step Guide to Smart Plant Choices and Four-Season Designs.* Portland, OR: Timber Press, 2010.

Easton, Valerie. *The New Low-Maintenance Garden: How to Have a Beautiful, Productive Garden and the Time to Enjoy It.* Portland. OR: Timber Press, 2009.

Hansen, Richard, and Friedrich Stahl. *Perennials and Their Garden Habitats,* 4th ed. Cambridge, England: Cambridge University Press, 1995.

Jekyll, Gertrude. *The Gardener's Essential Gertrude Jekyll.* Boston: David R. Godine Publisher, 1995.

Jekyll, Gertrude. *Gertrude Jekyll's Color Schemes for the Flower Garden.* London, England: Frances Lincoln Publishers, 2001.

Kingsbury, Noel. *Dramatic Effects with Architectural Plants.* New York, NY: Overlook Press, 1997.

McIndoe, Andy. *The Creative Shrub Garden: Eye-Catching Combinations for Year-Round Interest.* Portland, OR: Timber Press, 2014.

Mitchell, Henry. *The Essential Earthman: Henry Mitchell on Gardening.* Bloomington: Indiana University Press, 2003.

Roth, Sally. *Natural Landscaping: Gardening with Nature to Create a Backyard Paradise.* Emmaus, PA: Rodale Books, 1997.

Thomas, R. William, and the Chanticleer Gardeners. *The Art of Gardening: Design Inspirations and Innovative Planting Techniques from Chanticleer.* Portland, OR: Timber Press, 2015.

Wise, Barbara. *Container Gardening for All Seasons: Enjoy Year-Round Color with 101 Designs.* Minneapolis, MN: Cool Springs Press, 2012.

Photography Credits

All photographs are by Matthew Bartmann, with the following exceptions:

Caitlynn Webster, page 26

Elizabeth (Mimi) Castaldi, page 68

Elizabeth McWilliams, pages 2 and 21

Jeffrey Van Maren, page 167

Lila and Lou Bartmann, page 42

Laura Heindselman and Dave Roth-Mark, page 172

Lea Interholzinger, pages 127 and 173

Index

A

Acalypha wilkesiana 'Inferno', 108

Acanthus spinosa, 106

Acer palmatum, 232
  'Sango-Kaku', 74

Acer palmatum var. *dissectum* 'Atro-purpureum', 232

Achillea species and hybrids, 21, 23, 242

Aconitum species, 106

Aegopodium podagraria, 90, 113

aeonium / *Aeonium,* 204, 205

Aethionema schistosum, 126

agastache / *Agastache* species and hybrids, 27, 41–42, 67, 157, 171, 202, 248
  'Desert Sunrise', 41

Agastache foeniculum, 67, 172

agave, 63, 74, 218

aggressive plants, 30–31, 90, 113, 216, 248

ajuga, 113

Ajuga reptans, 113

akebia, 129

Akebia quinata, 129

Alberta spruce, 151

Alcea rosea, 29, 67, 126, 250

Allegheny spurge, 113

alliums, 140

Aloysia citrodora, 171

alyssum, 19, 38, 82
  'Carpet of Snow', 71
  See also gold / golden alyssum; sweet alyssum

Amelanchier arborea and hybrids, 109

Amelanchier species, 124

American beautyberry, 188

Ampelopsis brevipedunculata, 129

Anemone blanda, 81

angel's trumpet, 171

anise hyssop, 67, 171, 172

annuals
  in and around pots, 114, 207
  for blocks of color, 126, 248, 249
  budget considerations, 63
  drought-tolerant, 189
  filling in with, 25, 98
  growing from seed, 126, 249
  as independent of hardiness zones, 239
  for long-lasting color, 25, 30, 32, 45, 67
  as self-sowing, 30, 238
  for shade, 106

Antirhinnum majus, 29

aphids, 240

Aquilegia species and hybrids, 30, 67, 106

Arabis species and hybrids, 126

arbors, 166

arch, 51

arching / fountain-shaped plants, 60, 179, 198, 199, 231, 233

architectural plants, 221

Aristolochia species, 129

artemisia / *Artemisia* species and hybrids, 23, 63, 109, 187, 221
  'Lambrook Silver', 184
  'Powis Castle', 23, 63, 144, 145, 148, 184, 223
  'Seafoam', 23
  'Silver King', 216
  'Silver Mound', 23, 232

Artemisia schmidtiana, 232

Aruncus dioicus, 106

Asarum europaeum, 116, 117

Asarum species, 113

Asclepias incarnata, 165

Asclepias speciosa, 153

Asclepias syriaca, 153

Asclepias tuberosa, 140

Asiatic lily, 23, 45

aspens, 95

Aster ×*frikartii* 'Monch', 101, 232

asters, 38, 218, 232, 242, 250

  'Monch', 101, 155

  'Purple Dome', 60, 233

  'Wood's Light Blue', 154

Aster species. *See Symphyotrichum*
  species

astilbe / *Astilbe* species and hybrids,
  106, 109

attention-getting plants, 32, 63–64,
  74–76. *See also* focal points

Aubrieta deltoidea, 67

Aurinia saxatilis, 23, 45, 67, 155

  'Compacta', 186

azaleas, 80, 90, 108, 109

B

bachelor's buttons, 30, 126

balsam, 30

bamboo, 90

barberry, 24, 62, 124, 144

  'Crimson Pygmy', 145

  dwarf, 233

  Japanese barberry, 24

  'Sunjoy Citrus', 94

barrel cactus, 63

basket-of-gold, 23, 45, 67, 186

bayberry, 124

bearded irises

  for big flower effect, 45

  in boundary-line beds, 126, 129,
    130

  color uses, 44, 137, 154

  in combinations, 78, 156

  dividing, 148

  as dry-tolerant, 187

  dwarf, 93

  'Hello Darkness', 223

  leaves, 37, 74, 82, 184, 221

  for sidewalk strips, 177, 183, 191

  for slopes, 218, 222, 223

  as a workhorse perennial, 21, 23

  See also irises / *Iris*

bear's breeches, 106

beautyberry, 187

beauty bush, 232

beds

  enlarging, 149–151

  not built around something else,
    132–145

  shapes, 50, 88–89, 136, 143

  See also flower beds within lawns

beebalm

  as an agressive spreader, 95, 216

  cuttings, 248

  deadheading, 157

fragrant foliage, 171

  maintenance, 30, 218, 231

  uses for, 126, 134, 148, 218

begonia / *Begonia* species, 106, 114,
  200, 248

bellwort, 105

benches, 161, 165, 174

Berberis species and hybrids, 124

Berberis thunbergii 'Crimson Pygmy',
  145

bergenia, 23

Bergenia cordifolia, 23

Bidens 'Golden Goddess', 203

biennials, 28

bignonia, 129

Bignonia capreolata, 129

birches, 95

bird feeders and birdbaths, 53, 93,
  111, 157

bird's-nest spruce, 221

black-eyed Susans, 23, 45, 67, 68,
  121, 218

blazing star, 38

bleeding heart, 106, 107

blocks, landscaping, 215, 216

bloodroot, 105

bloom

  blue consecutive, 154

continual, 25, 153–156

early blooming shade plants, 105

extending the season with annuals, 155, 157

long bloomers, 67

perennials with overlapping bloom times, 155

spring-blooming shrubs, 80

yellow consecutive, 154

blueberry bushes, 53

blue fescues

for calming effect, 144, 145

for contrast, 33

dividing, 148

'Elijah Blue', 71, 130, 145, 235

for lamppost gardens, 56, 60, 71

as low-maintenance accents, 218

shapes, 233

for sidewalk strips, 148, 184, 186, 191

for softening eyesores, 232, 233

blue flax, 250

blue lobelia, 85

blue spruce, 24, 96

blue wood aster, 106

boltonia / Boltonia species, 232

borders, plants for, 126

Boston ivy, 129, 226

boundaries, marking,

borderline gardens, 125–127

fences, 92, 121, 123

garden plan, 130–131

hedges, 18, 122–123

plants for, 119, 126

Bowles's golden grass, 232

boxwood, 82

'Winter Gem', 233

breadseed poppy, 249

browallia / Browallia species, 106

Brugmansia species and hybrids, 171

brunnera, 23, 97, 106, 109

Brunnera macrophylla, 23, 106

'Jack Frost', 97

Buddleja davidii, 124

budget-friendly practices. See penny-pincher tips; purchasing plants

building block gardening, basic method, 33–34

bulbs, 80–81, 84, 107, 109

burning bush, 96, 124

bush honeysuckle, 124

butterfly-attracting plants, 153, 172, 219

butterfly bush, 124, 248

butterflyweed, 140, 218

Buxus microphylla 'Winter Gem', 233

C

cactus, 91

calendulas, 172

California bluebell, 192

California phacelia, 11

California poppy

as dry-tolerant, 187

as easy annual from seed, 249

as self-sowing, 30, 154

uses for, 41, 89, 154, 188, 189

"Call Before You Dig", 178, 228

Callery pears, 109

Callibrachoa 'Million Bells', 194

Callicarpa americana, 187, 188

calling before digging, 178, 228

calliopsis, 249

Callirhoe involucrata, 67, 126

Callirhoe species, 218

calming effects, 32, 40, 41, 144, 145, 184

camellias, 77

Campanula medium, 29

Campsis radicans, 69, 128

candytuft / evergreen candytuft, 23, 63, 126, 186, 218

cannas / Canna species, 122, 126, 127, 152, 156

Canterbury bells, 29

Cape fuchsia, 239

cardinal creeper, 129

cardinal flower, 24

Carex elata 'Aurea', 232

Caryopteris, 52

catchfly, 249

caterpillars, 240

catmint

  for big coverage, 148, 185

  for continuous color, 67, 155, 157, 202

  cuttings, 24, 247, 248

  dividing, 242

  as dry-tolerant, 187

  as foil for other colors, 182, 184

  as a quiet companion, 41–42

  for sidewalk strips, 177, 182, 185, 189, 191

  'Six Hills Giant', 148, 247

  as a workhorse perennial, 23

Centaurea cyanus, 126, 249

Centranthus ruber, 22, 23, 44, 45, 157, 250

Cerastium tomentosum, 23, 152, 223

cerinthe, 249

Cerinthe major, 249

Chaenomeles hybrids, 80

Chamaecyparis pisifera 'Golden Mop', 96

chaste tree, 248

cherry laurel, 124

chives, 172

chrysanthemum / *Chrysanthemum* species and hybrids, 232, 242

Claytonia species, 105

clematis / *Clematis,* 69, 89, 128, 167

  hybrids, 129

  'Jackmanii', 69

  'Princess Diana', 125

  'Ramona', 71

Clematis paniculata, 127, 129, 167

Clematis terniflora, 69

Clematis virginiana, 69

cleome, 30, 126, 249

  'Rose Queen', 249

  'White Queen', 249

Cleome hassleriana, 30, 126

Cleome houtteana, 249

climate. *See* hardiness zones

climbing plants. *See* vines and climbing plants

coleus

  'Burgundy Sun', 133

  as colorful shade plant, 105, 106

  in containers, 72, 201, 203

  cuttings, 108, 201, 248

'Electric Lime', 133

'Henna', 109

overwintering, 201

color palettes

  houses and, 46, 75, 77–79, 146

  inspiration for, 44

  See also garden plans

color(s)

  accent, 43, 182

  big bang effect, 40–41

  calming effects, 32, 40, 41, 144, 145, 184

  clashing combinations, 41, 184, 185

  designing with, 38–46

  mixes vs. single colors, 249

  neutral grays, 184

  for pop, 32

  purple as signature color, 12

  repeating, 34, 77, 93, 108–109, 153, 177

  secondary, 41, 43, 61, 79

  spotlight, 41, 43, 64, 68, 79, 111, 184

columbines

  difficulty of dividing, 241, 243

  as hummingbird-friendly, 11

  for long-lasting flowers, 67

  as seedling-producing, 250

  as self-sowing, 30

as shade-loving, 106

compost, 203, 253

concrete, broken chunks of, 216

concrete landscaping blocks, 215, 216

coneflower, 44, 45, 66, 67, 121, 155, 242

   'Hot Papaya', 108

   'Meteor Red', 217

   'Salsa Red', 108

   See also purple coneflower

conifers, 63, 66, 115, 221, 233

Consolida ajacis, 249

container gardens,

   choosing plants for, 197–202

   formal vs. casual style, 50

   maintenance, 202–208

   permanent, 199, 200

   planting pots within pots, 198, 200

   sowing from seed, 198

   watering, 202, 204–206, 208

containers / pots

   as accents, 192, 195, 199, 208

   choosing, 194–197, 205–206

   decorated, 198

   drainage, 197

   marking entrances with, 167, 168, 173

   for minimizing watering chores, 205–206

for outdoor gathering spots, 167, 168

placement, 79, 161, 195, 197, 201, 202, 206

potting mixes, 202, 206

raising, 196, 207

storing during winter, 202

using without plants, 199

Convallaria majalis, 106, 113, 117

copperleaf 'Inferno', 108

coral bells, 23, 148, 149

coreopsis / *Coreopsis* species and hybrids, 21, 49, 67, 229

   lanceleaf coreopsis, 23, 223, 250

   'Limerock Ruby', 29

   See also threadleaf coreopsis

Coreopsis lanceolata, 23, 223, 250

Coreopsis tinctoria, 249

Coreopsis verticillata, 23, 157, 242

   'Moonbeam', 145, 235

corn, 126, 170

corner gardens,

   around a streetlight, 232

   bed shapes, 88–89, 97

   corner-markers, 87, 92, 94, 163

   cost-saving strategies, 95

   existing corners, 96

   garden plan, 100–101

   pacing development of, 99

paired beds, 89–90

planting for clear visibility, 97

punctuation plants, 93–94

using spreading plants, 95

visual weight of design, 90–93

when not to plant, 97, 99

corn poppy, 249

Cornus alba, 124

Cornus sericea, 124

   'Kelsey's Dwarf', 187

Corsican violets, 150

Cortaderia selloana, 74

corydalis, 106

Corydalis aurea, 106

Corylus avellana 'Contorta', 74, 187

cosmos, 40, 126, 198, 218, 249

Cosmos bipinnatus, 126, 249

Cosmos sulphureus, 126, 249

Cotinus coggyria, 81

cotoneaster / *Cotoneaster* species, 232

cottage garden effect, 30, 35

creeping juniper, 63, 221

   'Blue Chip', 96

   'Blue Rug', 235

creeping phlox

   along a walkway, 82

   bloom time, 155

   for border gardens, 126

creeping phlox (*continued*)

　for corner gardens, 95

　dividing, 242

　for large coverage, 126

　for setting off other plants, 38, 152

　for sidewalk strips, 186, 188

　as a terrace planting, 220

creeping sedum, 49, 186, 211, 242

creeping thyme, 152, 186, 219, 221, 242

crocuses, 80, 81

culinary herbs, 248

cup plant, 90

curbside gardens. *See* sidewalk strip gardens

curly willow, 63, 75, 84, 85

cutting back plants, 198, 200, 241

cuttings

　as a cost-saving practice, 24, 108, 201

　easy plants to grow from, 124

　mint family plants, 248

　rooting, 247–249

　square-stemmed plants, 197, 247–248

cyclamen / *Cyclamen* species, 106

Cymbopogon citratus, 171

cypress vine, 127, 172

D

daffodils

　dividing, 245

　in formal and casual style, 50

　miniature 'Minnow' and 'Tête-à-tête', 81

　uses for, 45, 51, 70, 80–81, 154

dahlias / *Dahlia* species and hybrids, 24, 44, 45, 130, 247, 248

daisies, 21, 44, 63, 203

　'Golden Goddess' *Bidens,* 203

daisy-shaped flowers, 38

daphne, 12

Datura species and hybrids, 171

daylilies

　for big-flower effect, 44, 45

　for border gardens, 126

　dividing, 242

　lemon lily, 10, 235

　planting in multiples, 20

　'Red Ribbons', 21

　for slopes, 216, 218

　for softening eyesores, 232

　'Stella de Oro', 41

　as a workhorse perennial, 21, 23

　yellow hybrids, 235

deadheading, 155, 157

Delosperma nubiginum, 98

Delosperma species and hybrids, 152, 156, 186

delphiniums / *Delphinium* species and hybrids, 29, 93, 157, 218, 241

Delphinium tricorne, 105

Dendranthema species and hybrids, 232, 242

desert plants, 63, 64, 91

Dianthus barbatus, 29, 67, 157, 250

dianthus / *Dianthus* species and hybrids, 152, 184, 186, 219, 238, 242

　'Brilliant', 243

diascia, 27

Dicentra cucullaria, 105

Dicentra eximia, 106

Dicentra spectabilis, 106

digging, calling before, 178, 228

digiplexis, 106

Digitalis ×isoplexis hybrid, 106

Digitalis purpurea, 29, 250

Digitalis species and hybrids, 106

dinnerplate dahlias, 44

dividing plants, 148, 241–246

dogwood, 95, 109

　red-twig, 95, 122, 124, 187, 221

　yellow-twig, 95, 221

doors and doorsteps, 18, 51–52, 77–78, 79, 148, 149

Douglas firs, 110

dracaena, 197

dramatic effects, 81, 95, 126, 146

driveways, 97

drought / dry-tolerant plants, 187, 189, 205

dudleya, 205

Dutchman's breeches, 105

Dutchman's pipe, 129

dwarf apple tree, 53

dwarf barberry, 233

dwarf basket of gold, 186

dwarf bearded iris, 93

dwarf bleeding heart, 109

dwarf blue spruce, 39

dwarf gold alyssum, 186

dwarf goldenrod 'Sweety', 217

dwarf hollies, 221

dwarf iris, 19

dwarf Japanese maple, 232

dwarf larkspur, 105

dwarf red-twig dogwood, 187

dwarf rose, 151

dwarf sunflower 'Sungold', 198

dwarf threadleaf cypress 'Golden Mop', 63

dwarf winterberry, 187

E

echevaria, 205

Echinacea purpurea, 21. 23, 172, 250

Echinacea species and hybrids, 45, 67, 155, 242

  'Meteor Red', 217

edging, 90, 138, 141

edible flowers, 172

elderberry, 124

English ivy, 113, 128

English laurel, 124

entrance gardens,

  avoiding hazards, 77

  clearing shrubs, 61, 74

  doors and doorsteps, 18, 51–52, 77–79, 148–149

  garden plan, 84–85

  house color considerations, 77–80

  marking with containers, 167, 168, 173

  plant height and shape, 82–83

  steps, 57, 74

  suitable plants, 74–76, 80–81

  symmetry, 74

erigeron, 21

erosion control, 209, 214–215, 219, 220

Eschscholzia californica, 187, 189, 249

Euonymus alatus, 124

euonymus shrub, 78

European wild ginger, 116, 117

evening gardens, 170

evening primrose, 170

evergreen candytuft / candytuft, 23, 126, 186, 218

evergreens

  at entrances, 74, 77

  in formal style, 50, 63

  in lamppost gardens, 63

  planting near eyesores, 233

  shrubs, 37, 50, 74, 77

  in winter, 25, 66, 83, 95, 122, 233

ever-silvers, 25, 57, 63, 74, 95, 140, 221, 233

expanding gardens,

  changing the terrain, 153

  enlarging beds, 148–151

  filling space, 157

  perimeter plantings, 150–151

eyesores,

  clear access for utilities, 226, 228

  fire hydrants, 224, 229

  garden plan, 234–235

  plant color choices, 229, 231

  planting for distraction, 226–228, 233, 234–235

eyesores (*continued*)

  providing clear access, 226, 228

  softening with plants, 224, 231–232

  telephone poles, 234–235

  utility boxes, 227, 231

F

false sunflower, 45

fantail willow, 63

feather grass, 31

fences

  adapting for vines, 128

  as distractions for eyesores, 226

  house style and, 49

  privacy, 121, 181

  rose-covered, 124

  softening, 118, 181

  stepping down the height, 123

  types, 121

fennel, 172

ferns, 96, 103, 105, 113

fertilizers, 203

fescues, 62, 184. *See also* blue fescues

Festuca glauca, 186, 191, 232

  'Elijah Blue', 71, 130, 145, 235

feverfew, 30

fire pink, 106

Flanders poppy, 249

flower beds within lawns,

  adding vs. enlarging / reshaping, 143

  formal and casual style, 50, 136

  garden plan, 144–145

  laying out, 139

  maintenance aspects, 141, 149

  paths for, 134–135, 138–139

  placement, 134, 135–136

  shape and size, 136

flowering almond, 80

flowering cherries, 53, 104, 109

flowering crabapples, 73, 80, 109, 114

flowering groundcovers, 152, 184

flowering quince, 80

flowering tobacco, 106, 170, 171

flowers, edible, 172

flower shapes, describing, 38

foamflower, 106

focal points

  in design, 32

  human-made objects as, 32, 63, 83, 99, 111

  offset, 136

  See also attention-getting plants

foliage

  colorful, 25, 46, 105, 108–109, 148

  dark, 42

  fragrant, 171

  large, 126

  leaves and water needs, 205

  repeating flower colors with, 108–109

  in winter and off-season, 26, 31, 221, 227, 231

food plants, 52, 53, 163, 172. *See also* herbs

forget-me-not, 29

forsythia, 96, 124, 143, 232, 248

Forsythia ×*intermedia,* 124, 232

fountain grass, 90, 218, 232

four-o'clock, 171

foxglove, 29, 106, 250

fragrant plants, 171

freesia / *Freesia* species, 171

fuchsia / *Fuchsia* species, 106, 200, 248

G

gaillardia / *Gaillardia* species, 29, 250

Gaillardia ×*grandiflora,* 250

Gaillardia pulchella, 248

garden design, evaluating, 31–33, 69

gardener's shadow, 239–241

gardenia, 171

garden ornaments, 60–61, 64–65, 83, 142

garden plans
  boundary-line bed, 130–131
  corner garden, 100–101
  corner garden with bench, 174–175
  distracting from eyesores, 234–235
  entrance garden, 84–85
  flower bed in lawn, 144–145
  lamppost garden, 71
  shady spot, 116–117
  sidewalk strip, 190–191
  slope, 222–223
garden style
  all-natural, 48–49
  house style and, 49–50, 51
  informal / casual, 48, 50
  lamppost gardens as establishing, 58
  quiz to determine, 47
  semiformal / formal, 46, 48, 50
  style you already have, 24–25
gathering places and sitting spots,
  benches, 165, 161, 174
  connecting to the house, 160, 163
  corner garden with bench plan,
    174–175
  corners of, 163, 164, 168
  creating shade, 164, 166–167
  garden plan, 174–175
  outdoor rooms, 163–164

pergolas, arbors and gazebos, 159,
    166–167
separation from the street, 159, 164
views from, 164
gaura / *Gaura* species, 41, 126
gayfeather, 218
gazebos, 167
gentian, 212
Geranium maculatum, 105
geraniums
  bedding, 151, 175, 200, 234
  color uses, 41, 76, 85, 88, 93, 151
  in garden plans, 145, 175, 235
  in a perimeter planting, 151
  scented, 171, 200
  wild, 105
  See also hardy geraniums
Geranium species and hybrids, 23,
    106
gladiolus / *Gladiolus* species and
    hybrids, 45
goatsbeard, 106, 109
golden privet, 124
goldenrod, 216, 242
  'Fireworks', 154
gold / golden alyssum
  for blocks of color, 38, 45
  as a corner plant, 94
  dwarf, 186

for long-lasting bloom, 42, 67, 155
  as a low-maintenance plant, 218
  as a workhorse perennial, 23
  See also alyssum; sweet alyssum
goutweed, 12, 13, 90, 113
grape, 127, 129, 167
grape hyacinths, 42, 107
grass, ornamental. *See* ornamental
    grasses
grass, removing, 58, 213
Grecian windflowers, 81
groundcovers
  aggressive, 113
  as companions, 39, 78, 143
  for erosion control, 209
  herbs as, 219
  mosaic of, 147
  next to driveways, 97
  shade-loving, 109, 113
  for sidewalk strips, 184–186
  as spreading plants, 186
  for weed control, 213
ground ivy, 113

H

hardiness zones, 28–30, 239
hardy geraniums, 23, 65, 97, 154
  'Ballerina', 106

hardy geraniums *(continued)*
  'Brookside', 106
  'Rozanne', 67
Harry Lauder's walking stick, 74, 77, 187
hazels, 63, 77
heath, 59, 75, 188, 221
heathers, 59, 75, 95, 188, 221
Hedera helix, 113, 128
hedges
  for defining boundaries, 18, 123
  as distractions from eyesores, 226
  for a formal touch, 50, 82
  for noise control and privacy, 121
  shrubs for, 122–124
height in design
  borders, 125
  contrasts, 221
  entrances, 82–83
  height differences rule of thumb, 152
  how to add, 93
  incremental, 151–152
  for lamppost gardens, 59
Helianthemum nummularium, 33
Helianthemum species and hybrids, 187
  'Hartswood Ruby', 214

Helianthus annuus, 126, 249
Helianthus debilis, 126, 249
Helianthus maximiliani, 126
Helianthus species, 45, 126, 249
Helianthus tuberosum, 90
Helichrysum petiolare, 196
  'Licorice Splash', 175
Helictotrichon sempervirens, 81
Heliopsis helianthoides, 45
heliotrope, 80, 171
Heliotropium arborescens, 80, 171
hellebore, 106
Helleborus species and hybrids, 106
Hemerocallis flava, 10, 235
Hemerocallis species and hybrids, 23, 45, 126, 232
hens-and-chicks, 60, 156, 183, 187, 205, 219–220
herbs
  culinary, 172
  as groundcovers, 219
  oregano, 140, 219
  sage, 219, 221, 223, 248
hesperaloe, 22, 63, 65, 218
heucheras / *Heuchera,* 23, 105, 106, 108, 109, 115, 116, 132, 202
  'Fire Alarm', 108
  hybrids, 23, 106

  'Purple Palace', 108
  'Southern Comfort', 108
  'Sweet Princess', 108, 117
hibiscus / *Hibiscus* species and hybrids, 44, 45, 124
holly
  'Compacta', 233
  'Nellie Stevens', 134
  'Sky Pencil', 93
hollyhocks
  as accent plants, 74, 94
  avoiding in raised beds, 93
  for border gardens, 122, 126
  as companion plants, 143
  as a long bloomer, 67
  for privacy, 169
  as seedling-producing, 250
  as short-lived, 29
homeowners' association (HOA), 178
honeysuckle, 69, 119, 120, 129, 228
hops, 128
Hosta hybrids, 116, 117
hostas / *Hosta*
  for balance and contrast, 156
  foliage, 96, 108, 202
  hybrids, 116, 117
  in shade gardens, 103, 105, 107, 115, 117
  for visual weight, 90

houseplants, 168

hummingbird-attracting plants, 11, 69, 106, 120, 134, 172, 192

hummingbird feeders, 53, 164

hummingbird mint, 67, 171, 202, 248

Humulus lupulus, 128

hyacinth bean, 127, 129

hydrangeas / *Hydrangea* species and hybrids, 24, 25, 61, 124, 128, 227, 248

hydrogel granules, 206

Hymenoxys scaposa, 186

I

Iberis sempervirens, 23, 63, 126, 186

Iceland poppy, 29

ice plant, 98, 184, 186

'Fire Spinner', 152, 156

Ilex glabra 'Compacta', 233

Ilex verticillata

'Berry Poppins', 187

'Nana', 187

'Southern Gentleman', 130

'Winter Red', 130

Impatiens balsamina, 30

impatiens / *Impatiens* species, 105, 106, 109, 114, 200

Indian blanket, 29, 248

invasive plants, 124

Ipomoea alba, 129, 170, 171, 172

Ipomoea horsfalliae, 129

Ipomoea quamoclit, 127, 172

Ipomoea species, 129

irises / *Iris*

dwarf, 19, 154

'Hello Darkness', 223

hybrids, 23, 45, 126, 130, 187, 191

leaves, 142

Siberian iris, 23, 126, 242

sweet iris, 188

See also bearded irises

Iris pallida 'Variegata', 188

Iris reticulata 'Harmony', 154

Iris sibirica, 23, 126, 242

ivy, 110

J

Jacob's ladder, 106

Japanese barberry, 24

Japanese beetles, 239–240

Japanese maples, 61, 74, 83, 93, 187

Japanese willow, 124

jasmine, 171

Jerusalem artichoke, 90

Johnny jump-ups, 14, 80

junipers

'Blue Arrow', 130

'Blue Star', 71, 76

columnar, 59, 74, 93, 221

groundcover type, 25

mat-forming, 97

Pfitzer, 96

Juniperus 'Blue Arrow', 71

Juniperus horizontalis 'Wiltonii', 235

Juniperus squamata 'Blue Star', 71

Jupiter's beard, 22, 23, 44, 45, 157, 250

K

'Karl Foerster' grass, 63, 142, 166

kerria, 95, 124

Kerria japonica 'Pleniflora', 124

Kniphofia species, 20, 242

Kniphofia uvaria, 20, 23, 45, 126

'Knockout' rose. *See under Rosa* species and hybrids; roses, shrub

Kolkwitzia amabilis, 232

L

Lablab purpureus, 127, 129

ladybugs, 240

lady's mantle, 115, 148

lamb's-ears

cuttings, 248

lamb's-ears *(continued)*

 dividing, 148, 242

 in garden plans, 101, 191, 223

 'Helen von Stein', 184

 low water needs, 187, 205

 as seedling-producing, 250

 as a spreading plant, 31

 uses for, 15, 35–36, 78, 152, 154, 184

 as a workhorse perennial, 21, 23

Lamiaceae, 107, 248

Lamium galeobdolon, 113

lamium / *Lamium* species, 106, 115, 116, 185, 186, 248

Lamium maculatum, 113

 'Pink Pewter', 117

lamppost gardens,

 garden plan, 70–71

 plant shape and color, 60–63

 repeating colors in, 18, 66

 use of proportionate height, 59

 using vines, 59, 68, 69

lantana, 30, 152

larkspur, 137, 238, 249

lattices, 127, 170

Lavandula species and hybrids, 171, 187

Lavatera species, 126

lavender

 for edging, 148

 for entrances, 74

 fragrant foliage, 171

 as a hedge, 82

 low water needs, 187

 for marking corners, 86

 as a quiet companion, 41–42

 romantic style of, 35

 types, 219

 in winter, 57, 63, 74, 219, 221

lawns

 gardens vs., 139, 141

 as path surface, 138–139

 removing grass, 58

 replacing with gardens, 157–158

leaning plants, 74

leaves

 describing shape and size, 37

 fallen, 114, 253

 iris, 37, 74, 82, 142, 184, 221

 plant water needs and, 205

lemon balm, 171

lemongrass, 171

lemon thyme, 172

lemon verbena, 171

lettuce poppy, 249

Leucanthemum ×superbum, 23, 45, 67, 71, 85, 126, 155

'Banana Cream', 175

liatris / *Liatris* species, 38, 218

licorice plant, 175, 196

ligularia, 106

Ligularia dentata, 106

Ligustrum species and hybrids, 124

Ligustrum ×vicaryi, 124

lilacs, 25, 122, 123, 143

Lilium hybrids, 23, 45

Lilium lancifolium, 23, 30

lily-of-the-valley, 10, 106, 113, 117

limbing up trees, 114, 115

Linum lewisii, 250

Linum perenne, 250

liriope, 22, 113

Liriope muscari, 113

lists of plants

 for big-flower effect, 45

 for borders, 126

 early bloomers for shade, 105

 easy annuals from seed, 249

 easy annuals to sow in place, 126

 easy to grow from cuttings, 124

 flowering plants for shade, 106

 fragrant flowers and foliage, 171

 groundcovers for shade, 113

 long-lasting flowers, 67

 low growers for a sidewalk strip, 186

perennials easy to divide, 242

perennials for deadheading, 157

perennials that cover at least 2 feet, 126

perennials with overlapping bloom times, 155

seedling-producing, 250

short-lived perennials / biennials, 29

soft shapes, 232

tall and trouble-free, 126

vines, 129

workhorse perennials, 23

xeric, 187

lobelia, 133, 248

Lobelia cardinalis, 24

Lobelia erinus, 85

Lobularia maritima, 171

‘Carpet of Snow’, 71

Lonicera morrowii, 124

Lonicera sempervirens, 69

‘Blanche Sandman’, 120, 124

Lonicera species and hybrids, 129

Lonicera tatarica, 124

low-growing plants

containers for, 197–198

for lamppost gardens, 59

for marking boundaries, 119

near driveways, 97

shrubs, 59

for sidewalk strips, 184–186

for variety in height, 221

low-maintenance plants, 21, 31, 34, 126, 218. *See also* maintenance

lungwort, 90, 106, 109, 148

lupines, 29, 241

Lupinus hybrids, 29

Lychnis chalcedonica, 29

Lychnis coronaria, 29, 250

Lysimachia nummularia, 113

M

Macleaya cordata, 90

Magnificent Seven perennials, 155

Mahonia species, 199

mailboxes, 59, 68

maintenance

container gardens, 202–208

continual, 239–241

cutting back plants, 198, 200, 241

flower beds within lawns, 141, 149

paths for ease of, 157, 210–211

safety on slopes, 211

sidewalk strip gardens, 177, 180–181, 189

vines and climbing plants, 69, 129, 167

See also pruning; watering; weed control

Maltese cross, 29

manholes, 225, 229

manure tea, 203

marigolds

for big-flower effect, 45

color uses, 40, 45, 97

dwarf, 93, 149

dwarf ‘Gem’, 148, 149, 175

as easy to sow in place, 126

for edges, 93

in garden plans, 85, 145

‘Lemon Gem’, 41, 85

as low-maintenance, 218, 249

‘Safari Yellow’, 145

marjoram, 219

mat-forming plants, 31, 97, 242

Maximilian sunflower, 126

meadow garden, 137

Mediterranean plants, 218–219

Melissa officinalis, 171

Mertensia virginica, 30, 105

Mexican feather grass, 205

Mexican hat, 238, 250

milkweed, 153

Mimulus species, 106

mint family, 108, 247, 248

Mirabilis jalapa, 171

miscanthus / *Miscanthus* species, 74, 94, 170, 175, 242

  'Cosmopolitan', 95

  'Gracilimus', 232

  'Morning Light', 90, 100, 130, 232

  'Purpurascens', 232

  'Variegatus', 235

miscanthus grass, 232

Miscanthus sinensis

  'Cosmopolitan', 175

  'Morning Light', 100, 130

  'Variegatus', 235

Monarda species and hybrids, 126, 157, 171, 242

Monardella macrantha, 186

mondo grass, 113

moneywort, 113

monkeyflower, 106

monkshood, 106

moonflower vine, 129, 170, 171, 172

Morella pensylvanica, 130

morning glories, 94, 127, 128, 129, 163

moths, 170, 172

moving plants, 240–241, 247

mugo pine, 25, 147, 221

mulch

  around utilitarian objects, 224, 226, 227, 230, 231

  benefits of, 250

  for container plants, 206

  covering compost with, 253

  fallen leaves, 114, 253

  for finishing touches, 69, 141

  gravel, 34, 180, 182, 212, 231, 252

  for moisture retention, 180, 182

  rocks as, 182

  on sloping gardens, 217

  types, 251, 253

  for weed control, 14, 87, 125, 130, 180, 213

  when expanding gardens, 149–150

multiples, planting in, 20, 49, 238

mums, 24, 60, 218, 242

Myosotis sylvatica, 29

Myrica pensylvanica, 130

Myrica species, 124

N

Narcissus hybrids, 45

Nasella species, 31, 205

nasturtiums, 172, 192

native plants, 11, 104–105, 111–112, 121, 218

Nepeta ×faassenii, 24, 41, 67, 155, 182, 202

  'Walker's Low', 191

Nepeta species and hybrids, 23, 157, 187, 242, 248

New England aster, 126

New Zealand flax, 31, 95, 192, 202, 218, 232

Nicotiana alata, 80

  'Jasmine', 171

Nicotiana langsdorfii, 106

Nicotiana species and hybrids, 171

Nicotiana sylvestris, 106, 170, 171

northern bayberry, 71

O

oakleaf hydrangea, 227

oat grass, 81

Oenothera species and hybrids, 170

Onoclea sensibilis, 113

Ophiopogon japonicus, 113

opium poppy, 249

oregano, 219

  'Kent Beauty', 140

Oregon grape holly, 199

Oriental poppies, 23, 36, 67, 129, 152

ornamental grasses

  for borders, 126

for containers, 202

dividing, 242

for filling in quickly, 126, 157

in formal and casual style, 50

low water needs, 205

for special effects, 39, 88, 184

in winter, 25, 26, 77, 83, 95, 221, 231, 233

overwintering tender perennials, 200, 201

P

Pachysandra procumbens, 113

painted daisy, 29

palms, 76

pampas grass, 74

Panicum species, 242

Panicum virgatum 'Heavy Metal', 235

pansies, 86, 172

Papaver hybrids, 23

Papaver laciniatum, 29, 249

Papaver nudicaule, 29

Papaver paeoniflorum, 249

Papaver rhoeas, 249

Papaver somniferum, 249

Parthenocissus quinquefolia, 128, 129

Parthenocissus tricuspidata, 129

Parthenocissus vitacea, 129

partridge feather, 178

Passiflora, 69

Passiflora incarnata, 128

passionflower, 69, 128

paths and walks

for connecting sitting spots, 160, 163

for ease of maintenance, 157, 210–211

entrance, 51–52

establishing on slopes, 210–211

in formal and casual style, 50

lawns as surface of, 138

planting alongside, 81–83

purposeful and pleasurable, 134–135

on sidewalk strips, 179

surfaces of, 22, 138–139, 157, 163, 211

Pelargonium species and hybrids, 85, 171, 175

'Boldly Hot Pink', 175

red cultivars, 145, 235

pennisetum /*Pennisetum* species and hybrids, 60, 218, 232

penny-pincher tips

buying annuals, 63

buying wholesale, 158

coleus vs. perennials, 106

filling space quickly, 157

overwintering tender perennials, 200, 201

propagating coleus, 108

recycling broken concrete, 216

sowing seeds in containers, 198

substituting evergreens / ever-silvers for shrubs, 63

using corn as a patio screen, 63

using found objects as corner markers, 94, 163

using plants with large coverage, 148

using rocks, 182

using shrubs for color, 46

using sloped raised beds, 93

using sticks for plant supports, 163

penstemon / *Penstemon* species and hybrids, 187

peonies, 10, 74

peony poppy, 249

peppermint, 248

perennials

biennials mistaken for, 29

for deadheading / cutting back, 155

easy to divide, 242

with overlapping bloom times, 155

perennials *(continued)*
  overwintering tender, 200, 201
  for shade, 106
  that cover at least 2 feet, 126
  workhorse, 21–23
  See also lists of plants
perfumes, 171
pergolas, arbors and gazebos,
  166–167
perimeter plantings, 150–151
perky Sue, 186
Perovskia atriplicifolia, 50, 60, 67,
  126, 182, 187, 232
Perovskia species and hybrids, 56,
  100, 224, 248
Persian shield, 105
Persian stonecress, 119, 126
pest-deterrent aromas, 219
Petunia ×*hybrida* 'Purple Wave', 101,
  191
Petunia hybrids, 45, 171, 186
petunias
  'Coral Reef', 203
  pleasing fragrance, 171
  'Pretty Much Picasso', 147
  uses for, 19, 30, 40–41, 43, 100
  'Wave', 45, 95, 126, 148, 156, 190
Phacelia campanularia, 192
Phacelia tanacetifolia, 11

Phaseolus coccineus, 129, 172
philodendron, 168, 169
Phlox divaricata, 86, 106, 126
Phlox maculata, 23, 45, 67, 126, 155,
  157, 171
Phlox paniculata, 23, 45, 67, 126, 127,
  129, 155, 157, 171
Phlox stolonifera, 23, 126
Phlox subulata, 126, 155, 186, 242
Phormium species and hybrids, 31,
  192, 202, 232
photinia, 124
Photinia ×*fraseri,* 124
Phygelius ×*rectus,* 239
Picea abies 'Nidiformis', 221
plectranthus / *Plectranthus,* 106, 248
plume poppy, 90
pole beans, 53, 127, 163
  'Kentucky Wonder', 127
Polemonium species, 106
pollinator-attracting plants, 130, 165,
  172
poppy, 90, 249
porcelainberry, 129
prairie plants, 218
prickly pear, 63
privacy solutions
  fences and other structures, 51, 121,
   137, 162, 168, 170

  plants, 121, 125, 127, 166, 168–170
privet, 124, 126
propagation
  dividing, 148
  seedling-producing plants, 250
  self-sowing plants, 29, 30–31
  of shrubs, 123
  square-stemmed plants, 108,
   247–248
  See also cuttings
pruning
  container plants, 198, 200
  shrubs, 61, 63, 74, 77, 110
  trees, 114, 115
  vines, 129
Prunus caroliniana, 124
Prunus glandulosa 'Sinensis', 80
Prunus laurocerasus, 124
Pulmonaria species and hybrids, 106,
  148
punctuation plants, 93–94
purchasing plants
  buying in quantity, 158
  buying wholesale, 158
  from grocery stores and nurseries,
   201, 241
  from home growers, 171
  native plants, 112
  small pots, 23

purple coneflower
  as butterfly-attracting, 172
  in garden plan, 130
  as a native plant, 218
  as seedling-producing, 250
  uses for, 40, 45, 56, 60
  as a workhorse perennial, 21, 23

Q

quiet companions, 41–42

R

rain, 246–247
Ratibida columnifera, 238, 250
Ratibida pinnata, 121
redbud, 95
red cardinal flower, 248
red hot poker
  architectural features, 221
  dividing, 242
  planting in multiples, 238
  uses for, 45, 93, 94, 126, 218
  as a workhorse perennial, 23
red monardella, 186
red valerian, 250
repeating colors and forms, 34, 77,
    93, 108–109, 153, 177
retaining walls, 211

rhododendron, 63
rhubarb, 53
river birches, 95, 221
rockcress, 67, 126
rock garden, 212
rock rose, 33, 187, 214
rocks
  to fill space quickly, 157
  as garden accents, 64–65, 67, 100
  as mulch, 182
  placing for erosion control, 215
  as plant anchors, 220
rocks and gravel bed, 150
Rocky Mountain columbine, 243
roots
  checking before dividing, 242, 243
  digging and planting among,
    113–114
  of plants for slopes, 216
  running, 242
  taproots, 241, 243
Rosa rugosa, 124
Rosa species and hybrids, 45, 124,
    129, 171, 232
  'Double Pink Knockout', 100
  'Knockout', 124
  'New Dawn, 175
  'Oso Easy Lemon Zest', 235
  'Pink Knockout', 100

'Sunny Knockout', 70, 71
rose campion, 29, 250
rosemary, 82, 171, 172, 187, 219
roses
  for big-flower effect, 45, 49
  dwarf, 151
  in formal and casual style, 50
  in mixed plantings, 27, 37, 66,
    93
  'Oso Easy Lemon Zest', 235
  pleasing fragrance, 171
  propagation, 123
  for softening eyesores, 232
roses, climbing
  'Blaze', 124
  'Golden Showers', 124
  'Joseph's Coat', 124
  'New Dawn', 124
  'Paul's Himalayan Musk', 124
  as a well-behaved vine, 129
  'White Dawn', 124
roses, shrub
  for blocks of color, 148
  as fast-growing, 22
  growing from cuttings, 124
  'Knockout', 41, 61, 124, 125
  'Knockout' series, 44
  in mixed plantings, 35, 39, 90, 148
  planting near eyesores, 229

Rosmarinus species and hybrids, 171, 187

rudbeckias / *Rudbeckia* species and hybrids, 23, 45, 67, 68, 137

'Goldsturm', 216, 242

rule of thirds, 136, 197

rule of thumb for height differences, 152

Russian sage

for borders, 126

in casual style, 50

in corner garden plan, 100

as dry-tolerant, 187

for lamppost gardens, 56, 60, 63

as a long bloomer, 67

in sidewalk strips, 182, 184

for softening eyesores, 224, 232

starting from cuttings, 248

S

sage, culinary, 219, 221, 223, 248

Salix alba 'Flame', 124

Salix integra 'Hakuro-nishiki', 124

Salix matsudana 'Tortuosa', 84

salmon geraniums, 85, 93

salvia / *Salvia* species and hybrids, 98, 137, 152, 187, 229, 248

'Black and Blue', 154

'Caradonna', 38

'May Night', 71, 145, 223

Salvia ×*sylvestris* 'May Night', 71, 145, 223

Sambucus species and hybrids, 124

Sanguinaria canadensis, 105

santolina, 187, 221

Santolina chamaecyparissus, 187

scarlet runner bean, 94, 127, 129, 163, 172, 192, 198

scented geraniums, 171, 200

Sedum rupestre, 219

'Angelina', 223

Sedum spurium, 186, 220

'Dragon's Blood', 223

sedums / *Sedum* species and hybrids, 187

'Angelina', 60, 183, 185, 219, 221, 223

'Autumn Joy', 67, 172

creeping types, 49, 61, 186, 211, 242

dividing, 242

'Dragon's Blood', 60, 223

as dry-tolerant, 205

groundcover types, 88, 97, 152, 186

low water needs, 205

as a Mediterranean plant, 220

in mixed plantings, 36, 156

for slopes, 216

seedling-producing plants, 250

self-sowing plants, 29, 30–31, 238, 243

Sempervivum species and hybrids, 187, 219

Sempervivum tectorum, 60

sensitive fern, 113

serviceberry, 109, 123, 124

shade

for container plants, 206

gauging, 103

part-sun and part-shade defined, 105

removing branches to eliminate, 114

seasonal, 104

for sitting spots, 164, 166–167

shade gardens,

garden plan, 116–117

plants for, 90, 102, 105–110, 113, 114–115

shapes of plants, 36–38, 60–61, 63, 233

Shasta daisies

for big-flower effect, 45

bloom time, 67, 155

for border gardens, 126

companion plants, 152

deadheading, 157

dividing, 242, 244, 246

in garden plans, 71, 85, 175

for lamppost garden, 60

as self-sowing, 213

for showy effect, 40

on slopes, 213

white color, 16, 21, 212

as a workhorse perennial, 21, 23

Shirley poppy, 249

shrub roses. *See* roses, shrub

shrubs

    as all-season anchors, 149

    avoiding one-two planting pattern, 122

    with bright bark, 221

    with colorful foliage, 25, 46, 148

    evergreen, 37, 50, 74, 77

    fast growing and easy care, 123–124

    as hedges, 122–124

    low-growing, 59

    as pests, 124

    as potted plants, 195, 199, 200

    propagating, 123–124, 248–249

    pruning, 61, 63, 74, 110

specimen, 143

spring-blooming, 80

subshrubs, 219

in winter, 25–26, 77, 122, 140, 187–189, 221, 231

Siberian elm, 12, 112

Siberian iris, 126.23, 242

sidewalk strip gardens,

    in full sun, 186

    garden plan, 190–191

    HOA / local government restrictions, 178

    maintenance considerations, 177, 180–181, 189

    plants for, 182–189

    plants to avoid, 179

    providing clear passage, 178–179

    reducing damage potential, 180

    in winter, 189

Silene armeria, 249

Silene virginica, 106

Silphium perfoliatum, 90

silver plants. *See* ever-silvers

sitting spots. *See* gathering places and sitting spots

slopes,

    aesthetic aspects, 213–214

    calling a professional, 215

drainage, 212

erosion control, 209, 214–215, 219, 220

establishing paths, 210–211

garden plan, 222–223

maintenance, 210–211

plants for, 93, 216–223

preparing the soil, 213

raised beds on, 93

rocks and blocks on, 215–216

slope holders, 215–216

small plants, 23, 80, 95

smokebush, 9, 81

snapdragon, 29

snowdrops, 80, 81

snow-in-summer, 23, 152, 223

softening effects, 42, 88, 118, 181, 224, 232–232

Solidago species, 242

Solomon's seal, 105

spearmint, 248

specimen plants, 96, 114, 143, 221

Spiraea japonica 'Little Princess', 233

Spiraea nipponica 'Snowmound', 232

Spiraea ×vanhouttei, 80

spirea, 80, 143, 248

    'Little Princess', 233

    'Snowmound', 232

spreading plants
  aggressive, 30–31, 90, 113, 216, 248
  avoiding near utility objects, 231
  maintaining, 30–31
  for slopes, 216, 218
  space requirements, 186
spring-blooming plants, 80, 104–105
spring bulbs, 80–81, 84, 107, 109
squash, 52, 53
Stachys byzantina, 23, 101, 205, 223, 242, 250
  'Helen von Stein', 191
Stachys species, 248
stems, square, 108, 197, 247–248
steps, 57–58, 74
Stipa species, 31
stop signs, 230
Strobilanthes dyerianus, 105
Stylophorum diphyllum, 105
success in growing plants, 237
succulents, 61, 205
sunflowers
  annual, 44, 45, 59, 126, 170, 249
  in border gardens, 122, 126
  dwarf 'Sungold', 198
  height considerations, 152, 218
  at a lamppost, 68
  'Teddy Bear', 198
sunrose, 187, 214

swamp milkweed, 165
sweet alyssum
  annual, 149, 152, 171
  as edging, 43, 93, 148
  growing from seed, 198
  pleasing fragrance, 171
  See also alyssum; gold / golden alyssum
sweet autumn clematis, 69, 127, 167
sweet peas, 163
sweet potato vine, 72, 200, 201
sweet William, 29, 67, 157, 250
switchgrass 'Heavy Metal', 148, 184, 235
Symphyotrichum cordifolium, 106
Symphyotrichum novae-angliae, 126
Symphyotrichum species, 242, 250
Syringa vulgaris, 130

T

Tagetes patula 'Safari Yellow', 145
Tagetes species and hybrids, 45, 126, 249
Tagetes tenuifolia 'Lemon Gem', 85, 175
tall garden phlox
  for big-flower effect, 44–45
  for border gardens, 126

deadheading, 157
  as a long bloomer, 67, 155, 156
  pleasing fragrance, 171
  propagation, 245
  as a workhorse perennial, 21, 23
tall plants
  avoiding, 97, 218
  uses, 126, 152
  uses for, 59, 126, 143, 152
Tanacetum coccineum, 29
Tanacetum densum, 178
Tanacetum parthenium, 30
temperatures in hardiness zones, 28
terraces, 215, 216, 220
threadleaf coreopsis, 21, 23, 157, 242
  'Moonbeam', 145, 154, 235
threadleaf false cypress, 96
threadleaf golden cypress, 221
Thymus praecox, 186
Thymus serpyllum, 186
Tiarella species and hybrids, 106
tidy edges, 141
tidy plants, 40, 46, 59, 93, 218
tiger lilies, 23, 30
toad lily, 106
tools, 236
Torenia fournieri 'Catalina Pink', 117

torenia / *Torenia* species, 106, 114, 116
  'Catalina Pink', 117
  'Summer Wave', 109
tree mallow, 126
trees
  deciduous, 80, 90, 103
  incorporating, 16
  placement in beds, 113, 116
  planting under, 109, 111
  removing branches to gain sun, 114, 115
  ring-around-the-tree syndrome, 112–113
  roots and water needs, 111
  weight and balance in design, 99
trellises, 12, 50, 94, 128, 166, 169, 170
Tricyrtis species and hybrids, 106
trillium / *Trillium* species, 105
trumpet vine, 69, 128
tuberose, 171
Tulipa hybrids, 45
tulips
  for big-flower effect, 45, 80–81, 137
  in corner gardens, 86, 91
  dividing, 245
  repeating colors with, 73

U

USDA plant hardiness zones, 28–30, 239
utilities. *See* eyesores
Uvularia species, 105

V

variegated Japanese willow, 124
verbena, 30
Veronica spicata 'Red Fox', 175
veronica / *Veronica* species
  in garden plans, 145, 175
  'Georgia Blue', 31, 38, 154
  'Sunny Border Blue', 67, 145
  uses for, 37, 97, 126, 151, 185, 229
  as a workhorse perennial, 21, 23
vinca, 113
Vinca minor, 113
vines and climbing plants
  adapting fences for gripping, 128
  annual, 127, 163, 167
  in formal and casual style, 50
  for lampposts, 59, 68, 69
  light-weight, 128
  maintenance, 69, 129, 167
  nonflowering, 226
  supports, 128, 163, 167, 169, 172
  trouble-making, 128

  on utility poles, 228
  vigorous, 129
  well-behaved, 129
Viola corsica, 150
violas / *Viola* species, 14, 113
violets, 14, 80, 113, 150
Virginia bluebells, 30, 105
Virginia creeper, 43, 128, 129
virgin's bower, 69
Vitex, 248
Vitis species and hybrids, 129

W

walks. *See* paths and walks
walls
  building, 215
  containers against, 197
  as a focal point, 99
  in formal and casual style, 50
walls (*continued*)
  for privacy, 137, 170
  retaining, 211
  rock, 220
  sitting spaces and, 161, 162, 164, 173
watering
  container plants, 202, 204–206, 208

watering *(continued)*
  importance when dividing, 245–246
  plants for minimizing, 205
weed control
  in containers, 203
  groundcovers as, 213
  mulch as, 14, 87, 125, 130, 180, 213
  before weed seeds are distributed, 240
weeds
  grass as, 213
  in groundcovers, 221
  seeds in compost, 203, 253
weeping flowering cherries, 93
weeping Japanese maple, 60, 97
weeping trees, 63
weigela, 24, 124, 248
  'Wine and Roses', 144
Weigela florida, 124
white gardens, 16, 41, 50
wild geranium, 105
wild ginger, 113, 116, 117
willow 'Flame', 124
winecups, 67, 126, 218
winter and off-season beauty

bark, 74, 95, 97
character plants, 74
evergreens, 25, 66, 83, 95, 122, 233
ever-silvers, 25, 57, 63, 74, 95, 140, 221, 233
foliage, 26, 31, 221, 227, 231
ornamental grasses, 25, 26, 77, 83, 95, 221, 231, 233
shrubs, 25–26, 77, 122, 140, 187–189, 221, 231
trees, 95
winterberry
  'Southern Gentleman', 130
  'Winter Red', 130
wisteria / *Wisteria* species and hybrids, 69, 128, 167
woodbine, 129
woodland phlox, 86, 106, 126
woodland wildflowers, 104
wood poppy, 105
woolly thyme, 97
workhorse perennials, 21–23, 77, 153
workhorse shrubs, 123–124

xeric plants, 182, 186–187

yarrow
  color uses, 40, 185, 237
  dividing, 242, 246
  large size, 139
  'Moonshine', 154
  spreading habit, 95, 139, 216, 231, 237
  as a workhorse perennial, 21, 23
yellow archangel, 113
yellowbells, 105
yuccas / *Yucca* species
  architectural features, 221
  'Color Guard', 60
  companion plants, 152
  in corner gardens, 91, 94, 95
  for slopes, 218, 221
  spikey shape in design, 22, 32, 37, 39, 63, 74
  as a workhorse perennial, 22, 23

Z

zinnia / *Zinnia* species and hybrids, 45, 126, 172, 249
  'Envy', 80
  'Thumbelina', 80, 198